Dear Vic_____im,

Please enjoy my book, for it is all true. After you

THE
DERMINATOR
OR
Tales of a Lucky Dermatologist

hAve finished all 65 chapters, consider yourself :

DERMINATED

With fond regards,
" The Derminator "

ISBN: 1-4196-8585-6
ISBN-13: 9781419685859

Visit www.booksurge.com to order additional copies.

THE
DERMINATOR
OR
Tales of a Lucky Dermatologist

Douglas N. Naversen, M.D.

I dedicate this book to my wife Jane Naversen. She has put up with my antics all these decades. She is my best friend. I am glad it is a life sentence.

In addition, I salute the dermatologists of America, past, present and future. In particular, I praise our future doctors now toiling in medical school. I really appreciate our young physicians in training who are studying and working long hours as interns and residents. We welcome you to our ranks!

With an aging baby boomer turning fifty every eight seconds for the next decade, we hail you doctors as you join us in "the medical trenches." Our patients will need and greatly benefit from your hard work, enthusiasm, intelligence, altruism and fresh outlook on life. Get ready for a long, fun run. Your fascinating journey will take you to a wonderful destination.

— Douglas N. Naversen, M.D.
Medford, Oregon
January, 2008

*All profits from this book
will be used for dermatology
and skin cancer research.*

My father, a dermatologist in private practice in rural southern Oregon, has long been an inspiration to me for the strong relationships that he develops with his patients. I was first exposed to my dad's professional side when I was in high school and I worked in his office over the summers, filing charts and performing administrative duties. About once a day, when a willing patient presented, he'd invite me in to "assist" with a procedure (the removal of a suspicious mole or a cyst underlying the skin) or to observe a patient interaction. I wasn't struck by the gore of surgery as much as I was by the rapport that my father shares with his patients. I could sense the concern and empathy he felt for them, and the way that patients seemed drawn to his silly sense of humor and zealot-like passion for dermatology. My father was the first to teach me that medicine is not a purely scientific endeavor—it is also a human one, and an opportunity to have meaningful exchanges with others. He is one of the reasons that I decided to set aside an established journalism career at age 32 to enroll in medical school.

In this book, my father recounts his most unforgettable experiences with patients, collected over decades of practicing medicine (identifying details have been changed to protect patient anonymity). Each chapter represents a new adventure in dermatology and in life, and together they span patient encounters that are touching, sad, humorous, clinically challenging, and even scandalous; the medical school antics of a young man and his classmates; stranger-than-fiction duties in the emergency room; near-death experiences on southern Oregon's Wild and Scenic Rogue River; and murderous threats from a psoriasis-plagued patient living in the wilds of Alaska. Dr. Naversen's storytelling is at once folksy, heartwarming, and hilarious, with an appeal all its own. I hope you'll enjoy reading these very funny, very moving, very real adventures as much as I have.

— Laurel Naversen Geraghty
Former editor, *Glamour* and *Allure*
Student, New York University School of Medicine

Table of Contents

Chapter One: The Taxi Driver

I checked in for work promptly at 7:30 on a Monday morning in my Medford, Oregon, dermatology clinic. My trusted back-office assistant, Pat, motioned me to Room 3. As I walked in, I eyed a smiling woman wearing a long trench coat. "Hi, I'm Dr. Doug Naversen," I said. "Hi, I'm Sally the taxi driver," she said. Before I could even ask her about her chief dermatology complaint, she quickly unbuttoned her coat and it slipped off her broad shoulders right onto the floor. The woman was standing before me buck-naked. Her curves were sensuous. Her heaving breasts would have made a stripper proud. As I awkwardly stared at her nakedness, it slowly became clear to even me that this taxi driver had an agenda.

Quickly to the intercom I went. "Pat, Dr. Naversen needs assistance in Room 3, please." Pat rescued me, we were able to diagnose and treat the taxi driver's skin condition (she had pityriasis rosea, a ringworm look-alike, probably caused by human herpes virus 7), and I haven't seen her since. Was I the chosen one, or does she do this to all her doctors? (What did her husband Lino think about this?)

This was just another routine Monday morning in the life of a dermatologist.

Chapter Two:
My Two Minutes of Fame

I always wanted to be a dermatologist. My skin was so bad in high school; unsightly pimples ruled my life. Feelings of depression, embarrassment, and inferiority troubled me daily. I had some good dermatologists who treated me in high school and college, but my cure didn't arrive until 1982, when Accutane was approved by the F.D.A. My five-month course of therapy was miraculous, and I haven't hardly had a pimple in several decades. I figured that if I became a dermatologist someday, I could relate and empathize with my patients. I had been there myself, and I had shared their pain. If I could get their skin problems cured, they could blossom and move on with their lives, unhindered by their troublesome affliction.

While a college student at the U.S. Air Force Academy, I entered the Life Science (pre-med) major, hoping that I would someday be a skin doctor. At the time, the Air Force Academy was sending two percent of its graduating class to medical school, and I was lucky enough to be among them. Off to Ohio State Medical School I went.

The dermatology rotation was a prized elective. Only two medical students a month were chosen. For half a year, I sweet-talked the head assistant in charge of electives. (Assistants rule the world, don't they?). I even gave her flowers and candy. And sure enough, when the selections came out, I was in!

Fresh off my one-month dermatology elective with Dr. Ed Lowney and Dr. Eldred Heisel—two of the best dermatologists in the great state of Ohio—I felt I knew more dermatology than most doctors in the country; some actually told me that I did. Then came my two minutes of fame in the Ohio State Emergency Room at University Hospital.

My medical resident, Dr. Falco, and I were on duty late one night. In walked a black gentleman with a most peculiar gait. "Naversen, get in there and check him out," ordered Dr. Falco. Since this was one of my first clinical rotations, I was still green behind the ears. But I steeled my nerves, and in I went.

I briefly reviewed the gentleman's records, and I performed a history and a physical exam. I observed his most peculiar walking style. And since I was fresh off my dermatology rotation, I was acutely attuned to his rich black skin. I therefore did a quick check of his entire skin surface after my orthopedic evaluation was done. Since my findings were now complete, I excused myself from the room to check out with Dr. Falco.

"Dr. Falco," I said boldly, "this gentleman has an hysterical gait. He is faking it. No one walks like that. There is secondary gain involved here. And by the way, he also has secondary syphilis."

Falco raised his eyebrows and said, "Doug, I'll check it out."

Ten minutes later Dr. Falco came out of the room and grabbed me. "Doug, you are absolutely right about the hysterical gait. None one walks like that. He is faking it. There is secondary gain involved here. But about the syphilis—you are all wet!"

I replied "Well Dr. Falco, I appreciate your expert opinion. But I do believe he has syphilis. How about we get a VDRL (a blood test for syphilis), just in case? As a matter of fact, Dr. Falco, I will bet you one greenback dollar on it."

"Remember, Naversen, you're the lowly medical student, and I am the medical doctor. But let's get the blood test—I accept your bet." It was the last day of our rotation, so Dr. Falco went off to endocrinology, and I headed for general surgery.

Five days passed before I had time to track down the lab results. The VDRL was sky-high four-plus positive! It was bizarre—on the one hand, I felt extreme elation because my patient had V.D. and I had been the one to identify it. On the other, I felt very sorry for this gentleman's sordid plight. The epidemiology people were very good—they had tracked him down and pumped him full of penicillin, and they had already traced his contacts. He was all but cured of his disease.

It was a week later that I was able to link up with the good Dr. Falco. Greeting him with a huge grin, I said "Dr. Falco, you owe me a greenback dollar." Dr. Falco said, "Doug, what the heck are you talking about?" Since our bet had been made late at night, and since we were chronically sleep-deprived, he had completely forgotten it. I recounted the weird saga of our patient in the emergency room with the hysterical gait, and about our wager on the possibility of secondary syphilis. I then showed Dr. Falco the markedly positive four-plus lab slip. Dr. Falco's jaw dropped, and in sudden defeat he whipped out his wallet, and gave me my hard-earned greenback dollar. As he walked away, I heard him muttering, "Maybe I should take a dermatology rotation."

The next year, Dr. Falco was named the Chief Medicine Resident at the Ohio State University Hospital. This was quite an honor! He was and he is a fine doctor. I feel I did my part in teaching him the importance of the skin and dermatology. Thus ended one of the greatest moments of my life, and my two minutes of fame.

By the way, how did I know that the patient had secondary syphilis? Well, because I noted the faint papulosquamous rash on his torso, and the characteristic "nickel and dime" eruption on his palms and soles. With a big slug of intramuscular benzathine penicillin in the hip, our patient was cured of his syphilis. But at last report, I heard he still walks kind of funny.

Could it be I was developing the 'trained eye' of the dermatologist even as a medical student? I sure hoped so. But would I ever again achieve the exalted peaks of being both good and lucky?

Chapter Three:
The Evil Angels

One of the fine psychiatrists in Medford, Oregon, Dr. Jeff Thompson, phoned me one morning. "Doug, I have a patient you should see." Since I was an idealistic, young physician new to southern Oregon (and conveniently had an unexpected hole in my schedule due to a last-minute cancellation), I said, "Sure Jeff, send him over."

George was a large, calm, quiet gentleman about 70 years old. As I entered the room, he blurted out, "Doc, the evil angels are jamming me again."

"Excuse me?" I replied.

"Yes, Doc, the evil angels are jamming me again. They turn on the voltage every day at about 8 a.m., and the electrical current really gives me bad headaches. It's been going for months now."

He pointed to his crown where the point of maximum pain seemed to emanate from his cranium. In exactly that location I spotted a very black, irregular-looking mole. I reasoned to myself, "Perhaps he has a black skin cancer—a melanoma—that was invading beneath his skin surface and causing referred pain and headaches to the gray matter of his brain. I said to George, "I think we need to remove that black mole on the top of your head. Maybe it will help your headaches."

"Doc, if you can make my headaches go away, I'll do anything," he vowed.

My assistant Pat skillfully prepped his scalp with Hibiclens soap. (I prefer it to that darn Betadine prep, which stains my white coat brown and causes allergic reactions in some patients.) As I pulled on my size-seven vinyl gloves, I chose to use xylocaine with epinephrine and a 30-gauge needle. After a gentle injection into his skin, he was numb. I selected an 8 mm punch biopsy (cookie cutter), and I popped out the mole. I buzzed a bleeder with my trusty hyfrecator. I closed the wound with three 4-0 nylon sutures. George was amazed at how rapidly the black growth came out.

And here is the sweet part, the part I was really proud of. Secretly, I had slipped a pair of pliers into the side pocket of my white doctor's lab coat. After I was done with the surgery, I pulled out the pliers and smeared a little bit of George's blood on it. I made sure he saw the bloody pliers, and I said "George, I got the angels out."

"Are you sure Doc?" he questioned. "Yep, George I got 'em all." Luckily, no video camera recorded this surgery. Had my residency professors at U.C. San Francisco seen me pulling a pair of pliers out of my lab coat to cure an "angel" problem, they would have unceremoniously booted me out of the residency. Why, the American Academy of Dermatology might have even pulled my board certification. But I was feeling lucky that day.

When I reviewed George's skin biopsy slide under my Olympus microscope, I was relieved it was a benign nevus, or mole. I dictated my pathology report with my Sony Dictaphone—"benign compound nevus without evidence of malignancy." There is no black death—there is no melanoma here today on my watch, I thought.

George came in two weeks later to have the sutures removed. He beamed a wide smile and said, "Doc, the headaches are gone. You got the angels cured. They are finally dead. Thank you, thank you, thank you!"

Shucks, it twern't nothing, I thought. Every now and then, even the blind groundhog finds the acorn. We just happened to find our acorn with George that day. I admit our treatment plan was somewhat unconventional. Using pliers to rid George of his angel problem is not written up in any dermatology journals that I know of. And we proudly took credit for the cure.

Fortunately, we savored the moment. Because six weeks later George came back and slumped into his chair in Room 3. "Doc, they're back. They're jamming me again. They got deep down into my teeth."

Pat humbled me when she later said, mockingly, "Dr. Naversen, Oh great healer of people, how 'bout you pull out all of his teeth and cure him for six weeks. Then it goes to his gallbladder. We do a cholecystectomy, and he is good for another six weeks. Then it goes to his spleen. We do a splenectomy, and then it goes to who knows where." Okay, point well taken. Maybe our "cure" wasn't as good as we thought.

George was still very appreciative of our futile efforts to fix his problem. He came back the next week and gave me a nice thick brass belt buckle. It said "God, Guts and Guns made America great." It was one of the nicest presents I've ever received, because it was totally unexpected, and because it came from George's heart.

Well, what would I do if George was still alive and if he came into my office with a similar problem today? I have reflected on it, and I believe I have a cure. I would tell George, "Yes, the angels are jamming me too. What you have got to do is to go buy a new baseball hat. Next buy a fresh roll of aluminum foil in the grocery store. If it is not a fresh roll, it won't work. Every week you have got to pull out 12 inches of fresh foil from the roll. Carefully fold it on the inside of your ball cap, and then wear the hat 24 hours a day. It has to be shiny side facing out, or it won't short-circuit the angel power probes. George, it is OK to take off the cap for a few minutes a day to brush and shampoo your hair. Remember, it takes at least 10 minutes for their force field to build up. And if you don't change the foil weekly, the joules are just too great, and the laser beam will bore right through the aluminum, and I can guarantee you will get headaches again. But if you follow my instructions exactly, George, you will be cured." And now you know why Naversen gets the big bucks!

George has since passed on from natural causes. I am clueless as to why he had his fixation against those angels. What I did fail to tell you is what his psychiatrist told me the day of his initial phone call. For you see,

Dr. Thompson had diagnosed George with chronic schizophrenia. The patient was delusional in certain areas. He was also a functioning human being. He was never violent and he never hurt people. He shopped at the local Safeway, he paid his property taxes and he voted regularly. May George rest in peace.

Chapter Four: Infidelity?

A beautiful black woman entered my office. With the right lighting and a blowing fan to highlight her hair, she could have graced the cover of a magazine. But she had sad eyes, and her face revealed a look of profound depression. "What's wrong?" I asked. She immediately burst into tears. "I have V.D., and my husband has been cheating on me."

"Whoa, Nellie," I said in sympathy. "Tell me what's happening." After more sobbing, she related that a routine blood test for syphilis had returned positive. She was a faithful wife and she had never had an affair. She concluded that the sexually-transmitted disease could have only come from her husband Harold. "Has he been unfaithful to you?" I asked.

"Well, I don't know," she said. "I thought we were really in love, but this changes everything. I am devastated. My life is over."

I handed her three Kleenex tissues for her eyes. After a suitable pause, I said, "Let's move forward and proceed with your skin exam." There was a patch of hair loss on her scalp, with permanent scarring. She also had a fine, crinkly red plaque on her forehead. Further questioning revealed that she was now allergic to the sun, even though as a child and teenager her skin never sunburned or showed sun sensitivity. A skin biopsy revealed follicular plugging, an interface dermatitis and a superficial perivascular and perifollicular lymphoid infiltrate with plasma cells. Her antinuclear antibody (ANA) blood titer was markedly positive. These are all fancy words that point to one clear diagnosis: lupus.

Lupus erythematosus is an autoimmune disease that often strikes young women. Literally translated, lupus means "wolf." Sunlight sensitivity, rashes on the face, and hair loss with scarring alopecia are characteristic of discoid lupus erythematosus (discoid LE, or DLE for short). More active forms of lupus are associated with kidney problems, seizures, anemia, inflammation of the lining of the heart and lungs, arthritis, and other autoimmune phenomena. These more severe symptoms indicate systemic lupus erythematosus, or SLE. Some patients with lupus may even have a "BFP"—a biologic false positive test for syphilis. Bingo! Our depressed black patient didn't have an S.T.D.—she had lupus!

A few more blood tests confirmed absolutely no syphilis—and my patient was euphoric when I told her. She was willing to accept a diagnosis of lupus erythematosus far more readily than one of syphilis and infidelity. Her husband Harold had been true to her. Her marriage was saved. She left the office with bounce in her step. Surely, even a psychiatrist could not have done a better job in curing her depression, I thought. Just like the day I cured the man of his "angel" headaches, I felt I had made a significant contribution to dermatology. Could this possibly be worthy of the Nobel Prize in medicine, I wondered?

Six weeks later, the comely woman returned for a follow-up visit. Her sad eyes and old look had returned. Although she no longer had worries of infidelity (Harold was an OK guy after all.), I soon learned that she was almost always depressed. I guess I did not really merit the Nobel Prize for the brilliant diagnosis of lupus. But perhaps I gave her a few weeks of happiness, and maybe I even saved helped save her marriage. Savor the moment.

Chapter Five: Smokey Bob

Smokey Bob was 30 years old, 6-foot-2 inches tall and very athletic. With rippling forearm muscles and shoulder-length blond hair, he made a striking figure—even more so because of the obvious psoriasis all over his body. "I've got Agent Orange poisoning," he told me on his first visit to my office at Elmendorf Air Base in Anchorage, Alaska, where I lived and practiced in the late 1970s, after my residency. (By the way, I am not violating patient confidentially; all this became a matter of public record; keep reading)

"It looks like psoriasis to me," I replied.

"Doc, it's Agent Orange from Nam," he said, his voice beginning to take on a threatening tone. He told me he had served in the Special Forces in Viet Nam and Laos, and that's where he had been exposed to the toxin. I thought to myself, if he has Agent Orange poisoning, why did it take 20 years to show up? He had no evidence of chloracne—the severe pocking of the skin that the Premier of the Ukraine, Mr. Viktor Yushchenko, suffered when his soup was poisoned with the similar compound, dioxin.

After thoroughly examining Smokey Bob's skin, I noted he had typical psoriasis covering half his body surface. It flared after a strep throat, which is the classic trigger factor. A throat culture confirmed strep, and a skin biopsy was diagnostic of psoriasis. When I showed Smokey the biopsy report of psoriasis—not Agent Orange poisoning—he acted defiantly, and glared at me with a sinister look that made my backbone shiver. On the other side of my desk, he was getting so hot under the collar I could swear he was breathing fire. Was smoke actually coming out of his ears? That's when he secretly earned from me the nickname "Smokey." With his body language and evil tone of voice, he had me feeling defensive and vulnerable. He raised his voice so loudly that my trusty Air Force Corpsman Sergeant Canny Brown could hear the ruckus from outside the room, and buzzed me on the intercom: "Doctor Naversen, are you okay?"

I replied to Canny, "We are cool." I secretly hoped that we were in fact cool. Smokey could not accept my diagnosis of psoriasis. I was lucky enough to have trained at the prestigious University of California, San Francisco, dermatology program, where I was chief resident. I had recently passed my rigorous dermatology boards that had required me to travel from Alaska all the way to Chicago to take the exam. I felt like I was a crackerjack physician ready to cure the world of its dermatology ills. Despite my training, and despite being armed with high hopes and good-will for all dermatology patients and my fellow man, I felt that I'd come up against a solid brick wall when Smokey repeated, "Doc, it's Agent Orange poisoning."

So I did what I do very well: I played dumb. "Smokey, I'm not the only dermatologist in the great state of Alaska. Why don't you get a second opinion downtown in Anchorage?" (I said this knowing that I was the only board-certified dermatologist in the state.)

Since Smokey was "acting out" and displayed deeply smoldering feel-ings and delusions, I consulted a local psychiatrist. "Carla, I need help. Can you see this gentleman ASAP?" I was very happy when she did. She called me the next day after an interview with him and said, "Doug, I have bad news for you. You are number one on his hate list."

"Bummer," I thought. "That guy makes me really nervous." I actually feared bodily harm.

The next day, the psychiatrist called me again. "Doug, I have some good news for you. You're only number two today—I'm number one on Smokey's hate list!"

"Yes, Carla, thank you, that really makes me feel good!" I envisioned in my dreams that Carla and I would both go down, bludgeoned to death by the blond, athletic, axe-murderer who now hated both of us more than anyone else on the planet.

Smokey Bob continued to disrupt the hospital routine by offending other patients and the hospital staff. Carla discharged him, leaving both his psoriasis and paranoia untreated, since he dismissed all suggestions for medical care. He didn't feel he needed anything other than to rid his body of Agent Orange intoxication.

Several weekends later, I was pulling my 12-hour emergency room shift as medical officer of the day, a duty I served one night a month. Although I was a full-time practicing dermatologist, I had an internal medicine background. I had worked in lots of emergency rooms, so I felt I could handle most problems that might come through our doors. I took a call from Valdez, Alaska, where the pipeline flows 800 miles from Prudhoe Bay to its terminus in this charming port town. I was told that an active duty Air Force Tech Sergeant had been murdered when arguing with another camper over a camping spot! The excited voice on the phone described the suspect and the crime clearly; a tall, muscular blond-haired man had pulled out a gun and he had shot the sergeant dead. It was none other than our Smokey Bob!

Carla and I were number one and number two on his hit list, and he had just blown away number three. What would he do to *us*? A massive manhunt failed to collar Smokey. Fortunately, I had scheduled vacation time to take my family back to Dayton, Ohio, to visit my mother, Thelma, and my father, Enoch. I couldn't have been happier to jump on the plane to the lower 48. Smokey wouldn't find me in Huber Heights, Ohio.

Two weeks later, when I returned to the Great Land, I learned that I was safe. The murderer had slipped into Anchorage and holed up with his girlfriend. When she figured out what had happened, she ratted him out to the police. Smokey was tried and found innocent of murder by reason of insanity. He was sent to the Midwest for a very long stay in a prison for the criminally insane.

I learned from this case that, try as I might, it is impossible to cure every skin condition. Sometimes, the patient's belief system is their worst enemy. I'm just glad more people didn't get hurt (especially Carla and Naversen!).

Chapter Six: 30 Hours Without Food

My alarm clock reverberated at exactly 6:00 a.m. on July 1, 1973. I woke with a start. I hadn't slept well that night. For you see, I was now an internal medicine resident. Get up and cure the world of its medical ills, Dr. Naversen!

I ate a quick breakfast; I kissed my lovely wife Jane and my son Nathan, and I said, "Goodbye. I don't know when I'll be back. Don't wait up for me." Then off to Big Willy I headed—also known as Wilford Hall, U.S. Air Force Medical Center, San Antonio, Texas.

Promptly at 8:00 a.m., our hospital commander, a Brigadier General in the U.S. Air Force, welcomed and briefed us. "Doctors, you will learn more this year than any other year in your entire life. You will work harder than any year in your entire life. And be sure to keep your sense of humor." He was right on the first two counts, and I tried to keep my sense of humor during the next twelve months of grueling medical residency.

During my first month at Wilford Hall I was assigned to the cancer ward, known as hematology/oncology. We took care of sick and dying cancer patients who had been transported from all over the world. Our hope was that we could cure their cancer with surgery, radiation therapy or chemotherapy. Unfortunately, if we saw our patients later on in their disease course, cures were a lot harder to get. Death and dying were all too common that month. It was pretty heady stuff to be involved in their care. If Dr. Naversen, straight out of the three-year M.D. program at Ohio State Medical School, screwed up, he could kill some of his patients. Was he ready?

As fate would have it, I was the resident on call that night. I found a very brief moment to call Jane, "Hi Jane. The good news is, you don't have to fix me dinner tonight. I am on call. I love you and Nathan very much. The bad news is, I won't be home until tomorrow night."

The noon lunch went by in a flash. I was too busy curing and saving patients to be hungry. Besides, I had rounds with our professor at 1:00 p.m. I boned up on the individual patients, problems and their cancers instead of sneaking a lunch break.

Our afternoon clinic and rounds were fruitful—our staff doctor recommended ideas and medical studies that might solve a patient's problem or give them some relief from their cancer pain. Then dinner rolled around. I was far too busy evaluating a sick patient with a temperature of 103° to be concerned about food. As I worked through the evening, my epinephrine levels were surging.

We had a special midnight supper for the doctors and staff on call that night. It went from 11:00 p.m. to 12:30 a.m. It was a good time to sip on coffee to stay awake, and to wolf down a stuff-gut omelet. I could reflect on the day's activities with the corpsmen, nurses and doctors. Maybe I could get some advice on my difficult patients from the senior residents on call.

As I was sitting down in the hospital cafeteria getting ready to take my first bite of food since early that morning, I started salivating in keen anticipation of taking in a mouthful of bacon and eggs. Suddenly, the "code blue" sounding through the hospital pierced the air. We found there was electricity instantly running through all of our doctor spines. A patient on our ward had suffered a cardiac arrest.

I sprinted down the hospital corridor. As the doctors and nurses administered CPR, I found myself in the middle of it. After 40 minutes of CPR, we knew we had lost him. We tried multiple electric shocks to the chest wall, along with just about every cardiac drug in the crash cart, but all to no avail. He had been a chronically-ill, brittle-heart patient with multiple medical problems, including internal cancer. I figured it was just his time to go.

It was now 12:30 a.m. The cafeteria was now closed—no midnight snacks for Dr. Naversen.

I slept a few fitful hours in the doctor's lounge that night. Just as I would snuggle down for the night, a minor emergency would wake me. "Dr. Naversen," the nurse would sound, "we need you down on 2 West." The night's darkness passed quickly. I momentarily contemplated eating breakfast before another side of me chimed in. "Fool, what are you thinking? You have medical rounds at 8:00 a.m., and you need to bone up on your 12 patients!" And that's what I did.

Ward rounds lasted from 8:00 to 9:30 a.m. All the new residents, senior attendings and physicians were learning about their new patients. After all, it was now July 2, and a new day was upon us.

Breakfast quickly came and went. Unfortunately, I did not partake of the feast. I vaguely contemplated lunch at high noon, now just two-and-a-half hours away. At about 11:00 that morning, I started shaking; I hadn't eaten in about 30 hours! My adrenaline and fear had substituted for food. I tried to walk quickly, but I must have staggered like a zombie down the stairs to the dining room for lunch. I definitely felt hypoglycemic.

The ensuing meal was one of my top feasts of all times. After lunch, I savored a great cup of coffee. I tried to enjoy the moment of quiet and sustenance, for I knew it would not last.

Then it was back to the ward. I worked feverishly that afternoon to get my work done so that my patients would be taken care of. I didn't want to work late, but on the other hand, I didn't want to be one of those docs that leave the hospital abruptly at 5:00 p.m. with his patients crumping. The new doctor on call, who doesn't know the patients as well as me, is then stuck with them. Luckily, I got all my patients squared away, and I went wearily home, trying to stay awake as I got on the freeway.

Driving home in my hot 1969 yellow Camaro named "Pearl," I nearly did fall asleep. The only thing keeping me awake must have been the thought of seeing my wife after my two-day ordeal in the hospital as a newly-anointed medical resident.

Jane fixed me a wonderful dinner, and I remember briefly playing with my son Nathan. At about 8:00 p.m., I feel asleep on the couch. Maslow's physiologic hierarchy of needs was right-on. We need food, drink, sleep and shelter before we ascend to that plane of self-actualization. Sweet love would just have to wait for another day.

The next 12 months would be a challenge. I learned more in that one-year than at any other period in my life. But why are we wasting all this time on internal medicine? Bring on the good stuff—dermatology!

Chapter Seven:
Hansen's Disease

I had always wanted to diagnose a fresh case of Hansen's disease, also known as leprosy. It is one of the most feared and reviled of all human diseases. Although we think of it as a tropical disease, its cause was discovered in Norway in 1874. The great Dr. Armauer Hansen identified the rod-shaped mycobacterium that caused the condition. In his honor, leprosy was named after him.

Since my parents were born in Norway, I have had a special fascination with Hansen's disease. I'd studied with Dr. Paul Faisal and the excellent Dr. Axel Hoke in San Francisco at the old Marine Hospital (United States Public Hospital), which actually had its own leprosy wing. While a resident at U.C. San Francisco, I was able to travel to Carrville, Louisiana, to work with world experts and researchers at the largest leprosarium in the United States. I learned that the bacteria that causes the disease is mycobacteria leprae. That is a cousin of mycobacteria tuberculosis. They are both transmitted by airborne droplets and nasal secretions. Fortunately, the bacteria that causes leprosy is not highly contagious like chicken pox or the common cold. However, prolonged, intimate contact with family members or friends can result in infection. If one parent has it, there is a 20-percent chance the children will get it. If both parents are involved, there is a 50-percent chance.

The nine-banded armadillo is the only animal in nature that carries the leprosy mycobacterium. Drug studies done on such infected animals gives us hope in finding new and better medicines for treating this scourge. By the way, would you rather study an armadillo, an infected worker, a child, or your grandmother?

My delightful partner, Dr. Jeri Mendelson, trained in Arkansas. She discovered some patients who cooked up "road kill armadillo," and guess what—they got leprosy from the animals! So leave road kill for the buzzards.

Fast forward to Medford, Oregon, circa 1988. It was late on a Friday afternoon in my new office on Siskiyou Boulevard. I had suite B and my good friend and plastic surgery colleague, Dr. Ron Worland, had suite A. Ron caught me all alone—the staff had left for the day, and my feet were propped up on the desk as I signed off a large stack of charts.

"Doug, I want you to come over to my office and see a case of "granulomatous rosacea.""

That's not a bad diagnosis for a plastic surgeon to come up with, I thought. "Sure Ron, let's go," I said. "If you were two minutes later, I would have already been out of here."

Now in suite A, I spotted Jonathan across the room, I had two emotions. The first was of total elation. Here was my first case of lepromatous leprosy in the flesh. He had leonine facies, loss of the lateral eyebrows, and nodules on his ears and torso. Because of my training in San Francisco and Louisiana, I knew his appearance was classic for Hansen's disease. I felt like the surfer who had just caught the perfect wave—it is over, there is nothing left to live for! I am in Nirvana! My second emotion was that of sympathy, sadness, and profound despair. Before me sat a fellow human being who had contracted a potentially fatal disease that could scar and disfigure him for life. It would provoke revulsion from friends and family. He could lose his job as a pear-picker living in southern Oregon. He would probably be deported back to Mexico. If you think you have problems, think how Jonathan felt when I told him he had leprosy. His English was only slightly better than my Spanish, but I was able to educate him about the nature of his condition. I told him we needed to do a skin biopsy, obtain blood work, collect urine studies and obtain a chest x-ray. His condition was apparent to me on his skin and lymph node exam, but knowing the natural history of the disease, I realized the leprosy undoubtedly peppered the whole inside of his body. We had to document the extent of his internal involvement.

I got him free medicine from the U.S. Public Health Service Hospital in Louisiana, and we started him on a triple cocktail of B663 (lamprene), dapsone, and rifampin. I enlisted Dr. Rick O'Toole, an infectious disease doctor, to follow him with me. Although I felt confident we could control and cure him, various allergic reactions and toxic drug side effects could be triggered as the leprosy mycobacteria were destroyed inside his body. (For example, if Jonathan had been a Jenny—a female instead of a male—and if Jenny had been taking birth control pills, the rifampin would have increased the metabolism of the hormone so rapidly that if she was sexually active, the woman would have a high probability of getting pregnant.)

To make matters worse, some months later, I got a call from Immigration and Naturalization. They wanted to deport Jonathan since he was potentially contagious to other Americans. I said, "If you deport Jon back to Mexico, he is dead meat. He will die." Amazingly I&N consented to let him stay in the U.S., as long as he kept up with his medications and medical visits.

I never charged Jonathan a dime, and we got his drugs for free. But I did get paid. He would come in and say, "Dr. Naversen, I'm getting better, but I need more medicine."

I replied, "Jonathan, I'll order more medicine for you from Louisiana. Come back in two weeks with the biggest, juiciest watermelon you can find, and I'll have the triple cocktail ready for you."

Two weeks later Jonathan appeared with the biggest, juiciest watermelon I had ever seen. I never knew where he got his trophy watermelons, but they sure tasted good. We exchanged drugs for melons, and off he went. My wife, Jane, son, Nathan, and two daughters, Laurel and Leina, would devour the flavorful treat. Only when it was consumed would I reveal its true leprous source. "Oh, gross, Dad, I feel sick!" was the usual response. "But big juicy watermelons of the first order were hard to get," I thought. So sure enough next year, I'd trick the family with another Jonathan watermelon.

The other way I got paid was by watching his nodules, lumps and bumps regress. Jonathan was really getting better! His face and chest and skin all over still had lesions, but they were shrinking. If I could get Jon cured of one of the most dreaded of all diseases known on the planet, that would be pay enough.

Jonathan went off medication in 2001, 16 years after I first diagnosed his Hansen's disease. He is cured! His skin biopsies that were initially loaded with "red snappers" on our special Fite stains now are devoid of the mycobacteria. His disfiguring nodules and tumors are gone. He is a good-looking guy after all these years. It was very rewarding for me to help in the cure of his leprosy. We doctors sometimes forget why we got into medicine—to help people and to cure them. We face Medicare regulations, Blue Cross, CLIA, OSHA, the F.D.A., recertification exams, and numerous other regulatory bodies. Doctors are the most over-regulated people in the universe! We often get insurance denials for medically necessary work, but Jonathan is what it is all about—to stomp out skin disease, regardless of whether you get paid. Sometimes you have to step up to the plate and just do the right thing.

Whenever I see a patient here in Medford, Oregon, population 75,000, I feel we can do a great or better job compared with the high-powered doctors in big cities with their big medical centers. We have the personal touch, and we cut to the chase. I feel so lucky to have a job that I would do for free. But people pay actually me money to do it right. Life is good!

Chapter Eight: My First Day
of Medical School

I missed my first day of medical school. From afar in Norway, I wondered, would Ohio State kick me out? Well, I guess I would find out when I got back to Columbus.

How could I miss one of the most important days of my life? Well, it was a mail screw-up.

In the spring of 1970, I was happily in my senior year at the Air Force Academy in Colorado, looking forward to medical school and a few years of civilian life in September. My folks were living near Boston, Massachusetts, but for some reason, Ohio State kept sending my mail to Dayton, Ohio, where the family owned a house. Unfortunately for me, I didn't receive those letters in a timely fashion. Otherwise, I would have known that Ohio State had a new three-year plan. Instead of starting in the fall like every other medical school in the country, we would start on July 1st. Forget summer vacations. We would go "balls to the wall," and the great state of Ohio would have a new crop of badly-needed doctors every three years, instead of every four. "Great plan—*on paper*," I later mused.

Two hours before I was to jump on the plane for a dream trip to Europe, I opened the official letter from Ohio State. It said "Report for medical school promptly at 8 a.m. on July I. Tardiness will not be tolerated." Gulp. "Well, what if am not only tardy, but I don't even show at all?" I questioned.

The devil seized me and I openly blurted out, "No way I'm going to pass up a trip to Germany, England and Norway where I will visit my Viking roots. My parents were both born in Norway, for God's sake. They are not going to take this from me." Instead, I whipped out a quick letter:

Dear Ohio State University School of Medicine,

I will be on a once-in-a-lifetime trip to Europe, and I will not be back in Ohio until July 5th. Could I possibly start on July 5th, not July 1st?

Respectfully yours,
Douglas N. Naversen

Then I jumped on the plane for Europe. The trip exceeded my wildest expectations, racing by faster than a Viking ship in high seas during a maelstrom. Soon, July 5th loomed before me. I would have to face reality. Would I be penalized, would I be so far behind my classmates that I would never catch up, or would I be unceremoniously kicked out?

I wish I had an instant replay of July 1st, 1970, back at Ohio State Medical School that day. But I don't think instant replays had been invented way back then. My good friend and classmate at the USAFA (class of '70) was Mike Ballinger. We studied together in many pre-med classes, and our close-knit group of future air force doctors really bonded.

Mike was to be my roommate at OSU. When I didn't show on the allotted day, he was worried that I would be summarily booted. (Maybe, he realized that if Naversen wasn't there, he would have to pay the rent on the apartment on Stinchcomb Drive all by himself. Or even worse, to get a roommate, he would have to marry that gorgeous, hometown girlfriend of his after all, the very lovely Rhonda from La Rue, Ohio.)

Mike rapidly went through the medical school check-in line, he got his forms, he collected his books and papers, and he quickly hustled off to dump them in his locker. He then ran (not walked) to the back of the line again, this time to save Naversen's butt.

As Mike's turn came again (actually Doug's turn) in the queue, he told the head secretary, "Hi, I'm Doug Naversen, and I am here to register for medical school."

With a triumphant look, the authoritarian Buckeye administrator whipped out my letter. Waving it in the air, she practically shouted for all to hear, "Gee, Mr. Naversen, there must be some mistake. This letter says you are in Europe even as we speak!"

Mike turned five shades of red, and he began sputtering, "I'm sorry, I'm not Doug Naversen. I am really Mike Ballinger. I was just pretending to be Doug Naversen."

The secretary and all within earshot shared hearty guffaws at Mike's expense. He had been nailed to the wall by the efficient assistant. We have already established that assistants like her rule the world.

Because he tried to save my derriere, Mike exposed his human side. What a great guy to cover for me like that! When he related the story to me on July 5th (yes, I did finally make it to Columbus), I nearly split my pants laughing. Would I have done the same for Mike?

When I finally did officially show up at school, as you guessed, I didn't get kicked out of medical school. Ohio State's policy was that if you were good enough to get in, you were good enough to graduate. They would bend over backwards to help you become a doctor. Lucky for me!

I collected my books and filled out the forms. I took the psychological tests as requested. And yes, I did graduate from Ohio State Medical School in three years.

By the way, Dr. Mike Ballinger practices in the suburbs of Chicago. Amazingly, one year before graduation, he dropped out of medical school for personal reasons. But he is one heck of a veterinarian!

Chapter Nine: Dr. Worland, Stock Picker Extraordinaire

You met my good friend Dr. Worland in a previous chapter. Ron is an experienced plastic surgeon, and he does lots of charitable community service in southern Oregon. He even travels to Mexico every year and operates gratis on the indigent cleft palate kids who have no medical care. But what I really like about Ron is his investing prowess.

One day I wondered to myself, "What medical companies make breast implants?" Would any of them make a good investment for my office retirement plan? Normally I don't like to invest in medical companies if I thought it might influence my prescribing habits. Since I don't do breast augmentation surgery in my office, I felt there was no conflict.

I sought out Ron's nurse Julie. Nurses have great insight on what is good and bad, including medical equipment, supplies, and even medical doctors. Julie exclaimed, "Well, Dr. Naversen, my son is a business major, and he just did a study and found that Mentor Medical is a superior company. They formerly had a 10-percent share of the silicon breast implant market. Now that silicon implants are banned by the F.D.A., and because saline-filled ones are our only option, Mentor now has a 50-percent share of the entire U.S. breast implant market! I believe you could make a killing for your retirement plan if you bought their stock." I thanked Julie for her advice. (By the way, if you are woman who has had silicon breast implants, or if you have a friend or relative who have also had them, the latest studies fortunately do not show dire consequences or autoimmune diseases resulting from the procedure. The general health is the same as age matched controls who did not have breast augmentation surgery.)

I then sought out Dr. Worland. "Ron, I've have been researching it, and I think I will invest in Mentor Medical." Being somewhat impetuous, Ron reached into his desk and immediately pulled out several implants for me to squeeze. "Not bad," I said as I gently caressed both the silicon and the saline-filled implants. The silicon implants felt more natural, but the saline products were the only ones that were routinely available on the market in the United States at that time. They are expensive, and I didn't want to squeeze them too hard and rupture them. Worland would have billed me for the damage.

When I told him about my plan to invest, Ron said, "You're right, Mentor is a great company. I'm buying some!" He picked up the phone, dialed his broker, and blurted out an order: "Buy 500 shares of Mentor at the market."

"Hey, it was my idea!" I said. Here, I had a great stock pick confirmed by an expert surgical nurse and her son the business major, and the man bought it right out from under me. I had visions of a great bull market in Mentor, but by the time I could place my order the stock would have doubled in price. The next day, I too bought some Mentor Medical. I paid a different purchase price than Dr. W., but I figured I just got their too late for the bargain price he got. But I was still happy to own the stock.

One week later, Ron discovered he had mistakenly bought 500 shares of Mentor Graphics, a company based in Portland, Oregon—he did not own Mentor Medical, the great breast implant company. Upon hearing the news, I hastily checked my records. I smiled, for unlike Dr. W., I had purchased the correct stock.

Ron was able to have his order reversed by his broker, but my purchase price was better than his. Unfortunately, for Ron and me, Mentor Medical never did soar in price nor make us rich. It went up a little, and six months later we both sold our shares for a modest profit.

In the meantime, a Japanese company pumped over one hundred million dollars into Mentor Graphics. The Oregon-based company was going gangbusters. The stock was going off the chart. Had Ron stayed with Mentor Graphics, and had he sold at its peak, he would have made a small fortune. I guess sometimes you do better just picking stocks like throwing darts, just like the monkeys do in the *Wall Street Journal*.

Chapter Ten: Dr. Naversen, Stock Picker Ordinaire

Fresh from my experience with Dr. Worland and Mentor Medical, I decided I was no stock market guru. Maybe I would just do something good for a change. My wife was raised in Mentor, Ohio, right on Lake Erie. She had always liked the Cleveland Indians, and she usually got to go to some baseball games every summer on "good student" promos through her school. Even though we now live several thousand miles away from Ohio, in southern Oregon, Jane still follows the Tribe. She longs for another world championship, not seen since Bob Feller and the Indians won the World Series in October, 1948 (the year Dr. Naversen was born).

One October, I heard you could invest in the Indians for five or six dollars a share by buying stock through your broker. I would buy her 100 shares, get the certificate and frame it for her for Christmas. She would love the memento, and it would hang in her kitchen, reminding her of Cleveland and the Buckeye State. To boot, Doug would get big bonus points. Without telling Worland this time, I ordered 100 shares "at the market", and I asked them to please send me the stock certificate.

Just before Christmas, the package arrived. Inside was the certificate No. CI21279, dated December 3, 1998, for 100 class-A common shares of the "Cleveland Indians Baseball Company, Inc., incorporated under the laws of the state of Ohio." The red-and-white certificate showcased Jacobs Baseball Stadium with the green infield and outfield centered in the picture. In addition to the American Flag behind second base, you could see fans in the stands. You could even see multicolored ads touting Shell, Key Bank, Budweiser, MTD, and other businesses.

Since Jane now owned 100 shares of the Tribe, I figured the team would go the way of the Boston Braves, the Washington Senators, and the dinosaurs. Naversen could kiss this investment goodbye. The Indians were doomed. They were definitely heading for the cellar of the American League.

On Christmas Day, Jane absolutely loved the handsome framed certificate I had wrapped for her. Surprisingly, it was her best sentimental present that year. We hung it proudly in the kitchen. Amazingly, despite the Naversen Curse (almost as bad as the one that plagued the Boston Red Sox for decades, after trading Babe Ruth to the New York Yankees), and despite some pretty darned good teams in the late 1990s and early 2000s, the Tribe never did win another World Series. They were just one out from wining the world championship in 1997, when playing the upstart Florida Marlins. The Marlins rallied in the late innings, and won. And in October, 2007, the Tribe had a commanding three to one lead over Boston for the American league pennant. But in a home game in Cleveland, the Ohio team just could not put the Massachusetts club away. Boston swept the next three games to win the pennant, and then swept four from the Colorado Rockies to win another world series.

After owning the stock for what seemed a relatively short time, Jane got a letter in the mail. The owner, Old Man Jacobs, was selling his interests in the Cleveland Indians and in the stadium that bore his name, and did Jane care to sell her hundred shares for $24 each? We thought, why that is a "four bagger." We buy at six dollars and we sell at $24. That is the best stock Naversen ever picked! You know, classic "buy low, sell high" Wall Street stuff. (By the way, Mr. Richard Jacobs bought the team in 1986 for $35 million. He sold in 2000 for $323 million. That is almost a 10 bagger!)

The letter further stated if you wanted the certificate back, just enclose an extra five dollars. They would cancel out the certificate and then mail it back to you. I thought, "All I ever really wanted was the darn stock certificate in the first place." Faster than Bob Feller could fire a fastball to home plate, we sold the stock for a nice long-term capital gain. We paid a few dollars of tax on the gain, but we all have to pay our fair share, don't we! When the cancelled certificate returned in the mail, it went back into the frame, and then we returned it to its rightful place on the kitchen wall.

We have since relegated that wonderful certificate from the kitchen to the pantry to the computer room upstairs. It hangs proudly on the wall, so we can see it daily when we go to check our email. We still have great hopes that the Cleveland Indians will win it all again someday. If not Cleveland, then how about the Cincinnati Reds? And, while we are at it, let's get greedy. How about the Browns or the Bengals take the Super Bowl?

Cleveland just suffered another crushing defeat. LeBron James and the Cavaliers got swept by the San Antonio Spurs in June, 2007, in four games. (The Spurs coach, Greg Popovich, was my classmate from the class of 1970 at the US Air Force Academy.) Cleveland fans, do not give up hope, I suspect LeBron and company will be back.

.

Chapter Eleven: Ten Ways To Remain Loyal To The Most Pathetic Teams In Sports

The Ballad of a Beaten-Down Fan

A special chapter by Bob Albrecht (University of Oregon journalism student, writer for the Medford Mail Tribune, and my friend)

When it comes to sports, no city has it worse than Cleveland.

During 21 years of faithfulness, many bad moments in Cleveland sports have stuck with me like recurring nightmares. There was the time, in 1986, when quarterback John Elway of the Denver Broncos became famous for "the drive" against the Browns, destroying Cleveland's Super Bowl hopes. In 1989, Michael Jordan knocked the Cavs out of the NBA playoffs when he hit "the shot" — a painful moment that Gatorade recently memorialized in a particularly hard-to-watch commercial. Seven years later, Baltimore stole the Browns (literally) and went on to win Super Bowl XXXV. Worst of all, in 1997, manager

Mike Hargrove and closer Jose Mesa of the Cleveland Indians joined forces to gift-wrap the World Series' deciding game for the Florida Marlins.

I'm not a Cleveland fan by choice. Honestly, who would choose such torture? The burden of rooting for these teams was placed upon me at an early age. I blame it on my Gramps. He is from the great state of Ohio, born and raised in Geneva, 50 miles from Cleveland. In high school he would cut class and head into the city to watch the Indians play. Although he moved his family out west a few years before I was born, he passed his sports allegiances onto me. Maybe it isn't his fault. Perhaps my fate in sports purgatory was pre-ordained.

Despite all of the pain, I've remained loyal. As my reward, I've learned how to deal with heartbreaking losses the same way a young child recovers from the loss of a puppy. Now, after surviving 21 years of sports ineptitude, I'd like to offer my services to anyone having a hard time dealing with his or her own beloved and struggling sports team. Here they are—ten ways you can remain loyal to even the most pathetic franchises in sports.

1. *Buy lots of apparel.* I probably own over $2,000 worth of Cleveland t-shirts, hats, sweatshirts, and other paraphernalia. If I were to give up on my favorite teams, I'd need a lot of new clothes. If multiple afternoons of shopping in some overcrowded mall to replace an entire wardrobe aren't sufficient incentive to stay on track and keep believing, I don't know what is.

2. *Show your allegiance.* During the Cavs' ill-fated 2004 playoff run, a couple of members of the team grew "playoff beards." In their honor, I did too. Jessica Simpson's probably capable of growing more facial hair than I am, but I tried. At least this way, when the Cavs went down, I went down with them.

3. *Find teams to hate.* Every year, when the Indians are inevitably knocked out of the playoffs, I'm still able to enjoy baseball's postseason. Why? Because I can root against the Yankees, the team I loathe just as much as I love the Indians. Not only does this hatred nurture and reinforce the love I have for my team, but it keeps me going when they fall into hard times. Rooting for the Yankees would be like rooting for the house

in blackjack—what fun is that? Instead, I choose to wait for my Indians to catch some cards.

4. *Remember those who came before you.* The Boston Red Sox broke an 86-year-old *curse* to win a World Series. If they can do that, anything's possible. I firmly believe that the Indians could take a team of minor league castaways and over-the-hill major leaguers to an American League pennant like they did in the 1989 film *Major League.*

5. *Hope that parity continues.* The three biggest leagues in professional sports are in a rare state of equality. The NFL, for example, is so well-balanced that teams can go from worst to first in a single season. Exhibit A: The New Orleans Saints. One year, they were at the bottom of the league. With a new coach, a new quarterback, and a high draft pick, the next year they finished their season in the NFC Championship game. Repeat after me: "If they can do it, we can do it."

6. *Don't grow up.* This one's important. Through all the losses, I've remained more naïve than a 14-year-old who still believes in Santa Claus. Even with mounds of overwhelming evidence to the contrary, I'm convinced that one of my teams will break through. Unfortunately, this skill is not all that coachable—you just gotta believe.

7. *Use this phrase: "We'll get 'em next year." Repeat.* This expression comes in handy in a number of scenarios: When your team comes tantalizingly close to winning a championship (like the Indians did in '95 and '97); makes a trade or free-agent signing; replaces a bad manager or head coach; or drafts a budding superstar, like the Cavs' LeBron James. Each of these occasions presents fresh hope and optimism for seasons ahead.

8. *Focus on the upside.* When you root for a historically-bad franchise, you have to find the silver lining. Take the 2002 Cavaliers—they were awful. But the reward for their ineptitude was the number-one pick in the NBA draft. "Ladies and Gentlemen, with the first pick in the 2003 NBA Draft, the Cleveland Cavaliers select…LeBron James!" That moment ranks among the greatest in my life. All sports fans would have been happy if their team acquired such a star, but I was giddy for weeks.

9. *Force yourself to watch the post-game celebrations of other championship teams.* It can be painful, but it can also serve as a reminder of what you're working toward. Seeing other fans enjoy a championship will only

make you crave victory that much more—and make it that much sweeter when your team finally takes home the trophy.

10. *Find a bond that ties you to the franchise.* This one is different for everyone. For me, the thought of celebrating a championship win with my Gramps is enough to keep me going. The only problem — he's not getting any younger. You're on the clock, Cleveland.

Beyond these pointers, I'd like offer one last line for every tortured fan to live by: "All good things in life, are worth waiting for." Or so I'm told.

Chapter Twelve: Gang Tattoos

The 17-year-old lad walked awkwardly into my office. He wore black Chuck Taylor Converse All-Star high-top tennis shoes. The handcuffs and leg irons slowed him down greatly. The accompanying guard kept a sharp eye on the youth. The juvenile delinquent teenager was our first patient from the Rogue Valley Youth Correctional Facility in nearby Grants Pass, Oregon. He had a number of gang tattoos on his skin, and he wanted them off.

How did I have the unique opportunity to help Nathan better his life at no financial cost to himself? One afternoon a few weeks prior, I'd gotten a call from his father. He related how his son was now incarcerated, and he had become a model inmate. He wanted to better himself, and that included ridding himself of multiple, visible gang tattoos on his hands and arms—he knew he would be unemployable because of them. He had three tattooed "dots" on his right hand, the number 13 on his left forearm, and an "Irish Pride" tattoo on his elbow. A prominent skull-and-bones tattoo disfigured his right biceps.

I have talked to local police in Southern Oregon about gangs and tattoos. They don't really know how much gang activity is in our community. But tattoos can be tip-offs of gang activity, particularly the "three dots" and the number "13." The 13th letter of the alphabet is "M," which stands for a Mexican gang. (It also stands for marijuana.) The police explained to me that a Hispanic gang based in L.A. broke off and moved to Las Vegas. From there, some of the gang members moved to Southern Oregon. Since only 10 percent of the population here is Hispanic, the gang recruited Caucasians to the group.

Watch out for "Irish" and "Irish Pride" tattoos as well. Apparently the Irish and Hispanic gangs in the inner city areas respect each others turf. In honor of that, the Hispanics often anoint their bodies with Irish tattoos. In prosperous east Medford some years ago, exactly 13 houses were graffitied with spray paint and Irish tattoos on the doors and sides of houses. The *Medford Mail Tribune* reported the incident, but did not mention the association with gang activity. You and I know that "13" and "Irish" insignias are hallmarks of gang activity.

Nathan's dad loved his son, and wanted the very best for him. He started crying as he related his son's circumstances, and if the lad could just get those darn tattoos off, he might have a chance for a normal post-penitentiary life. I told him we would do whatever we could for his son. At Dermatology and Laser, we are blessed with nine cutting edge lasers that will vaporize tattoos without leaving a scar. However, we couldn't help a patient who did not voluntarily choose to have the tattoos removed.

Nathan's crude amateur tattoos responded nicely to the laser treatments, and he was the first graduate of our "Dermatology and Laser Associates of Medford Last-Chance Program." Nathan would agree to leave gang activity forever, and in return we would use the most modern lasers to cure his skin. If we could help get a wayward youth back into the mainstream of life, we would be doing our job. We issued him a diploma, we took a handsome photo of his face, and his warden placed both in the permanent file at the correctional facility.

Our gang tattoo program has greatly expanded now to include non-incarcerated patients. With the good help of Nancy Payne and Jackson County Community Service, we screen the candidates. If they have gang-related tattoos in visible places, such as on the hands, arms, face, lower legs or neck, they are eligible for the program. Swear words and other objectionable marks that would cause a gang fight with a rival gang, or preclude employment in a local business, also qualify. The tattooed candidates do

32 hours of community service before we ever see them. They can do this for any of 120 non-profit, charitable organizations in Jackson or Josephine Counties here in Oregon, or in Siskiyou County in Northern California.

When we see them at Dermatology and Laser, we do their consult for free. For appropriate candidates, we will laser their tattoos at no charge. For every session, we bill them 10 hours of community service, so the three-county area gets thousands of hours of public service. They can pick up trash along the local interstate I-5, they can work in the library, and they can mow and weed-eat in local cemeteries. It may take one to six sessions to cure the tattoos.

I have found that if we do these laser sessions without charging a patient in cash or in volunteer labor, the patient does not value it. But, if they pull weeds, mow grass or work hours at the Access Food Share warehouse aiding the poor and hungry, they appreciate their treatment all the more.

If your son or daughter has such a tattoo, or if they have a profanity emblazoned on their skin, there is a problem. Talk to them. Be a parent. Be empathetic and supportive. Get them in for counseling. Salvage his or her life before it is too late. A violent death, suicide, incarceration, drugs, alcohol addiction or dropping out of school may become painful realities for your child.

But tattoo regret is not limited to teenagers and twentysomethings. We had the opportunity to treat an older gentleman named Brett, who was in his late thirties. Brett appeared to be 20 years older than his stated age. He had obviously lived a hard life. He also had a noticeable, large teardrop tattoo on his right cheek. A teardrop symbolizes profound depression, for a loved one has been murdered. If the teardrop has been filled in with India ink, the murder has been avenged. It dawned on me when I saw him: You are looking directly at a murderer!

But Brett was much more than that. He related to me that his brother had been murdered. While in a Michigan penitentiary, in the laundry room, he had killed the convict who had taken out his little brother. Brett was ultimately discharged from the prison, but a good civilian job was tough to obtain with the disfiguring tattoo on his face. Although he was employed when I first saw him, he worked as a short-order cook in the humid bowels of a sweaty restaurant kitchen without air conditioning. He wanted to better himself. (By the way, ethical tattoo artists do not tattoo anyone's face.) After just a few sessions—crude amateur tattoos respond best to lasers—his large black tattoo was now gone, and Brett has other options in his life.

I gained more perspective on tattoos after treating a female prison guard from Pelican Bay in Crescent City, California. This is a penitentiary for the worst of the worst. Al Capone would have gone there if he was still alive. Even Charles Manson did time there. Erika sported a "Pelican Bay Prison tattoo" on her right upper chest. She bonded with her tattoo, and so did we at DLAM. Remember, if you like your tattoo, so do we. If you don't like it, we don't like it either. That is when we fire up our fleet of lasers.

Erika related her perceptions of jailhouse tattoos. There is no autoclave for prisoners, so their needles are easily contaminated with bacteria and viruses if they tattoo themselves or a fellow inmate. She would give them alcohol wipes to use on their skin before and after the tattoo was placed, and the convict would also use it to clean the needle. Unfortunately, isopropyl rubbing alcohol does not prevent the transfer of hepatitis B, hepatitis C and HIV (the AIDS virus). Later in life, even if discharged from prison after having paid their debt to society, the hepatitis virus could destroy their liver and cause an agonizing death. Getting a tattoo in prison is truly one of the worst gambles a convict can take.

Chapter Thirteen: The Mighty Rogue River

We are blessed with three great rivers in southern Oregon. The Applegate, the Illinois and the mighty Rogue are wonderful for fishing, swimming, boating, rafting and just having fun. With its wild and scenic designation, the lower Rogue is the most famous of the three. It is so incredibly beautiful that many motion pictures and TV shows have used the river as a backdrop. As far back as 1954, George Montgomery and Martha Hyer starred in *The Battle of Rogue River*, fighting Indians along the riverbank. John Wayne filmed *Rooster Cogburn* because of its riparian splendor. I once saw an old episode of the hit TV show *Route 66* filmed near Grants Pass, Oregon, starring Joey Heatherton in her cinematic debut. Meryl Streep and Kevin Bacon filmed whitewater scenes from *A River Wild* there. And remember when Butch Cassidy and the Sundance Kid were relentlessly hunted by the law? They escaped capture by—you guessed it—jumping into the Rogue River at Hellgate Canyon. Even the American military now uses the Rogue to train their whitewater river combat teams.

One cold May day, I discovered just how mighty the Rogue River really is.

On that day, six rafts launched from Grave's Creek, at the beginning of the "wild and scenic" section. By taking the three-day, two-night trip in

May, we could depart anytime, no permits required. In the summer, you needed to mail in a request for a permit and send in a non-refundable check, and you usually weren't successful in getting one.

We were going to have a wonderful wilderness experience. Never mind that I'd read in the *Medford Mail Tribune* that the river was running at 10,000 cubic feet per second. The previous September, I ran the river at one-twentieth that flow. "No problem," I thought. "We are river men." Besides, our float trip party consisted mainly of doctors and other medical professionals.

In my raft was a crackerjack podiatrist named Dr. Pat Code. One time in his office, he "laid on the hands" and cured the plantar fasciitis plaguing the soles of my feet. He was my next-door neighbor, and we'd always had fun on our adventures.

As we began our float down the Rogue River, we didn't have a care in the world. The riverbanks were beautiful, and we enjoyed unique views of the hills and mountains surrounding us as we negotiated each bend and turn. There was no easy highway access in this remote section. We were bound to see deer, river otters, turtles, osprey, bald eagles, king-fishers, and my favorite bird, the majestic blue heron. We were likely to spot black bears, and if we were lucky, maybe even an elusive cougar.

Zane Gray, in his heyday, had a cabin on the Rogue River and wrote some of his famous western sagas there. When we got further down-stream, we could take a rest stop at his cabin on the starboard side of the river. Although he had long ago passed on, Gray's cabin still stands, and it was well maintained by the heirs to Levi Strauss. In addition to the lodge, we knew we would be passing the exact sites of some of the bloodiest battles of the Indians wars in the 1800s.

As Pat and I drifted along, enjoying the view, we noticed a weather front moving in. Gray clouds grew more sullen by the minute. The skies soon became completely overcast, rain was threatening and a chilly wind blasted the bow of our 13-foot inflatable raft. Pat was at the helm rowing easily, while I acted as an unwitting (dimwitted?) windbreak for him as I sat in the bow while the waves constantly splashed and chilled me. The other rafts were downstream from us as we cluelessly drifted in last position. Aside from the marginal weather and the high river flow, we had high expectations for fun. Adventure and camaraderie was what it was all about. Why, we are Oregonians. We'd take whatever the river could give us, we'd laugh, and then we would spit it back out again.

As it happened, the spitting-it-out part was not far from the truth.

Pat interrupted my meditation with nature by suddenly blurting, "Doug, you are the greatest dermatologist in the world."

"Pat, it is nice of you to say that," I replied.

Then Pat said, "Doug, loan me $200 right now."

I said, "Pat, are you crazy? We are in the middle of the Rogue River on a float trip. Why do you need $200?"

"Just give it to me, Doug!" he snapped. So I pulled 10 crisp Jacksons out of my pocket, and I carefully handed them over to Pat so the wind would not whip them overboard into the rapidly-flowing river.

Not 30 seconds after he put the bills in his wallet, I said, "Pat, there is a big rock ahead. Go left." But Pat went right. I felt my pulse quicken. We were at Tyhee Falls. Although not in the class of Rainie Falls, the Coffee Pot and Blossom Bar—three of the river's notoriously fierce sections—some experienced river guides felt this deceptive riffle could be the trickiest section of the wild and scenic Rogue.

Suddenly I was ejected from the bow of our inflatable boat, catapulted by the sudden force of the rapids pounding on our raft. I felt my body being propelled as if in slow motion through the air as I screamed out, "Sheeeiiitt!" Just before I splashed into the cold, cold water, I thought, I'm sure glad I have a good life vest on. I bobbed up to the surface, and although I didn't see Pat, I instantly started swimming for the left bank of the river. Suddenly, I saw my bright red dry bag floating by on top of the water. It contained my wallet and my valuables. "Do I want my wallet or my life?" I instinctively thought. I let it float on by and I kept swimming.

Next, the devil really began testing me. Out of the corner of my eye, I saw bobbing on the river's surface my bag of freshly made brownies, thoughtfully prepared the night before by my wife. As it cruised by, I thought, "Doug, let them go." I guessed I would never savor a bite of them, and I was right. (I later heard the rafts men downstream found them to be quite a tasty snack.)

After what seemed like an eternity, I finally got to the shore, looking somewhat like a drowned rat. I was shivering violently. The sky was overcast, and even if the sun had been shining, I was on the riverbank in the shadows of tall trees, so I never would have felt the warmth of the rays anyway. Suddenly I spotted Pat for the first time, out in the water. Blood was gushing down his forehead. He wasn't swimming. The Rogue River was rapidly powering him down to the next set of rapids below, where he would be helpless in his dire condition.

Pat had been knocked unconscious when his head connected with the oarlock. He must have spun around and around in a vicious whirlpool. If not for his life vest, he would have been steelhead bait.

I screamed at him, "Pat, start swimming! Kick!"

I felt a chill go up and down my spine when he muttered, "Doug, keep talking to me." I knew at that moment he was in serious trouble. He was clearly hypothermic and bleeding, and maybe he had significant head trauma. He still wasn't swimming. With the other rafts far downstream, they could give us no help. Naversen and Code were left alone to face the wrath of the cold, gray, churning, boiling river.

I shouted encouragement to Pat as he was swept downstream. I had to run along the riverbank to stay up with him. If I would have tried to swim, I never would have reached him in time, as he was caught up in the powerful current in the center of the river surging onto the next set of rapids.

I had just purchased a new pair of Nike Air Deschutes sandals, which fit like a glove. I would often raft without shoes for the freedom and comfort, but that day I'd slipped the sandals on. Without them, I would have slowly hobbled through the stickers and brambles and rocks. There is no way I could have stayed up with Pat unless I had been in a full sprint along the river bank, wearing those Air Deschutes.

Pat began kicking a little and struggling through the frigid water, and eventually came within 10 yards of the bank. I waded into the chilly water, stumbling over the many rocks hidden beneath the river's surface. I lunged for him, and luckily, snagged him.

Once ashore, Pat shivered violently from hypothermia, with a big gash on his scalp that was gushing blood. We were all alone at the base of a cliff. Pat told me, "Doug, I saw nothing but stars, and all I could think of was my two kids, Doug and Caitlin."

We needed to get downstream, and we needed to get help fast. But the river's edge was thick with trees, bushes and rocks, and was nearly impassable. In our party happened to be a neurosurgeon, Dr. Jeff Louie. If I could just get him to Jeff, I felt Pat would okay.

Pat tottered up the steep hill we needed to climb to make our way out of this mess. It was dark in the shadows of the trees and the cliffs as we walked through the woods, and we were never as cold as at that moment. Pat was unsteady of gait; he was still reeling from the head gash, the blood and the near drowning. As I looked down from the cliff we had just ascended, I thought, "With this rocky footing, Pat may not make it." But I kept my mouth shut, and we kept grunting and toiling, each step seemingly more laborious than the one before.

As we slowly made our way on the rocks, I yelled positively, "We are going to make it! You will be fine. Just keep on moving." Although it seemed like hours before we made it downstream, it was probably only 30 minutes since the accident. We didn't know why the other boaters hadn't found us yet. As it turned out, we took the high road in the cliffs, and they took the low road along the river. They had punched through the brush and the trees along the riverbank. They missed us since we were 100 feet directly above them. Finally, we stumbled into the makeshift rafting camp. I was never so happy to see rafts and friendly faces.

We stripped off Pat's shirt and dried him off as he shivered on the sandy beach. Dr. Louie examined Pat and placed a very professional field dressing on his head. We strapped Pat to the front of Dr. Fred Nora's raft, and Fred transported him to the Marial Lodge downstream, with the rest of us floating nearby.

Pat said it was mighty cold as waves broke over the bow of the boat and constantly soaked his body, a body already depleted of energy by the near-tragedy upstream. Despite being propelled downstream at 10,000 cubic feet per second, it still took us one very long hour to reach the lodge, and the safety of a hot shower, a warm bed and a dry roof over our head. We put on dry clothes and had a family style dinner—all except for Pat. With his head trauma, nothing by mouth was allowed for him until he was medically cleared. It took three long hours for the rescue car, driven by his friend Rose, to wind its way through the narrow back roads and arrive at the lodge.

Since the river was so powerful, we all volunteered to take Pat home. (Perhaps there was a little cowardice in our reputedly-tough group of mountain men?) That way, we wouldn't have to face the Rogue River again tomorrow. Blossom Bar, and the Picket Fence and the Coffee Pot would definitely be a challenge to our nerves. Therefore, pretending to act courageously and with great nobility, I said with authority, "I am Pat Code's best friend and his next door neighbor. I will take him home."

It was Rogue River, one, Doug and Pat, zero. We dropped back 10 yards and we punted.

On the long drive back to Medford, Rose and I talked to Pat and I kept my eye on him. I didn't want him going south on us now. An epidural or subdural hematoma pressing on the brain could be a killer. Rose took us all the way to the hospital, a three-hour drive. Pat was released from Providence Medford Medical Center ER at midnight on what had turned out to be a mighty long day. The scans were all negative, and Pat would be okay. As we checked out of the hospital, he said to me, "Doug, thanks for hauling my carcass out of the water."

I felt lucky to be in the right place at the right time. I knew Pat would have done the same for me.

When Pat had fully recovered from the gash, I started asking him for the $200 I had loaned him 30 seconds before the accident. Since he still had near-total amnesia about the accident, and since his wallet was washed downstream by the rapids, he had no proof of the loan. (Don't tell Pat, but he never told me I was the greatest dermatologist in the world, and I never really loaned him $200).

Twelve months had passed when a coed from the University of Oregon in Eugene called up Pat out of the blue and said, "Are you Pat Code? Have you been murdered?"

Pat replied, "Reports of my death have been greatly exaggerated. Why do you ask?"

"Well, some of us college kids from U. of O. volunteered to clean up the banks of the lower Rogue River." She had found Pat's wallet buried deep in mud. Finding a wallet like that, she suspected foul play. She was ecstatic to learn Pat was still alive. She graciously agreed to FedEx Pat's wallet to his home in Jacksonville, Oregon.

One Saturday afternoon, I heard a loud knock on my door, as Pat came running triumphantly inside. Without saying a word to me, he opened up the moldy wallet. He quickly displayed his credit cards, his driver's license, his business cards and his Blockbuster card. But there was no $200! Pat thought he had nailed me on this one, and he blurted out, "You never really loaned me the $200, did you, you lying piece of Naversen dung?"

I looked at the empty wallet and I calmly replied, "Pat, that starving college kid stole your $200." And can you believe it, the man still hasn't paid me my $200 to this very day!

Chapter Fourteen: The Seven-Year Allergy Shot

As I walked into room Number 2, Geri sneezed violently three times in a row. "I am miserable with hay fever. I need another seven-year shot!"

"A seven-year shot?" I replied quizzically.

"Yes, doctor, the first allergy shot I got lasted seven whole years. I probably did not sneeze more than three times in all those seven years. You can do that for me, can't you?"

"Well, Geri, I assume you had a cortisone shot," I said. "We can use Kenalog injections two or three times a year, if you have severe allergies. Even though it is good stuff, at best, it will wear off after four weeks. But tell me more about your shot."

"Well, I lived in Washington State. My grass allergy in early June was killing me. The doctor did give me a cortisone shot of some sort in the hip. It cured me for all those years."

"Tell me more, Geri," I questioned.

"Well, shortly after the injection, I moved up to Anchorage, Alaska. After seven years, my husband and I moved to southern Oregon. It was then that the shot finally wore off."

I began laughing. "Geri, you didn't have a seven-year shot! You moved to Alaska where they don't have those allergies. There are different grasses, weeds and trees up there. It is too cold for the plants that made you allergic. When you moved back to the lower 48, you were exposed to pollens here in Oregon that are similar to the ones in Washington State. There is no seven-year allergy shot!"

Well, I just saw Geri in the office again today for her annual check. I can't give her the seven-year cure, but we have it down to the one-a-year shot. Since her peak allergic time is only three weeks long, one Kenalog shot seemingly cures her for the year.

Say, if anyone really does have a seven-year allergy shot, please let me know. It would greatly help our patients!

Chapter Fifteen: Medicine the Old-Fashioned Way

Half-way through excising the abnormal mole on Linda's right leg, the office lights went out. A freak daytime thunder-and-lightening storm must have done it. It was early in the morning and still dark outside. The rain and dark clouds covering the gray sky didn't help our vision, either.

Just then, our emergency backup light popped on. It must have been all of one candela of energy. I thought back to when I'd built the office in 1985, and made the mistake of calling this room an operating room. Building codes fired off, and they required us to have this emergency backup light since it was considered an operating room on a par with the fanciest such hospital facility. Seven years later, as the power went off, I was reassured that the light and batteries still functioned. But the unit was so dim it was totally useless!

I flashed back to my childhood, when I saw the movie *Boy Genius* about Thomas Edison. When his mother had to have an emergency appendectomy at night, young Tom went downtown to the local store, broke in, and stole a dozen large, hanging-wall mirrors. By shining the lantern into the mirrors, their country doctor had enough light to proceed with the appendectomy. Tom had saved his mother's life!

Inspired, I spewed forth orders to Sharon, "Get me some mirrors and a flashlight." The resulting light was like a bright beacon. Thank you, Thomas Edison!

"Linda, do you feel comfortable with Sharon and me finishing your surgery?" I asked.

"Go for it, Dr. Naversen. I am having fun," laughed Linda.

Although not like a hospital operating room, we did the best we could with what we had. No whining from us. Fortunately, we had no deep-down bleeders in the inner recesses of the dermis and fat that would require precise visualization. We closed the wound uneventfully. The mole was benign, and Linda ended up with a favorable surgery mark.

Later that morning, the rain had stopped, the sun was out, but still there was no power and no light. There is only so much one can do inside a dermatology office in darkness. What the heck, I thought, let's hold clinic outside beneath the Buckeye tree.

I was reminded of grade school in the late spring, when the weather was beautiful, usually in the 70s and 80s. "Miss Sharp," one of us would inevitably ask, "Could we hold reading class under the oak tree today? It is so pretty outside, and it is so hot and stuffy inside our classroom."

Miss Sharp would reflect for a moment, and then grudgingly say, "Well, okay, just this once." What we students didn't know at time was she wanted to go outside just as much as we did.

Just as the school class met outside that day, so did we hold clinic outside in the courtyard that morning. It wasn't quite in the 70s, more like the high 50s. I examined teenagers with facial acne, housewives with psoriasis of the elbows and knees, and lumberjacks with foot problems. A complete skin exam was difficult. As you know, we do not do "peephole dermatology" here at Dermatology and Laser Associates of Medford. But it was a quiet neighborhood, and we were shielded from peeping Toms on the street by a fence, bushes, and the aforementioned Buckeye tree. The patients didn't mind if we examined their scalp, face, arms, legs, back and abdomen. We did nothing X-rated in these outdoor sessions. An exam of the delicate part of the anatomy would have to wait until we got back into the privacy of our office. My assistant, Sharon, the patients and I actually had more fun outside that day than we would have inside. By mid-morning, we were actually disappointed when the power came back on. "Bummer—let's go back inside, Sharon," I said.

I like to think back how it must have been a century ago, when the horse-and-buddy doctor made his rounds. During the day, he was probably okay with the illumination. At night, he had no bright operating lights, no laser pointers, no batteries and chargers, and no backup emergency power sources. The old docs probably had to squint to see that rash or those bad tonsils. Don't even consider emergency abdominal surgery unless you are operating on Thomas Edison's mother.

It is easy to get caught up in the world's problems, but we have much to be thankful for with modern advances: new technology, new drugs, biologicals, new surgical procedures, and new medical and laser breakthroughs. But that morning, I kind of felt like an old-time, horse-and-buggy doctor.

Chapter Sixteen: Hives

Angela bitterly complained of itchy welts on her skin. Whenever she took a hot shower, got in an argument or exercised, her skin would flare. To make matters worse, she was a newlywed. Whenever she took a hot shower with her husband, her reward was 30 minutes of unbearable itchy hives on her torso, arms and legs. Even worse, whenever she made love to her partner, her climax was blunted, because she knew that the result would be a total-body rash. This dermatology consultation could be a marriage breaker—or maybe, if we were lucky, a marriage saver.

As I listened to Angela's tale, within minutes, I knew she had a less common type of hives known as cholinergic urticaria. Even though I was still a lowly dermatology resident at U.C. San Francisco, secretly, I felt urticaria was my forte. I had assisted Dr. Bill Akers in an in-depth seminar on urticaria held at the yearly American Academy of Dermatology meeting. This may well be the number-one medical meeting in the world, and it is attended by thousands of dermatologists from all the continents.

Angela's hives were a type of physical urticaria, triggered by some activity that would raise her core temperature. It made sense that hot showers, exercise, arguments and sex made her break out. They all quickly raised her core body temperature.

If a patient has one form of physical urticaria, he or she may have another. As I walked Angela outside in a cold, stiff San Francisco breeze on Parnassus Avenue at UCSF, she hived up on her face, ears, neck, hands and arms. But her covered body regions were not affected. This meant that not only did she have cholinergic urticaria, but she also had cold urticaria. While not only a nuisance, this could be fatal! We have all heard stories of strong swimmers who drown in water they should not have drowned in. If they had cold urticaria, jumping into a cold stream, lake or ocean could cause a massive release of histamine. The swimmer could faint in the water, and if someone was not nearby to haul them out, they would drown.

Being the budding scientist I was, I knew about passive transfer of cold urticaria. We could draw some of her blood, spin it down in the centrifuge, decant the straw-colored serum, and inject it into a volunteer's skin. If we were lucky, we could induce cold urticaria in that exact spot!

Not having a list of volunteers, and not having a human experimentation review board available, I decided that I would be the guinea pig. I injected Angela's serum into the skin of my forearm. Thirty minutes later, I held an ice cube on the injected site on my skin for five minutes. Sure enough, itchy welts swiftly appeared, and I found myself violently scratching my forearm. My experiment was a success—I had passively transferred her hives to my body through her serum.

I guess I was lucky. This type of testing is rarely done now. I could have contracted hepatitis B, hepatitis C, or even the dreaded AIDS virus from her serum. But the gods were smiling that day.

Now that we knew what her problem was, how could we help her hives and save her marriage? We decided on disease-modifying behavior. No hot showers or baths—just tepid ones. Angela would exercise in a temperate (not cold) environment, and she would not jog in the hot, humid, summer air. She avoided red wine and alcohol, since they would dilate her surface blood vessels and make her hive-up more readily. She also shunned histamine-releasing foods such as strawberries, shellfish, and medicines containing codeine.

We carefully titrated Angela's dose of anti-histamines. She would take them daily without fail. If we could get the anti-histamine to bind to the receptor sites in her blood vessels and her skin before the heat or the cold stimulated her mast cells (allergy cells) to degranulate, the histamine generated would wash downstream without causing hives. If the chemical could not glue onto a receptor site, the histamine's power to cause itching and welts would dissipate. That would be great for her—no hives.

There are many anti-histamines out there. Benadryl (diphenhydramine) was the first one on the market, circa 1934. It is over-the-counter and it is effective, but it can also knock you out. Take it a half-hour before bedtime, and by the time it kicks in, you are sound asleep. It only lasts four to six hours, so it must be taken four times a day. It shouldn't be taken before a drive, or you might fall asleep at the wheel.

Atarax (hydroxyzine) is my favorite sedating anti-histamine. (Sedating ones were all we had in the old days.) It comes in 10, 25, 50 and 100 mg doses. I have seen some people get goofy and lethargic on only one 10 mg pill, and I have seen others that can take 100 mg four times a day and come back and say, "I thought this was supposed to make me drowsy?"

Angela tolerated 10 mg with breakfast, lunch, and dinner. We dosed her up on 50 mg at bedtime. She slept soundly at night, but was able to wake up just fine in the morning. Some people feel like walking zombies in the morning, and that is not good. I like to fine-tune the dose to avoid this side effect.

But what about sex? Should we forbid it? Would our edict be a marriage-killer? Would Angela and her husband even listen to us? Instead, I decided to be proactive. "Angela, intimacy with your husband is a very important part of your marriage. I want you to take Atarax 25 mg by mouth one hour prior to intercourse. Let me know how it works."

One week later, Angela reported, "Dr. Naversen, your treatment plan is working. I get only mild hives after intimacy. There are no major volcanoes on my skin, and sex feels good again."

I was ecstatic she was doing so well. But in case the medications fail, we did have a few aces in reserve. Doxepin has 75 times the anti-histamine powers of Benadryl. A bedtime dose can do wonders for itchy skin.

In the new millennium, we are blessed to have non-sedating anti-histamines. Zyrtec, Claritin, and Allegra have revolutionized therapy. As a matter of fact, Allegra is so safe that a Delta Airline pilot (and brother-in-law of mine) can fly a Boeing 777 across the ocean, even with 300 passengers on his jet, while he is taking Allegra. The secret: it does not cross the blood-brain barrier, so it will not cause drowsiness.

If I would see Angela in my office tomorrow, I would use Allegra 180 mg in the morning and Atarax 25-50 mg at bedtime to curb her symptoms. She would slowly but surely outgrow her tendency to have hives. But even today, patients like Angela do not get better overnight. It might take a decade before the hives burn out. Time is our ally.

One out of five people develop hives at sometime in their life. They usually last just a few days. If they do last for over six weeks, please check in with your dermatologist or allergist for relief of your symptoms.

Chapter Seventeen:
The Heartbreak of Psoriasis

Psoriasis is a genetic disease that arises when the skin tries to replace itself too quickly. Instead of taking a month to form normally, the skin is "turned on" and grows ten times too fast, morphing to the strateum corneum (outer layer) in only three or four days. Since the skin doesn't have time to form properly, it is often itchy and scaly. Three percent of the population will develop psoriasis at some point in their lives.

Most patients with psoriasis have a localized plaque—it looks like dry, red thickened skin topped by abundant white scale—on their scalp, elbows or knees. Psoriasis often develops on the umbilicus and the lower back, too. It may even cause pits and yellow oil spots on the fingernails.

For most patients with psoriasis, the disease is only a minor nuisance, leaving them itchy and perhaps self-conscious. "Dandruff" falls on their clothing, requiring extra time to shampoo, and to clean off the clothing with a brush. It loves to go to bumped or injured skin, so ladies have to be extra careful not to cut their legs when shaving, otherwise psoriasis will erupt in the laceration some weeks later. But in a few rare cases, the disease can be the source of true heartbreak. Let me tell you of three tragedies I've seen in my practice.

Sue was a grade-schooler in Denver, Colorado, in the 1950s. She developed troublesome psoriasis of the scalp, arms, and legs. Her teacher noticed it one day, and Sue was unceremoniously kicked out of school.

A big pow-wow took place the following week. The atmosphere was charged with emotion as the principal, the teacher, and the parents met in the classroom. The mom and dad felt their daughter was being expelled for no good reason. The teacher was fearful of contagion to his students. The principal tried to be the diplomat, and he was proud when he forged a truce between parents and teacher.

Sue would be allowed back in school only if she wore long sleeves and pants (even if it was 80 degrees-plus!). And her desk had to be at least one yard away from the other students' desks. Poor kid—talk about giving someone a complex! Little did they know, psoriasis is not contagious. They must not have consulted with any dermatologists.

Sue returned to school the next week, but she had deep-seated feelings of depression and inferiority from that day on. Those feelings continued well into midlife.

Today, after decades of suffering, Sue has finally come to grips with her disease. She no longer has a complex about it. Her skin is in remission due to modern treatments not available 50 years ago. She even talks to fellow psoriasis sufferers, and she really motivates and inspires them. She is a ball of energy, and she peps them up. Good for her!

Kristina was a self-described hillbilly from Appalachia, born and raised in Kentucky. In the third grade, she erupted with psoriasis all over her body after a strep throat (just like Smokey Bob did in Alaska). The kids ridiculed Kristina so severely that her mom yanked her from school. Kristina suffered both physically and emotionally with the disease throughout her youth. (Her mother noted that the emotional baggage was far worse to deal with than the red, cracked, scaly psoriasis that greeted Kristina day after day.) She never went back to school!

Despite her psoriasis, she developed into a comely lass with a wonderful smile. Some people with a perceived defect compensate by being more compassionate, friendly, and understanding of the misfortune of others. Such was the case with Kristina. She eventually met a great guy who loved her, psoriasis and all. When he joined the Air Force, they were transferred to Elmendorf Air Force Base in Alaska, where I first saw her.

I had started the first hospital-run "tanning salon" in the state, and Katrina's skin soon bronzed as a result of the ultraviolet rays shining from the light box. She developed a nice tan, and her psoriasis involuted for the first time since the third grade. It helped that she was a faithful, compliant patient. She also soaked in oatmeal baths to gently soothe and cleanse her skin. Next she moisturized to fight dry skin. (Dry skin is itchy skin.) She then applied potent but safe cortisone creams to help slow the rapid proliferation of her psoriasis, and to thin the skin back down to its normal thickness. Finally, she used therapeutic shampoos to remove the scaly buildup and to fight the itching.

I was excited for Katrina when she enrolled in night school. She soon succeeded in earning her high school degree! I was struck by her emotional and intellectual growth. It had taken a decade and a half to overcome her childhood misfortune, and yet she had regained her life and transformed into a confident, unashamed young woman right before my eyes. How wonderful it was to see this beautiful woman take her rightful place in the sun. I was very proud of her.

Kathy was a vivacious lady from Rogue River, Oregon. She erupted with severe psoriasis at age 27, which is the average age of onset. She tried every treatment she could find, all to no avail.

Kathy read an article, which said that if you just wrap your skin for two weeks, your psoriasis would go away. She and her husband got excited, raced down to the drugstore, and bought $30 worth of tape that very afternoon. That night, as advised in the article, he wrapped her entire body with sticky, white medical tape. She stayed at home for two full weeks, looking like a mummy. (Since she couldn't bathe, and since the occlusion from the tape made her sweat even more than usual in the hot Oregon summer, in a house devoid of air conditioning, she probably smelled considerably worse than a mummy.) Nonetheless, Kathy and her husband had high hopes. Would her psoriasis be knocked out?

Two weeks later, her husband laboriously, but gently and lovingly, unwrapped the tape. It was very, very, sticky medical tape, and as he stripped it off, she cried out in pain. It was excruciating to watch as her skin and hair came off with the formerly white tape, now soiled from two weeks of use. They were anxious to see her improvement! They both were stunned to see that nothing at all had happened. Her psoriasis was as bad as ever. Adding salt to her wounds, she now had to deal with peeling, painful tape marks and raw, tender skin inflicted by the adhesive.

The final blow came two weeks later. At a tanning salon, she lay on the table. The proprietor spotted her red, peeling, scaling, unsightly skin, and she unceremoniously kicked Kathy out. "Never come back again," she was told. Kathy was totally crushed and devastated. She later told me that this was the absolute low point in her life. "It doesn't get any worse than this," she thought.

After visiting my office in Medford, I prescribed three weekly outpatient sessions with narrow band ultraviolet therapy, for one month, and they proved to be the magic bullet for her skin. The wavelength at 311 nanometers is the sweet spot for psoriasis, and it stops the rapid overgrowth of epidermis so that the skin can heal. She is now in remission. Kathy knows that she is not cured, and her skin could flare again after an infection, an increase in stress, bumping her skin against a door or even chronically leaning her elbow against her oak desk at work. She takes things one day at a time, and she is thankful for her clear skin.

A number of treatments now exist to help send psoriasis into remission. Most localized cases respond to soaks in water, tanning, and lubricants applied to the skin. Topical cortisones, Dovonex, tar, and intralesional Kenalog can be helpful. The F.D.A. has even approved lasers, which beam onto the plaque, and send it into remission.

For generalized psoriasis that cannot be treated with creams and salves, narrow band ultraviolet light sessions are a godsend. They are replacing the older broadband UVB wavelength (at 290–320 nanometers, it would often burn before healing the condition). They are also replacing the more cumbersome PUVA treatments. With PUVA, expensive capsules had to be taken two hours before the UV treatment, and they often caused nausea. The patient would now be allergic to the sun for the rest of the day until the pills wore off. They needed to stay indoors, and to wear good sunglasses to protect their vision from burning.

Systemic medications, although potentially more toxic than creams, can also be very useful. A new class of "biologics" is revolutionizing the treatment of psoriasis and its associated arthritis. Five are now available, and the list is growing. My favorites are tumor necrosis factors (TNF) inhibitors that can be injected by the patient in the privacy of their home.

Simplistically put, psoriasis may have an excess of TNF in the skin and joints. Thick, itching, inflamed peeling skin and tender arthritis may result. The biologic is self-administered by the patient with a foolproof, easy-to-use auto-pen injector. Delivered into the fat on the front of the thigh, a patient might have to do this twice a week, once a week or even only every other week to bring their skin and arthritis into a beautiful remission. It is like insulin for the skin. Just as insulin does not cure diabetes and it is required for long-term control, so a biologic does not cure psoriasis, but it may be helpful for keeping the skin free of unsightly plaques and the joints free of painful symptoms. In a properly chosen patient, side effects are minimal to non-existent.

Although these medications are expensive, insurance will often pay for a good deal of the cost. For those lacking health insurance, without the means to pay for a biologic, many pharmaceutical companies have programs to provide patients with the medication for free, or at a reduced cost.

If you or a loved one is troubled by psoriasis, I urge you to go see a dermatologist. But beware of various ads and publications trying to sell miracle cures for psoriasis. Many are junk! If it seems to be too good to be true, it probably is. One good resource is the National Psoriasis Foundation, based in Portland, Oregon (503-244-7404 or www.psoriasis.org). The foundation is very reputable, and has a great newsletter with a wealth of information and useful tips.

There is a tremendous amount of research being done on psoriasis, and we have better and safer treatments coming down the pike. If you have psoriasis or arthritis, don't give up hope!

Chapter Eighteen: Cardiology Rounds

Heart rounds at the Ohio State Medical School stimulated me. Although I knew even before entering medical school that dermatology was my first love, I always enjoyed the inner workings of the heart. I loved practicing on my newlywed wife, Jane. She was a willing patient, and I was a willing doctor-to-be. By the end of my exam, we were usually both hot and bothered. (To tell you the truth, sometimes I never made it to the end of the exam before passion seized us.)

Heart rounds obviously excited my fellow medical student, Dave, too—especially one day on the ward. Our head cardiology professor chose Dave to examine our first patient of the day, Kathleen, while on rounds. It just so happened that Kathleen was a stunning blonde. Long, shiny hair draped down to her chest. Her smile revealed a beautiful face and a perfect mouth with dazzling white teeth. An expensive-looking gold necklace and matching earrings adorned her body. She was a cross between Marilyn Monroe and Angelina Jolie. As she untied the front of her hospital gown for her cardiac exam, Dave was struck by her loveliness.

He leaned over Kathleen's chest to begin the exam. Dave knew that listening to the heart would be an important part of this general physical. And since everyone has a heart (except a few lawyers I know), the cardiac exam would be a key part of every exam he did.

The head cardiologist, internal medicine resident, medicine intern, heart nurse, and four medical students (including me) circled around the bed to watch Dave's progress. He carefully placed his Littman stethoscope on either side of her neck searching for bruits (noises indicating constrictions in the carotid artery). Then he knowingly placed the end of the stethoscope on four key areas of Kathleen's chest: just to the left of the lower side of her breast bone, three inches above that site, several inches further to the left, and finally to the point of maximal intensity (PMI) of the heartbeat, on the outside of the breast below the nipple. We all thought Dave must have found a good murmur or gallop because he was so intent on his exam, and because he was taking such a long time. A bead of sweat appeared on his upper lip.

Kathleen and Dave's audience stood like Stonehenge rocks around the bed—tall, still and silent, for what seemed like an eternity. We didn't want to cause any unnecessary noise or movement that would impair Dave's obviously expert cardiac exam. I thought to myself, Wow, for a second-year medical student, Dave really knows what he is doing.

Finally, the patient quietly and mercifully grabbed the far ends of Dave's stethoscope still wrapped around his neck, and put them into Dave's external ear canals. For you see, Dave had forgotten the most important part of the heart exam—to put the darned ends of the stethoscope into his ears.

Dave's face abruptly turned beet red, and our head professor chuckled to himself—he had been enjoying the spectacle from the beginning, when he noted the obvious flaw in the young medical student's ausculting technique. To her credit, Kathleen laid there like a mummy and did not make Dave feel like more of a fool than he already was. We fellow medical students felt so sorry for Dave that we didn't let out a peep or a laugh or even a chortle. We knew, but for the grace of God, that could have been one of us performing the exam instead of Dave. The head doctor briefly examined Kathleen, and off we went to the next patient on cardiac rounds.

This is why we have medical school. To get the kinks out of our history and physical techniques while we are under the close supervision of doctors and nurses much older and wiser than we are.

As we finished rounds that morning, I just felt thankful that Dave, not Doug, had performed that memorable exam!

Chapter Nineteen:
Malignant Melanoma

One reason I like dermatology is because my patients don't die of skin disease. At least, most of them don't. As an internal medicine intern at Wilford Hall U.S. Air Force Medical Center in San Antonio, Texas, it was painful to watch my oncology (cancer) ward patients drop like flies from lymphoma, leukemia, lung cancer, and Hodgkin's disease. And as an emergency room doctor, death from auto accidents, drug overdoses, and heart attacks could come storming through the hospital door at any moment. But my dermatology patients don't tend to die. I like them—they are interesting, they are fun, and they are sometimes more like old friends rather that patients. But then there is melanoma.

Laura had been my patient for a few years now. She was very nervous, and she had a bad habit of excoriating her skin. She had a compulsion to just pick and gouge any blemishes on her skin. She felt she just had to extract the core, and then and only then, would it heal. (In actuality, there is no core!)

"What are you so nervous about?" I asked Laura when she visited my office, honestly wanting to know. "Why do you pick at your skin so much?"

She said, "I have lots of issues, but the one bothering me most now is my husband. He has a funny mole on the right side of his upper back. It itches and it tingles, and his shirt was even tinged with blood last week. But he is a pig-headed man, and he just won't come in to see you for a checkup."

Corbett was retired military, and he could see me at the Air Force Dermatology Clinic for free. But as Laura said so emphatically, we men are pig-headed. As far as our health, we are like ostriches with our heads buried in the sand of life. Women are usually the health-care authorities in a family, and we need to listen to them more. They seem to have a sixth sense; they know when the medical problem is serious, and when the husband and the kids need to get in to their doctors.

When Corbett came in to see me six months later, he was the picture of health. He volunteered in the National Ski Patrol at Mt. Alyeska in Alaska, and he was a bush pilot and fisherman and hunter to boot. At age 45, his vigorous frame could have passed for 20 years younger. But that day in the office, he had a worried look on his face. "Doc, my wife, Laura, says I need to get my back checked out."

"I am glad you came in, Corbett," I said warmly, shaking his hand. I like to touch all of my patients. Some of them feel contagious or unworthy of kindness or human compassion, because of their perceived infectious or unhealthy skin disease. If a doctor touches them, they can't be all that contagious or worthless now, can they?

Corbett took off his shirt, and I noted severe scars all over his back from a bad childhood burn. His plastic surgeon had done a beautiful job of placing multiple skin grafts over the defects. But on the right upper back, I spotted a "funny mole"—not black like a melanoma, but red and inflamed. It had a bit of dried crusted blood where he had toweled off that morning. It was **A**symmetric, it had an irregular **B**order, it had variation in **C**olor, and it had a **D**iameter bigger than 6 mm--about the size of a pencil eraser. It was a mole that was **E**volving.. Those are the classic "ABCDE" warning signs of melanoma skin cancer.

"It itches a little, and every now and then it will spot some blood," Corbett told me. "I am pretty darn healthy, so I didn't feel I needed to get in. But my wife was troubled by it."

"Well, let's check it out." I replied. As I looked at the mole on his back, I didn't know what it was, but I knew I didn't like it. Any mole that bleeds should be examined and biopsied. We took a skin sample that very afternoon, and our pathologist called me later that week. "Doug, we got a bad one. The tumor is over three millimeters thick, and it extends to the fat. It is an amelanotic melanoma."

My heart skipped a beat. So *that* is why it had no black pigment! An amelanotic melanoma is a skin cancer that is hard to diagnose because it lacks the dark color characteristic of most melanomas.

The pathology exam revealed its true malignant colors. Since only one percent of all melanomas fall in that category, to diagnose it clinically, we remember the mottos "non-healing sore" or "the changing mole that itches or ulcerates or bleeds." We have to biopsy it.

Summoning the couple to my office the next day, I gave them the grim news. "Corbett, you have a thick, high-risk malignant melanoma. You have a significant chance of dying from it. With your permission, we will have our general surgeon widely excise the area this week to get it locally cured." At the time I was uttering these words, I wondered to myself, "Have the cancerous cells already spread through the blood stream and lymphatics to distant body sites?"

In 1907, and for many decades afterward, the surgical standard for melanoma was to remove five centimeters all around, resulting in a four-inch hole. Removal of such a large section of skin would often result in an unsightly, mutilating scar. Present guidelines call for only one or two-centimeter removal all around, so a graft or flap is seldom needed, and neither is a disfiguring scar. The cure rate for melanoma back then was only 50 percent, and now it is 85 percent and climbing, thanks to early diagnosis and prompt surgical excision.

During that office visit with Corbett and his wife, I said something that I usually don't say to any of my patients. "This could be a tough one. Keep your life insurance paid up, and if you want to take any trips, go ahead and take them. Try to live each day to the fullest."

I thought to myself, he has less than a 50-percent chance of living five more years. Ironically, if he would have been burned with the hot oil on that spot, his scarred skin would have been grafted, and he never would have developed melanoma in the first place.

Our surgeon did a nice job of re-excising the melanoma. Corbett was cured—locally. We could only hope the melanoma would not metastasize to a distant body site. The lymph nodes, the lung, the liver, the brain, and other areas of the skin remained high-risk sites. The best hope for cure of melanoma is to excise the abnormal mole early before it spreads to the rest of the body. Alas, chemotherapy, x-rays, vaccines, and immunotherapy still don't work very well for melanomas. Early local surgical cure is our best hope.

Well, Corbett did take that trip he had always wanted to take. He and his two boys skied the pants off of Colorado's best mountain slopes. For a month, they had a ball. Forget that darn melanoma. Let's have fun. And they did.

When Corbett and the boys got back to Alaska, they were ecstatic. Dad was too healthy to die of melanoma, they all thought. Maybe Naversen and the pathologist had made a mistake.

One year after I first saw Corbett, he complained of a lump in his right neck. I palpated an enlarging lymph gland. "Bad," I thought to myself. I did an immediate biopsy, and my heart sunk when our pathologist reported it positive for a melanoma metastatic to the lymph gland.

Six months later, a nodule surfaced on the top of Corbett's scalp. The pathologist again replied, "Doug, it is positive for metastatic melanoma to the skin."

Two years from the day I first saw Corbett, he was lying moribund high up on the sixth floor of the hospital. He had showers of black buckshot melanomas peppering his entire skin surface.

We had just had a big blizzard in Anchorage that night. After the storm ended, his kids put on their heavy winter boots, and they went out into the peaceful, beautiful, Alaskan winter night air. They stomped out large, bold letters on the virgin snow of the hospital lawn for their father. He would be able to see it from his hospital window the following morning, they thought. The message read in ten-foot-high snow writing, "WE LOVE YOU DAD!"

Well, he never got to see the message. He was too weak to get up to the window. And the next day, he was gone.

Corbett didn't get the message, but Dr. N. wants you to get yours before it is too late. Get that mole or non-healing sore checked sooner rather than later by your dermatologist. Your life could depend on it. According to the American Academy of Dermatology website (www.aad.org), almost sixty thousand new cases of invasive melanoma are diagnosed every year in the United States, and over 8,100 Americans die every year of malignant melanoma. In America, a person dies of melanoma almost every hour of the day, 24 hours a day, 365 days a year. Unfortunately, the remaining productive life of those dying is 17 years—these victims are taken in their prime.

Risk factors include blonde or red hair, easy freckling or sun-burning, a surplus of moles on the skin or moles present from birth, many large freckles (liver spots) on the upper back, a history of two or more blistering childhood sunburns, working outdoors three or more seasons, and a family history of melanoma. Fifty years ago, melanoma was called "The Black Death." Today, the cure rate is so much better so that nickname is no longer appropriate. But we in dermatology are greedy. We want a 100-percent cure rate.

Do yourself a favor. Enjoy the great outdoors, but protect your skin. Wear a hat with a three-inch or wider brim, and wear long sleeves and gloves. If it is hot and muggy, and long sleeves don't hack it, use a SPF 30 waterproof (or water resistant) sunscreen. Reapply it every hour if you are sweating, swimming, or toweling it off. Ideally, the sunscreen should contain Parsol 1789 (avobenzone), Mexoryl, zinc, or titanium. Don't throw out your present sunscreen—it is still good. Use it up, and the next time buy one of the more modern sunscreens that blocks both UVB and UVA. Try and do your activities early or late in the day, and stay out of the noonday sun if possible. Stay in the shade instead if you are chatting with someone. Instruct your kids and grandkids about common sense in the sun. Be sure to examine your skin all over every month after a bath or shower. And be sure to examine your significant other's back and the back of their legs where they cannot check themselves out. Be sure to keep a sharp eye out on your children's skin also. Treat yourself to a dermatology exam yearly! Remember, Ben Franklin said, "Prevention is always better than the cure."

And remember what Dr. Naversen says: "If at least one of your grandparents was black, you will probably never have to worry about skin cancer."

Chapter Twenty:
The Garden Isle

Kauai is one of my favorite places in the world. Beautiful beaches, lush rainforests, great hiking on the Na Pali Cliff Trail, snorkeling, boating, jogging, shopping, and helicopter tours entertain you, and they can just plain wear you out. It is the "tired feeling" that you really like. The phone never rings. Early morning walks on the beach with your significant other inspire you. Tasty lunches at Brenneke's Beach Restaurant restore you. "Polynesian paralysis" sets in and you take one of the top-ten naps of all time during the heat of the day. And then it's back to the sun-drenched beaches of the south coast later in the afternoon.

Why, I have even heard of people jogging on the Hyatt Regency Poipu Bay Golf Course just before sunset, when all the golfers are gone. Joggers are strictly prohibited on the course. And, personally, I would never violate such a rule and run at the Hyatt. But the rolling hills on the green grass at the far edges of the turf are gentle on your legs. Beautiful vistas include the pounding surf below the cliffs, the old sugar cane mill off in the distance, extinct volcanic cinder cones nearby, and the beautiful tropical colors as the sun sets in the west. As my daughter Leina once said, "There are no pastel colors in Kauai."

Nearby Poipu is a delight. "Dr. Beach" recently rated Poipu as the number-one beach in the United States. (Funny, despite its great beauty, it is not even the best beach on Kauai—try Lumahai, where they filmed the movie *South Pacific*.)

This leads us to our next exciting adventure. My wife, Jane, and my good friends, Jim and Jan, and I had just arrived at Poipu Beach. I had on my swimsuit, and I was taking off my shirt and my Nike Air Deschutes sandals, the same ones that came in so handy on the Rogue River trip with Dr. Pat Code. Suddenly, I heard some kid out in the ocean yelling, "Help!"

"There ought to be laws against these kids crying wolf," I thought. But then, "Help!" pierced the air a second time. It was even louder and more frantic. Since I was at the edge of the beach, I had a great view, and it turned out I was the closest person to the swimmer.

"Help!" punctuated the air, and I found myself hearing a blood-curdling scream for the third time. I was in the exact right place at the right time. It was not a kid, after all, but an overweight, middle-aged, balding man in trouble. He was a very tired swimmer, and the ocean waves were severely buffeting his body. He looked like he would soon sink like a large hunk of lava rock beneath the beautiful aqua ocean and the frothing white surf to the bottom of the sea. The man was getting ready to drown in beautiful Poipu Beach!

I began running through the surf towards him as I simultaneously gauged his distance, about 50 yards out. I flashed back to Boy Scout Lifesaving Class at Woodland Trails Boy Scout Camp, in Ohio, three decades earlier. I thought, "Maintain eye contact at all times, be confident when talking to the victim, and above all, watch out because he might get a death grip on you, and you will both death-spiral to the depths of the ocean."

After sprinting in a few feet, the warm, roiling surf was now too deep to run in. I started swimming as fast as I could in his direction. I kept my head above the water at all times so I could monitor his location. He was getting weaker and more panicky. Although there were a lot of people on the beach that day, there was no lifeguard on that stretch of sand—except me. My heart was racing as I closed in on him. I was glad I was in marathon shape. "Get ready for his death grip," I thought. "You might soon be sinking to the ocean floor in a two-man death tête-à-tête."

As I swam up to him in the turbulent water, I yelled confidently, "You are going to be just fine. Grab my arm and I will tow you in." We linked arms, and I started hauling him to shore. "He sure is heavy," I thought, "and this surf is no fun." My swimming form was not pretty; just call it "controlled panic" as we laboriously struggled to shore. To my great surprise and relief, 60 seconds later, a stranger from heaven swam out of the twilight zone and grabbed his other arm, and we pulled him slowly but steadily to safety. A large crowd had gathered to watch the near-drowning. His wife was hysterical on the sand. After a few minutes of grunting, kicking and arm pulling, and lots of heavy-breathing labor, we finally pulled him to shore and he collapsed sobbing on the sand. The intense physical exertion in the water made the seconds seem far longer than they really were.

The man's wife was crying uncontrollably. The crowd closed in around the couple. She said that they were vacationing from New York. She stated the obvious: "He is not an ocean swimmer."

Two hotel employees appeared out of nowhere, and they helped the husband and wife off the beach. In the blink of an eye, the couple was gone. The crowd melted away. The guy and his wife were too rattled to thank me for saving his life. And I never saw them again.

But my good friend, Jim McClure, came to the rescue. Jim is known to serve the coldest beer in the world. He must have a Ph.D. in beer refrigeration. He somehow keeps the bottle at the perfect tempera-ture—not too cold, and not too warm. You know, when the beverage is not frozen, but when the ice crystals are just starting to form on top, and the beer tantalizes your taste buds.

Jim opened his cooler and said, "Good job, Doug. This Bud is for you." He put the precious cargo in a blue foam cooler, and then he passed it to me with gusto. "You know, friends like you only go around once in life. It doesn't get any better than this." It was one of my top ten beverages of all time! It was a just and adequate reward for my brief swim in the ocean. Any debt owed to me by the tired swimmer was now paid in full.

But as we headed back to the condo after an eventful day at the beach, I vowed in the future to stay away from all lakes, rivers, oceans, and other large bodies of water. Pulling people out of the Rogue River and the Pacific Ocean was getting old.

Chapter Twenty-One:
Runner's High

I strained my eyes and squinted to see what the small white sign lying ahead said. The number six soon clearly came into view as I raced along the narrow country two-lane highway surrounded by giant coast redwoods. "No way, I couldn't have run six miles already," I thought. I was doing the Avenue of the Giants 10K Run, on May 3rd, 1992, at Humboldt Redwood State Park in northern California. I didn't realize it at the time, but I was having an "out of body experience," also known as an "in-the-zone experience." Whether you call it a "Zen-like state," "nirvana," or the classic "runner's high," if it ever comes knocking at your door, embrace it.

The marathon had started at 9:00 a.m. sharp. Along with several hundred other 10K runners, I toed the line at 9:10 a.m. I felt I was in good shape, but I was not in great shape. I noted the weather conditions were perfect for a 6.2 mile road race—cool, sunny, with minimal wind. Even if the bright sun did try to sap our strength, 85-percent of the course was shaded by the massive, noble giant coast redwoods, Sequoia sempervirens, towering 200 feet, and even as high as 360 feet, above the road surface. I was in awe as I thought, "Some of these huge trees are over 2,000 years old!"

The blow horn sounded, and off we went. Before I knew it, I saw the one-mile marker. "Easiest mile I ever ran," I thought. What made it particularly good was that the 14-mile mark for the marathon was right next to the one-mile mark for the 10K; both races were underway. Glad I hadn't just run 14 miles en route to a 26-mile marathon! I seemed to be running down hill the whole way. And if I got the slightest bit tired, I would just stare at the powerful redwoods growing thickly on either side of the race course. The trees seemed to mystically restore my energy.

Soon, I spotted the two-mile marker and the 15-mile marathon mark. Before I knew it, I had rushed past the three-mile mark, and I sure was glad I hadn't just run 16 miles, like the marathoners.

Quickly, the turnaround came at 3.1 miles, and I was already halfway done with my run! "Whoever said running was hard?" I thought. "I am cruising." But I know what goes downhill eventually must go uphill. I envisioned some brutal stretch ahead that might tire and cramp my legs, and even give me a bad stitch in my side.

Wonderfully, it felt like I was still running downhill. This made absolutely no sense to a rational person, a scientist, a laser specialist, a dermatologist, or a physician—and technically, I am all of these things. I had taken a lot of physics courses in college, and I know the physical laws of nature. This just can't happen short of an earthquake, a lava flow, a tidal wave or some other catastrophic event (excepting maybe at the Oregon Vortex, near Gold Hill, but that's another story?).

Then an amazing metaphysical event ensued. As I watched myself race faster and faster downhill, I felt my head leave my physical body, and it levitated 25 feet above my shoulders. At first it gazed to the left of the highway, and then it causally looked to the right of the highway. My cranium saw in a blur the beautiful greenery of the forest with the handsome red-brown bark of the giant redwood trees with their slender, irregular crowns going rapidly by. My body seemed to be sprinting. From my lofty vantage point 25 feet above the ground, I saw unmistakably and clearly that I was in fact still running downhill. I thought, "No way is this happening, but if you think you are running downhill, you are running downhill. Just enjoy it, run fast, and have fun."

Next I felt my skull bone slowly descend from on high. My head effortlessly reattached to my shoulders down below. That is when I saw the six-mile sign. I guess I had been distracted, and I must have missed the four- and five-mile markers.

"I am not even breathing hard, my muscles are fresh, and it feels more like the start of the race rather than the end of the race," I thought as I ran up and over the bridge crossing the majestic Eel River. My body surged with power as I sprinted across the finish line. I felt my spirit was in a time warp, and it barely registered on my brain when they called out on the P.A. system, "Runner, Doug Naversen, from Jacksonville, Oregon, finishing, time of 38 minutes 49 seconds."

I was astounded! Although it was not my personal record (35:50 is my best), this was the easiest sub-40-minute 10K I have ever run. I felt I could have immediately run another 6.2 miles, and I could have gone just as fast. It suddenly dawned on me, "You have just had an out-of-body experience," like the time Michael Jordan hit six three-pointers in the first half of the NBA championship basketball game against the Portland Trailblazers. They had three Trailblazers hanging on him every time he shot, but the ball still went in. Or like Tiger Woods charging from way behind and demolishing the golf field with perfect shot after perfect shot. Or like Nadia Comaneci when she scored a perfect ten in the Olympic gymnastic competition.

As a dermatologist, I tend to be a concrete thinker. If someone says I itch, I look for dermatitis with primary lesions. If there are only non-specific scratch marks, but no hives, blisters, infected hairs, or boils as skin markers to give a clue as to the cause, they either have a metabolic itch (caused by diabetes, thyroid disease, kidney failure, internal cancer, or the like), or they have neurotic excoriations.

I don't rely on unproven holistic health powers. I prefer things that really work. For example, I might prescribe an antibiotic by mouth for a bacterial infection, a steroid cream for contact dermatitis, a cortisone shot to break an itch-scratch cycle, or an anti-fungal cream for ringworm.

So when I say it was an "in the zone" experience, it was just that. You athletes out there, if you can train with people who help you get in this Zen-like state, you will have incredible workouts that will greatly enhance your stamina and endurance. If you can get "in the zone" in the Olympic finals, the gold medal will be yours.

I am looking forward to my next "in the zone" experience. Unfortunately, they are few and far between. I just experienced another Avenue of the Giants 10K run in 2004, this time with my good friend Dr. Bruce Mendelson. Even though it was the same course I completed in 1992, and even though I was still greatly in awe of the towering redwoods, this time on the run back to the finish line, there seemed to be lots of hills. An during the battle I found myself getting tired, and at the finish line my Nike watch said 40:41, almost two minutes slower than my "in the zone" time. At age 55 and twelve years later, I know I have got to be losing a step or two. But I just have the feeling if I could have found the zone, I would have had another sub-40 10K run. Keep on running!

Chapter Twenty-Two: The Beer-Drinking Poppy Man

Dwight always seemed down on his luck. He was overweight, and he was lethargic. His chief dermatology complaint was, "I got something going on down in man-land."

"How did you get it," I asked?

"Well, it is a long story, and I would rather not go into it today," he replied.

We did repeated treatments on his problem, and we were on the verge of a cure when he came to the clinic one day all beaten up. He had a swollen, purple-colored eye, bruised ribs, and black and blue marks all over his body. I sutured some facial lacerations. I sensed this was a drug deal, but again, Dwight didn't want to go into it. I didn't press him on the details.

Dwight seemed very lazy, but he sure had an interest in fertilizers, plants and horticulture. Since he was lacking any money for his office visits, he suggested we make a trade. In return for his dermatological visits and what he owed me, he would landscape my house. With his knowledge of plants and gardening, it looked like a win-win situation.

When my wife Jane answered the door at our house, she was surprised to see Dwight. He introduced himself to Jane, and he said he was here to landscape the Naversen residence. (I guess I failed to mention it to her.) So Dwight proceeded to do his good work, or so I hoped.

When I got home that night, Jane's sixth sense hit the nail on the head. "Is this another trade, dear?" she asked with a smirk on her face. She remembered that every trade I had ever made went south—perhaps with the exception of a few good watermelons. One time I traded office visits for a new custom hot tub cover. All I got was a flimsy temporary one that was a hideous green and two sizes too small. The trader skipped town on me without delivering the one we had agreed upon.

I know old-time family doctors often got paid in bread, eggs, potatoes, and chickens for office visits. Well, all I seemed to get were delays, lies and deceit. I usually got nothing for trading dermatological expertise for would-be services from patients. Would Jane be right about this one, too?

Dwight worked about 30 minutes by shoveling some red lava rock along the garden. Being a hot summer day in southern Oregon, he was sweating profusely. He decided to help himself to one of my cold ones. My wife was shocked to find him in her kitchen knocking down a Budweiser that he had grabbed out of our refrigerator. Jane kicked him out of the house.

Dwight seemed very slow to complete his gardening plans. He made lots of promises, but he did very little work. I pushed him for a final deadline.

That weekend, we were in Beaverton, Oregon, for a swim meet at Tualatin Hills, where they have a wonderful 50-meter pool. I drove our 29-foot Itasca motorhome north on I-5 for the five-hour journey from Medford to Portland. We usually would haul half a dozen kids to the meet. (Fortunately, only three of them were mine.) The others were swimmers were kids who needed a ride, since their parents couldn't make the trip that weekend. They would sleep in the back while I drove. Saturday morning, they got up early for warm-ups. My reward for staying up late and driving the night before was sleeping late the following morning. When I woke up, I could leisurely sip coffee and have breakfast while reading *The Oregonian*.

Imagine my surprise that morning when I looked at the front page and read, "Medford Man Busted for Opium Poppies." Dwight had been busted for drugs! No wonder he liked horticulture so much. He had secretly been growing marijuana and opium plants inside and around his house. The Federales had finally caught up with him. It looks like my landscaping is not going to get done for a while—maybe in five to ten years with time off for good behavior? Jane was shocked at the news, and then she laughed and laughed. "Another trade blown up in your face," she cracked.

Six weeks later, I got a call from the County Jail. Dwight's public defender said he needed character references. Therefore, Dwight asked me, "Would you give me one?"

"Yes, Dwight, you are the laziest person I know. You are a Budweiser thief, and you got all that free dermatology care, but you completed less than half of your proposed landscaping project. You are extremely knowledgeable about grass and opium poppies—and no, I'm not going to write you a letter." I gently hung up the phone hoping that I would never hear again from this poor, sad, unfortunate human being.

Dwight was tried and convicted on drug charges, and he was sent "up river." Actually, although we do have the lovely Rogue River, the Applegate River, and Bear Creek nearby, the jail is a mile from water, so I guess he was just sent to the County Jail, not actually up river.

Some months later, I started getting weird, threatening letters from Dwight. He claimed to have planted pot and opium in my garden, and the Feds would seize my property under RICO statutes. My wife showed the letters to our psychiatrist neighbor, Dr. Jeff Thompson (the same physician who sent me the patient complaining of being "jammed" by evil angels). Jeff confirmed our fears when he said, "The guy is wacko." Don't you psychiatrists have any fancier words than wacko, I wondered? Maybe this person had a character disorder, or was a pot-head, an opium addict, or a drug dealer.

It has been quite a few years since that excitement. I finally got my landscaping done. After a number of years, Dwight showed up at my front door looking pale and anemic from all that time prison. He wanted to let me know he had been sprung from prison, and he reached out his hand to shake mine.

It is a sign of disgust and disrespect when you refuse to shake another man's hand. Seldom have I refused. But there was no way I could shake with him. I just told Dwight he needed to leave, and please never come back.

By the way, the pot, and opium poppies never grew in our garden, so to date the Feds have not taken our house away under RICO laws. As for other trades I have made, I finally made a good one with a licensed massage therapist. I did a complete skin check for cancer, I removed a few suspicious moles, and I did free laser work. In return, I got half a dozen of the most glorious massages a human being could experience. I thought I had died and gone to heaven on most of them. A good masseuse is worth his or her weight in gold. At least one of my trades turned out well. Thank you Vicky!

Chapter Twenty-Three: Alopecia Universalis

Ben had a shoulder injury that had nagged him for months. His orthopedic doctor injected cortisone right into the hotspot of the painful bursitis. And then a miracle happened: Not only did his pain resolve, but he sprouted hair for the first time in 12 years! For you see, Ben had the worst form of alopecia areata, known as alopecia universalis. It had resulted in a dramatic loss of not only his scalp hair, but also his arm hair, leg hair, chest hair and back hair. Even his eyebrows and eyelashes were gone. He would have loved to have had nostril, armpit and pubic hair, just like anyone else, but they too had fallen out, along with every other stitch of hair on his body surface.

Usually in the summer, Ben noticed his scalp burned very easily because of his loss of top cover. He kept a dozen hats in his closet to use for every occasion. But with his newly erupting scalp hair, maybe, he wondered, he could go hatless for the first time in years.

Truth is, most of us take our eyebrows and eyelashes for granted. Ben was tortured when a speck of dust fell through the air and landed right on the surface of his eyeball; it was 2.5 on the Richter scale of pain.

A normal person's eyebrow or lashes would have trapped the particle and prevented the impact on the delicate cornea.

He also suffered from allergies, sneezing and nasal irritation. He didn't have nose hairs to filter out dust, gunk and pollens from the air and prevent particles from entering the respiratory passages.

When Ben came into the dermatology clinic, my colleagues and I were impressed with his history of total and complete hair loss, and the results of the Kenalog injection. The cortisone's anti-inflammatory effect on the white cells attacking his hair follicles (like a swarm of African killer bees attacking the hair shaft) caused the lymphocytes to dissolve away. Without all the inflammation, the intact and otherwise normal hair follicles could grow again. He sprouted hair on his scalp, beard, eyebrows, eyelashes, nostrils, ears, torso, arms and legs, and everywhere a grown man should normally have hair. He felt euphoric!

As I evaluated him, I knew if he had one autoimmune disease such as alopecia areata, he was at risk for others. I carefully screened him for pernicious anemia, diabetes, thyroid disease, Addison's disease, and pituitary growth failure, and searched his skin for the white patches of vitiligo. Fortunately, all findings were normal or negative. I breathed a sigh of relief. It would be simpler to deal with a hair loss problem rather than a systemic illness and multiple autoimmune phenomena.

Ben wanted to grow his hair and keep it as long as possible. I decided on a tapering dose of prednisone by mouth. I discussed the risks to benefits in great detail with Ben, explaining that we would try to "prime the pump." We would get his hairs to grow out, and then we would slowly taper down his prednisone doses. Due to its potential side effects, he could not stay on the drug forever.

We started him at 60 mg a day the first month, and then we began decreasing the dose. Ben's hair grew luxuriantly. He marveled at his transformed appearance. And he thought, "For being such an impressive wonder drug, prednisone is as cheap as dirt."

As his hair grew longer and longer, he visited friends and relatives. Everyone was astounded by his dramatic turnaround. Ben had photographs and portraits taken, just in case. After all those "bad hair days," it was nice to have some good ones for a change.

As Ben's prednisone dose was lowered to zero over four months, reality set in. All of his hair fell out again! Ben was depressed, but philosophical. He knew it was too good to last. He was appreciative that he had had the chance to experience "hair" again. He gained local fame, and was moved by the heartfelt sympathy expressed by his friends and relatives. His hair never grew back. At least his bursitis was gone forever, too.

Chapter Twenty-Four:
Alopecia Areata

Liz was a black model with a bright future. One day, she noticed a circular bald spot on her crown. Within six weeks, all of her scalp hair had fallen out! "Help! I don't like this!" she exclaimed.

As I examined Liz's scalp, I let her know she had alopecia totalis. It was worse than simple alopecia areata, but it not near as bad as what Ben had. Fortunately, Liz did not lose any other body hair except that on her scalp.

Standard treatment was to inject dilute cortisone into the scalp with a tiny 30-gauge needle. We used the same Kenalog, but in a less-concentrated strength, than what the orthopedic doc had used for Ben's bursitis. I told Liz we would inject her scalp monthly until the alopecia resolved. Unfortunately, there was no way we could inject her whole scalp with steroids. That would be too painful, and it would require too much drug.

"Liz, what we are going to do is experimental. The F.D.A. has not approved it. If you decide you want it done, we will use immunotherapy. We will make you allergic to a chemical not found in nature, called DNCB. It is as potent an allergen as poison oak and poison ivy. Poison oak extract would also work, but since you have never had poison oak or poison ivy, I don't want to make you allergic to it. If you touch poison oak or poison ivy when walking in the woods, you would curse Dr. Naversen if you got that itchy, miserable condition. The beauty of DNCB is that since it is not found outside the laboratory, you will never be exposed to it except from your bottle from the pharmacy."

After thorough informed consent, Liz agreed to DNCB therapy. I swabbed a quarter-sized patch on the front of her bald scalp with a two-percent concentration. Two weeks later, she developed a spontaneous cluster of blisters at the exact application site. "Great, we're in!" I thought. She was now allergic to the chemical. A few weeks later, she started growing a dark shock of hair exactly where I had applied the chemical.

Once or twice a week, Liz applied a dilute-strength solution of DNCB in acetone with a cotton swab all over her bald scalp. We only used a 0.1-percent concentration. She reported a mild tingling dermatitis on her scalp two days after each application. Fortunately, it was only mildly itchy compared to a case of poison oak. She also noticed mild swelling of the lymph glands behind her ears. If her hair would keep growing out, she could endure these minimal side effects. And slowly but surely, hair began to appear on her scalp. We kept our fingers crossed. She was getting good cosmetic growth.

The result of DNCB was awesome. Within six months, she grew 95-percent of her hair back. I injected the bald portion left on her crown with intralesional Kenalog to complete her cure. She felt gorgeous again, and she put all of her wigs in the back closet. Liz moved out of state, and I lost touch with her. I hope she maintained her good hair growth forever without the alopecia totalis. If she came in to see me today, I would use a more modern chemical known as SADBE. Time has proven it works as well as DNCB, and it may be slightly safer.

Alopecia areata, alopecia totalis and alopecia universalis are autoimmune diseases that afflict up to one percent of the population. Five percent of those cases may be triggered by acute psychic trauma (death, divorce or financial problems). Most are associated with focal inflammation of the scalp, and a good percentage of patients may have other autoimmune diseases, especially thyroid disease. If the hair loss is localized, we use potent topical cortisone solutions, intralesional Kenalog, local irritants, immune modulators such as Aldara, and occasionally even phototherapy with ultraviolet light.

But we need a few more magic bullets to turn off the disease process. Can you imagine how devastated a college student might be if he or she suddenly lost all of their hair within the space of a month? Or how a third grader and her parents would feel if the child suddenly developed alopecia areata?

By the way, we have all heard about a person whose hair has turned gray overnight. Medically speaking, they developed an acute case of alopecia totalis. The disease causes loss of only pigmented hair, and it spares white or gray hair. This is a valid scientific explanation of why this phenomenon really does happen to some people. It may especially occur after a severe emotional shock.

If you suffer from the condition, or if a friend or relative is troubled with alopecia areata, the National Alopecia Areata Foundation (415-472-3780, website www.naaf.org) is a very reputable organization with a great consulting staff of board-certified dermatologists. My "hair and nail" professor at UCSF, Dr. Vera Price, was founding chairman, and she has been a great supporter of the organization. I urge you to join the Foundation and learn more about the disease in the quarterly newsletter. Please contribute dollars for dermatology research, so we can conquer this common and baffling condition.

Chapter Twenty-Five:
Beware of Moles That Move

During my dermatology residency, there was an ongoing joke between me and my colleagues: "Beware of moles that move." One afternoon, years later, at the Dermatology and Laser Associates of Medford (DLAM) clinic, a 70-year-old gentleman returned for a six-month follow-up visit. I had previously treated a basal cell carcinoma on his face, along with some precancers on his ears and hands. I wanted to make sure the cancer was not coming back, and I wanted to check for any possible new ones that were forming.

Pete took off his shirt, and I was startled as he suddenly turned around. Just inches from my nose and right smack-dab in the middle of his back between his shoulder blades, I spotted a bloated, blood-sucking tick. Hello!

"Pete, why did you come here today? Is there anything new or different going on with your skin?"

"Nope, I'm just here for my regular six-month checkup. I don't know of anything else going on with my skin. I have no bleeding moles; I have no new growths to report. As far as I know, my skin is good."

The big, fat tick's anesthesia was so good when it bit him, Pete didn't have a clue about the predator's intimate relationship with the skin on his back. Judging by the massive, engorged size of the critter, it had been on his skin for days, or even as long as a week. But its presence was a surprise to Pete.

Without using additional anesthesia, other than what the tick had already provided, I grabbed the intruder with my trusty hemostat, and gently twisted it around and off. Next, I flicked out the deeply-embedded proboscis with a #11 Bard-Parker blade. This sore would heal in just a week.

"Pete, do you want Doxycycline for possible incubating Lyme disease?" I asked. I told him only three out of every 1,000 tick bites in Oregon resulted in Lyme disease. (The tick would normally have to attach itself for over 24 hours to transmit Lyme.)

He replied, "No." He told me his girlfriend would check him carefully for a bulls-eye rash around the central punctum, the opening in the skin where the tick had been. I know the girlfriend will keep a sharp eye on him. Although they are both 70 years old, they were set to be married in a few months. Good for them!

I plopped the tick in a specimen bottle containing formalin. The ectoparasite died instantly. "Eat shit and die," I thought. (Sorry about my French, but I hate ticks, lice, scabies and other blood-suckers that feed on poor unsuspecting humans, not to mention my dogs.) And I thought of the old line, "Beware of moles that move."

Chapter Twenty-Six:
Contact Dermatitis

Sharon complained of a severely itchy rash on her forearms. It had nagged at her for months, coming and going without apparent rhyme or reason. It was now the major malady in her life.

As I talked to Sharon and examined her skin, it became apparent to me that she was a saint. She cared for her invalid husband almost 24 hours a day. He had suffered a severe stroke, and so they just stayed at home. Once a week, she would shop for food and supplies. Then, back to the three-bedroom homestead in east Medford, Oregon, where they lived. There were no movies, no restaurants, no trips to the nearby Rogue River or Crater Lake, no Hawaii and no foreign travel. No nothing. A lesser woman would have been bitter and resentful for her sorry lot in life, cooped up in her house all day with her ailing husband. But on her wedding day 25 years ago, when she said her vows, she really meant, "For better or for worse, in sickness and in health." Well, for her, it was definitely, "for worse," and it was decidedly "sickness" and not "health." That is why I felt she was a saint.

I noticed blistering occurring equally on both of her forearms, extending up the inside of the arms, up to her biceps. "Looks just like poison oak," I said. I noted linear blisters and scratch marks—pathognomonic (diagnostic) of contact dermatitis. In southern Oregon, it is almost always poison oak that causes rashes with this appearance. Back east and in the Midwest, it is almost always poison ivy (the same chemical, urushiol, a pentadecacatechol, is found in both plants).

"But I never go out in the woods," replied Sharon. "I barely ever get out of the house. You know how ill my husband has been lately."

I always like a good case of contact dermatitis, because it is interesting, like a challenging detective story. A careful history, a thorough examination, and some sleuthing are required. If the history is not obvious for the cause, patch testing is a powerful tool to uncover the culprit. We could tape "postage stamps" containing 24 or more chemicals on the patient's back on Monday. We could remove and read the results on Wednesday, and we could do a delayed reading on Friday. We often test a shopping bag full of the patient's toiletries, perfumes, fragrances, sprays, creams and salves. A positive test is a red, itchy, blistered dermatitis beneath the patch. A negative test reassures us there is no allergy to that product, and it is safe to use on the skin.

I prescribed cool soaks, a potent cortisone cream to be applied four times a day, and prednisone by mouth. I was confident this would cure her. And it did—for exactly one week. Sharon was frustrated when the dermatitis reappeared the next Friday.

"Okay, let's take off the kid gloves," I thought. I scheduled formal patch testing on her back, and after the Wednesday and Friday readings, we were disappointed. She was negative to everything! Strike out! I'd said she had poison oak, and she never gets in poison oak. I'd said she had contact dermatitis, and all her patch tests are negative. If you are so good, I thought to myself, why can't you cure this angel of a woman?

Well, it turned out, every Friday, her arms would flare. It always occurred in the same place—inside the forearms and up the sides of the biceps.

"Are you smearing any creams, salves or perfumes on your arms?" I asked Sharon.

"Nothing," she responded. She slowly scratching at her arms as she wracked her brain for any miscellaneous products she could have used. "Only what you prescribed for me, doctor."

"Sharon, something is touching your skin and trashing it," I observed. "I want you to go home, and as you live your 24-hour day, be aware of anything, anything at all, that might be touching your skin. Call me if you think of what it could be."

A month later, I got an excited call from Sharon. "Dr. Naversen, I have it!" she exclaimed. "I know what I am allergic to."

"Tell me," I said excitedly.

"Well, every Wednesday night my lady friends come over for bridge. It is my only social outlet. The ladies are so nice. They know of our situation here, and they come to my place to help relieve my boredom. We use our dining room for the card table, so I have to move a large plant from there to the kitchen. The leaves brush against the inside of my arms, exactly where the dermatitis is."

"Bingo!" I thought. "What kind of plant is it?"

Well, I checked with the florist, and it is the English primrose, or primula obconica plant."

"Eureka! That is a known allergen, and it can be equally as bad on your skin as poison oak. You have developed, over the year, an allergic rash. Formerly, you were not allergic, but upon repeated exposure, now you are highly sensitive. Whenever you are exposed to the leaves, you will erupt two days later, just like poison oak would. You touch it Wednesday night, and you will break out every Friday. The puzzle is solved." Sharon got my full credit and praise for resolving the mystery. She threw the plant out, and her rash was cured forever.

In addition to poison oak and English primrose, Peruvian lily (alstremaria) is another potent plant allergen. If you are a florist, and if you get allergic to it, it can be a career-ending malady. The reactions can be so severe that blisters form on the fingertips, just from plucking off old petals when touching them only for a few seconds.

If you have an ongoing, troublesome, persistent case of eczema or dermatitis, get examined and tested by your dermatologist or allergist for a contact dermatitis. If you don't know, or you can't avoid what you are allergic to, despite the best medicine on earth, you are destined to suffer chronic, itching, miserable skin.

Chapter Twenty-Seven:
April Fool's Joke?

L ife is stranger than fiction. I didn't really like my stints in the emergency room as medical officer of the day, up in Elmendorf Air Force Base, Alaska, in the late 1970's. But it did allow me to see some great cases and great rashes that I wouldn't have seen otherwise.

One night I was getting "killed," as the hospital staff would often put it. Kids with earaches, adults in auto accidents, a lady with a seizure, and a teenager with an acute abdomen dominated my night. It was like a war zone. Finally, at 3:00 a.m., we had a lull in the action. I hoped I might grab a few winks of sleep in the doctor's lounge. Just as I was nodding off, the corpsman buzzed me on the intercom. "Doc, we got one for you," he said.

Well, this was unusual. Most often, he would start with, "We got a kid with a sore throat," or "We have a knife wound." But he didn't give me any clues this time.

I wearily put on my white doctor's coat and shuffled off to the exam room. A minister sat there, and he meekly said, "Hello." His wife was in the room, but it was clear who the patient was. The minister was in obvious pain, but seemed reluctant to talk about it. He had arrived in

Anchorage after a very long eight-hour drive. The time delay seemed to have greatly aggravated his pain. For some reason, he did not seek medical care in his hometown.

After several minutes of avoiding the subject, he suddenly revealed the reason for his pain when he blurted, "I have a Clairol shampoo bottle up my rectum."

But I was no fool. Since it was past midnight, it was now April 1st. The staff was obviously playing an April fool's joke on young Dr. Naversen. Maybe I had been gruff with one of the corpsmen, or perhaps I had unintentionally insulted the staff?

"Well, I'll fix them," I thought. I'll just send "Mister-Clairol-Shampoo-Bottle-Up-The-Rectum" for an x-ray. The hoax would be revealed, and I would get 20 minutes of precious sleep while he was next door getting "rayed."

Exactly 20 minutes later, the corpsman rang out, "Doctor, we've got your x-ray." I was feeling even sleepier than before the first time they woke me up. "I am never going to get any sleep tonight," I lamented.

I held the x-ray before the bright light. Just inside the rectum was an opaque object about 12 inches long, shaped exactly like a Clairol shampoo bottle. It looked big enough to be a convenient, family-sized container. That's when it dawned on me: This is no hoax, no April fool's joke—this guy is for real!

He sheepishly revealed that he and his wife had been playing around in the privacy of their bedroom. She shoved the plastic bottle up too far. Instantly, it was sucked up inside him and became stuck. It wouldn't budge. It was "Pain City." Whenever he tried to evacuate the bottle, paroxysms of hurt doubled him over. And he couldn't show his face in his hometown, being a minister and all. It was a small town and word would get out!

I tried to keep a straight face, and to be very nonjudgmental. Hey, the guy was happily married. The accident happened with his wife, not with some hooker. I guess each person to his own devices—in this case, a Clairol shampoo bottle.

I told them confidently, "Don't worry—I'll get it out for you." But try as I might, the massive swelling and the secretions in his rectum made it impossible to grasp the bottle with a tenaculum. The undersurface of the plastic was a sloppy blob. Every attempt to pull resulted in severe pain. It seemed that with every try to extract the bottle, there was even more swelling.

After some time struggling, the night was over. My shift was almost done, and I could soon go home to bag some serious sleep. My eyes were bleary.

But what about the minister? "I'll just send him up to Dr. John Garcia," I thought. Dr. Garcia was a super surgeon. Like the doctors in the movie, M.A.S.H., he wasn't very keen on being in the military. He longed to set up his private practice in Washington State when his Air Force hitch was over. But his aversion to the Air Force didn't keep him from being a true professional in his surgical clinic.

Despite my exhaustion, I couldn't help but smile as I wrote out an official United States Air Force Patient Consultation Form for John. "Dear Dr. Garcia, This 55-year-old white male has a Clairol shampoo bottle wedged up his rectum. Kindly remove it." Then I left for home.

I wish I had a video of Dr. Garcia reading my consult when he was up close and personal with our patient.

I had to wait until the next week to find out what happened. It was now Friday, and since I already pulled the all-nighter, I had a glorious three-day weekend coming.

It was not until the following Monday that I collared Dr. Garcia. "Had any interesting consults lately?" I asked while trying to suppress my laughter. I tried to play dumb. (It is easy for me to do.)

John told me that he couldn't get that darned shampoo bottle out either. Finally, after exhausting all other options, the surgical team had taken him to the operating room. The anesthesiologist placed the patient under general anesthesia, which knocked him out, thus relaxing him "down south." Without any pain to deal with, the nimble-fingered Dr. Garcia plucked out the slimy, glistening white plastic shampoo bottle, easy as can be.

The minister was fine. After a week, his sore derrière healed uneventfully. Thank goodness he had no permanent scarring or damage to the delicate mucosa.

I just have a sneaking feeling that he and his wife changed their brand—or at least their bottle size—of shampoo.

Chapter Twenty-Eight: Druggies, or How I Got Had

"Dr. Naversen, will you fill this prescription for Percodan on your patient?" the pharmacist asked on a phone call late on a Sunday afternoon.

My wife, Jane, replied, "My husband, Dr. Naversen, is out on a jog. Can I have him call you back when he returns to the house?"

I had a great jog. They were all great ones. I hadn't missed a day running in over six years. Once back at the house, my wife gave me the message, and I said, "Actually, I wouldn't refill Percodan because I never prescribe that particular narcotic."

Even though I called the pharmacist right back, they had closed for the day. I puzzled about the mysterious weekend call for a narcotic that I didn't use from a town that was a five-hour drive from Medford.

First thing Monday morning, I called the pharmacist. She stated that a very forceful young lady demanded that the pharmacist fill her prescription. Without batting an eye, the patient stared the druggist right in eye and said, "Dr. Naversen wanted me to have this for my severe menstrual cramps." Because I was temporarily unavailable, the pharmacist went ahead and filled the prescription for the patient who appeared to be in pain.

I said, "Could you please fax me a copy of the prescription blank?" When I got it a few minutes later, it was a clear forgery. The signature was not mine. I called the pharmacist back and said, "We have been had. I didn't write that prescription. Although Percodan is a good painkiller, I never prescribe that one. I know the young woman. Her mother used to work for me. What can we do?"

"Unfortunately, there is not a lot we can do," said the pharmacist. I can't really check with other pharmacies in Portland. I would be violating her privacy rights. And we can't really get the pills back at this juncture—it is too late."

"I know what we can do," I exclaimed. "I know her dad, and I will call him and let him know that his daughter is a druggie. He will straighten her out faster than the plodding arm of the law will."

The young woman used to visit her mom in our office. Becky was a wonderful and trusted employee. She never would do drugs, and she would never condone her daughter's use of drugs. The youngster Stephanie must have come over one time rifled through a medical drawer and stole a prescription pad. Somehow, she was able to get my official narcotics number, and then she forged the prescription. She figured by presenting it late on the weekend to the pharmacy in Portland, it would be hard to verify. She succeeded in extracting drugs from the system using an "inside job."

Dad straightened her out. He put the fear of God into his daughter. She gave up drugs, she later got married, and one day she brought her lovely baby by the office. We didn't bring up the drug incident, but I know we were both thinking about it. I hope the young lady learned her lesson. Her baby needs a drug-free mom!

Some years later, I removed five cysts from a woman's face, scalp and torso. They came out uneventfully, but I knew that with five deep cysts, there could be some pain and bleeding. "Do you need some pain pills?" I asked Keri. Since I wasn't on call that night, I wanted to keep my house in order. I wanted to make sure my partners were not called late at night for pain pills on a surgery I had done.

"Tylenol No. 3 doesn't work on me; how about some Vicodin?" Keri asked. She was a heavy-set, big-boned lady so I wrote her for #20 Vicodin.

I don't usually give quite that many for outpatient surgery, but I guess I was trying to be extra compassionate that day.

The next day we got a call from Keri's husband. He told my assistant, "This is amazing. We had a fire in our house, and it burned up our master bedroom and our two bathrooms. It was my daughter's defective curling iron. We could have lost our whole house. We might have all got burned up. We are okay, but the pain pills were in the bathroom. Is there any chance of another prescription for Vicodin?"

When I heard the request, I smelled a rat. Twenty Vicodin yesterday, 20 more today, I don't think so! I told my trusty assistant Sharon, "It has been over 24 hours since the surgery. Let's just use intermittent ice packs and Extra-Strength Tylenol, and tell her to avoid aspirin since that could cause bleeding.

On Saturday, I happened to be on call. The husband notified the answering service, "My wife is having bleeding, and she is in a lot of pain. Can the doctor call in some more pain medications?"

I called the husband within the hour. I gave the family a pep talk. "Rest the injured part, and take it easy this weekend. Use intermittent ice packs and dose up on Extra Strength Tylenol. I am not calling in any more pain meds. I would like to have your wife stop by bright and early Monday at 8:00 a.m. for a wound check and dressing change." (I thought of the Percodan junkie in Portland, and I vowed not to be had by a druggie again.)

My partner, Dr. Igelman, harassed me the next week. "Dr. Naversen, you cold-hearted bastard, the woman was in pain. Her house burned down, for God sakes. You didn't even have the common decency to give her more Vicodin when she was bleeding from the wounds you inflicted on her. You are a barbarian! I wouldn't treat a dog that way!"

Keri never showed for her dressing change Monday morning. We saw her later in the week. The wounds looked fine, there was no bleeding and I saw no infection. She was pain free.

Sharon removed the sutures and expertly Steri-taped the wound. "By the way," she asked, "how bad was the fire in your house?"

Keri said, "What are you talking about? We didn't have a fire in our house."

Sharon covered up someone's big lie when she said, "Oh, sorry, I must have mixed you up with another patient."

So the husband was the druggie in the family. He tried to use Keri's surgery as an excuse to pump me for more narcotics. He never told her about the dressing change on Monday. That's why she missed it. They were obviously not in cahoots. Had Keri been trying to get drugs, she, too, would have lied about the fire! I've learned by now to beware of narcotic refills on nights and weekends, especially when you are on call for patients unknown to you!

Chapter Twenty-Nine: Dr. Ig

God brought me Dr. Igelman via a multi-specialty clinic in Medford. Although correctly pronounced "Ig-el-man," he is variously known as " Dr. Eye-gull-man," "Dr. Inglewood," "Dr. Englewood," or just "Inglenook." Maybe "Dr. Piggleman" would be best, since no one can mess that one up. (Or would that be "Dr. Piggelman"?)

It makes matters worse that his name is Jon David Igelman, but he goes by Dave. No one ever gets it right. But after over four decades, you would think Dr. Igelman—let's just call him "Ig"—would have mellowed about his name pronunciation by now. He still gets upset when someone butchers his name, and it happens all day long. Even his diploma from the American Academy of Dermatology was misspelled. I have offered to pay the legal fee of $75 dollars to have his name legally changed to something non-controversial like "John Smith" or "Fred Jones," but he wishes to keep persecuting himself with "J. David Igelman."

After he honorably served his commitment owed to the U.S. Air Force Academy in the 1980s, Ig separated from military service, where he was the base dermatologist at the academy in Colorado Springs. He knew I was looking for a partner, but he chose to go with a local multi-specialty clinic here in Medford. The clinic was well-run (or so he thought), and they had been in existence since 1946, so why align forces with a fly-by-night solo practitioner named Naversen? Although I was disappointed that he joined the other clinic, I decided to keep the lines of communication open with Ig before he moved to Medford. I have learned not to burn bridges. Who knows what the future will bring?

Ig worked in Medford a total of four days when he found out his clinic was going down faster than the Titanic. Although their doctors were excellent, mismanagement, too many employees, and poor medical contracts with insurance companies caused their doom. The clinic would soon be closing its doors forever. Surprisingly, Ig didn't even get the dubious honor of being the last doctor to be hired by the clinic. That distinction belongs to a hard-working, family practice doctor in Medford, who is also a very fast runner. Who could he be?

Luckily for me, and no so lucky for the clinic, Ig gave them a pink slip before they could gave him one. He moved three miles across town to join me in my practice. For the first time, Naversen had a medical doctor as a partner.

From that moment on, the practical joke index soared greatly at Dermatology and Laser Associates of Medford. One day I came to work, and as I tried to put on my white coat, my hands wouldn't fit through the sleeves. Someone had stapled both arms shut.

Another day, Ig showed me a leak in our roof. (Leaky roofs were a sore point—our roof had leaked freely over the years despite thousands of dollars in repair work.) Rumor had it Ig had put a soaking wet rag on the ceiling with a bucket full of water on the floor, just beneath the supposed leak. He raised my blood pressure on that one.

Another day I came to work, and some skateboarders had supposedly shot a BB hole in my office window. Ig called them "punks on plywood." We have had quite a few run-ins on the office property. Our concrete ramps attract skateboarders like bums to the I-5 overpass. Well, it took me three months to discover, it was a fake bullet hole made with glue. I nearly fell off the ladder and killed myself trying to scrape it off.

Ig was particularly proud of his "heavy red brick trick." I am known at D.L.A.M. for my heavy black briefcase which I cart religiously to and from the office. It is my peripheral brain, where I temporarily store valuable articles, magazine reprints, business receipts, files, pens and my daily jogging log, among many other things. Now I admit that I may not look at the bottom of my briefcase every single day. I like to prioritize things—first things first, and last things last. Do the important things first, and the other stuff can wait until a later day. My desk is deluged with an incredible amount of junk mail, throwaway journals, ads, credit card statements, and personal mail that has to be taken home in the briefcase.

But I must admit my black briefcase seemed awfully heavy one week. Ig had secretly sneaked a red brick into the bottom beneath lots of paperwork. When I didn't discover it, the next week he put another one in next to the first one. Well, then even I could figure out that something was wrong. I laughed when I spotted not one, but two bricks, hidden in the bottom! I've since switched to a streamlined attaché case.

Some months later, a six-inch plastic Mickey Mouse appeared sideways outside my window. Mickey is up too high for me to safely remove it without risking life and limb. So Mickey stares at me day after day when I am working at my desk. I guess he will stay there until glue failure five or ten years hence.

The females on the staff can't escape Ig's practical jokes, either. One day a sign mysteriously appeared in front of our staff bathroom boldly indicating "Doctors Only." The sign over the other staff bathroom said "Men Only." Since, at the time, we had only two staff bathrooms and only male doctors at D.L.A.M., our ladies were out of luck when they felt the call of nature.

One day, in honor of our only Russian- born medical assistant, "Russian toilet paper" showed up in the bathroom. In the tissue dispenser, we found rolled up cardboard with embedded metal tire studs. (Talk about hemorrhoids!) Then we had an economy movement. Instead of regular tissue paper, Ig replaced it with a large box of leaves from our Buckeye tree outside in the courtyard between our two clinic buildings. But the man did have a heart—no poison oak leaves could be found in the basket.

As I did my business in the restroom on another day—"Blam!"—a loud noise sounded like a bomb. I thought al-Qaida had attacked. Really,

Ig had slid a bubble wrap under the bathroom door. He stomped on the material with his heavy shoe just outside the door that transmitted the loud popping sound, mimicking a bomb. Rumor later held that I was so startled that I wet my pants. (It's a lie!). Ig was particularly proud of that stunt.

Ig assisted me in a laser procedure on the delicate portion of a man's anatomy. We vaporized growths with our state-of-the-art our carbon dioxide Ultrapulse laser. Due to fumes and the fear of viral contaminants from the laser plume, standard procedure was for our trusty assistant Georgia to suck up all the vapors with a loud and powerful Buffalo filter held right next to the surgery site on the skin. In the heat of battle, I accidentally sucked up the patient's testicles, not once, but twice, into the tubing (great balls of fire!). Ig and Georgia are my witnesses. I think the patient kind of liked it.

Shortly after he started working at DLAM, Dr. Igelman remarked to his assistant Lisa that he had just gone to a new dentist. In the **Medford Mail Tribune** that day, we all read the dentist had been unfortunately busted for sexual improprieties. Ig remarked that it was the first time in his life he had been gassed with nitrous oxide for a routine dental cleaning. When he woke up from the procedure, he felt a little funny. He couldn't figure out why that night when he got undressed, he found his underpants on inside out, and backwards.

Lisa's eyes grew wide in shock at the revelation. Ig had gotten her, bigtime. He never had nitrous oxide after all. Had he told that same story only six months later, the gullible Lisa would have just laughed knowing that it was just an Ig joke.

But once in a while, Igelman gets some payback. I bought a great book called **How to Sound Smart** by Vincent and Conway. This quick and witty guide has over 200 foreign phrases, literary and philosophical references, and some wonderful English words that allow a person to sound as smart as they think they are. For a three month period, I peppered Ig with many such high-minded, tongue-in-cheek phrases. The poor man didn't know what hit him. He either thought Naversen was extra smart, or Ig was extra dumb!

One summer, Ig went to visit his in-laws in Korea for two weeks. When he got back, he saw a large "For Sale by Owner" sign planted on his front lawn. The phone number given on the sign was actually that of the local strip club. I wish I could have seen Ig's face after his 18-hour flight from Korea, through many time zones, only to discover that someone had put his house on the market.

Dr. Ig, we are dozens of tricks behind you by now. But someday, maybe not tomorrow, maybe not even next month, you are headed for a big fall. You will be nothing more than low-hanging fruit on the tree of life. The conspiracy will involve us all; it will be total. You are going down, my man.

But perhaps it is best left to karma. Some people would say a dark cloud already follows our Dr. Ig. He worked for the local clinic for only four days, and it went belly-up after over 50 years of operation. On Ig's trip to South Korea, a North Korean gun boat opened up and fired on a South Korean boat, sinking it to the bottom of the sea. War was eminent, and an international incident could have developed. And what about the time he vacationed in Kauai? The day he got there, a shark bit off a local, high school surfer's leg. The south beaches were closed for 48 hours, for the first time in recorded memory. I knew that somehow, in some way, Ig was to blame for these unusual calamities.

But in my mind, Dr. Igelman is a delight. It is great to have a well-trained, board-certified dermatologist to share problem patients with. We read lots of skin biopsy slides together and we keep each other out of trouble. Ig keeps us all from getting too serious about life. It is also nice to have someone at the clinic that I can regularly win beer bets with.

"Mrs. Jones has lichen planus," I said one day.

"No, she has lichen simplex chronicus," Ig replied. Another delightful partner, Dr. Dwight Tribelhorn (just call him "Dirt"), goes in the room and serves as the tiebreaker. Dirt's verdict returns in Naversen's favor, and the good guy (namely me) wins another beer from Dr. Ig. I tell him I want a Caldera beer. He runs all over town looking for it before he realizes they only sell it by the keg.

To summarize, I hope you liked chapter Twenty-Nine, the "roast" of my good friend and colleague Dr. J. David Igelman. But I don't think we have seen the last of practical jokes at Dermatology and Laser!

Chapter Thirty: Viagra

We all have a Viagra story. One of my favorites is from a friend of mine from Steamboat Springs, Colorado, who had a dinner engagement. An hour before he and his wife had to leave for the party, he popped a Viagra and they started playing around. His "quickie" was successful, so he took a shower and got dressed in his formal wear. Only one problem, it wouldn't go down! His wife gamely suggested he just drape a bath towel over it. Maybe no one at the party would notice his erect manhood covered with a terrycloth towel?

But I heard my all time best Viagra story in a local Bi-Mart department store in Medford. An elderly patient (and also a friend of mine) related his experience as we chatted by the shoe department. A 19-year-old clerk down the aisle was within earshot, and I knew she soaked up every word.

"Doc," Tom confided in me, "go ahead and take the pill, but it doesn't work by itself. Wait 60 minutes, and then have your partner stimulate you any way she knows how."

Tom's wife was about 70 years old. She was a foxy lady, even though she was now old enough to be on Medicare. Due to aging and some medical issues, Tom had not been able to have sexual relations with his lovely wife in some years. They had high hopes for the joy that the magic, blue, film-coated, rounded, diamond-shaped tablet might bring them.

Suddenly, with the pill, things went gangbusters! Tom related to me (and the 19 year-old-girl down the aisle) that he enjoyed the mightiest erection he had experienced in years. His prow was standing tall and erect, like a thick, solid wooden mast holding up a large sail on a Yankee clipper ship. (It wasn't holding up a sail, just his satin, white bedsheet.) They had the best sex he could remember in a decade. Then he felt like he was going into shock. He developed a pounding headache and his face felt flush. His eyes blurred, his vision turned blue-tinged and shadowy, and he could not otherwise perceive colors. He collapsed back into bed, his heart palpitating faster than a hummingbird's wings racing in mid-flight. After 30 minutes or so, he dragged himself up and went to the bathroom. He was still erect like a horny 16-year-old high school boy. When doing his business at the toilet, his stimulated proboscis made aiming difficult so he whizzed all over the floor.

"Was I embarrassed by the accident? You bet I was," he told me. "Of course I didn't want my wife to see the mess I had made. Imagine me, a totally naked man, with a totally erect penis, half in shock, on my hands and knees, hurriedly scrubbing the floor with a towel before my wife found out what I had done." Tom dragged himself back to bed and again he collapsed in exhaustion. He slept fitfully until morning. Finally, it shrunk down to its normal size.

Tom called his family doctor first thing in the morning. "I feel real bad, can I come in for a check?"

Sixty minutes later, Tom was in the examination room. He was so embarrassed by the night's events that he failed to mention the Viagra and his dynamite sex. Without this key piece of medical history, the doctor found only a slightly low blood pressure. "Tom, go home and get some rest. You look like crap," said his doctor.

At this juncture, I saw the 19-year-old female clerk straining to catch every morsel. Just then, Tom pulled out his pack of Viagra. "Doug, if I take any more of these, they will kill me. Here, *you* take 'em!"

I could barely contain my laughter all through Tom's saga of erectile dysfunction, love and the little blue pill. I found myself biting the inside of my cheeks throughout the story. I didn't want to seem disrespectful since Tom was baring his soul to me. And also, I didn't want to interrupt the great story that flowed from his lips.

I took the Viagra home and showed them to my wife, Jane. She said, "Doug, you don't need those things. Why don't you give them to one of your jogging buddies--maybe they could use them?" The perfect idea, I thought.

Chapter Thirty-One: Ronda, Is There Anything New and Different in Your Life?

Ronda was an attractive woman in her mid 20s. Her skin disease was not the issue; it was how she got it that shocked me. She stated she had gradually been picking up "infected hairs" on her arms and legs and, yes, the itching had been gradually been getting worse. When she went to bed at night, she went crazy with scratching.

An exam revealed burrow marks of the finger webs, wrists and abdomen—a slam dunk! These are classic signs of scabies. A scrape and a microscopic exam of a few of these skin tracts revealed the adult mite and eggs, confirming the diagnosis.

"Ronda, you have scabies," I told her. "That does not mean you are a dirty person, it just means that you were exposed to it. I want you to apply Lindane lotion tonight and in one week, all over your body. You will be cured." (Today, we might use Elimite cream. It is a more modern, but a more expensive medication.)

But the diagnosis was only part of the puzzle. I always like to know where the scabies came from. It always is good to trace the close personal contacts to find out from whom Ronda caught this ectoparasite.

Maybe we could provide them some relief from their itchy symptoms sooner rather than later.

To try and determine the source, I inquired, "Ronda, has there been anything new and different in your life?"

"Dr. Naversen, funny you should ask," she replied with a pained look on her face. "Have you read the **Medford Mail Tribune lately?**" At this point, Ronda's eyes got really wide, and then she began sobbing. "I am the lady that was abducted by that weirdo. He held me prisoner as his sex slave for five weeks." Her words rushed out in a torrent, as if the dam had just burst. "I am so lucky to be alive. I was able to escape through the hotel window one afternoon when he was asleep. I raced for help on the highway, and thankfully the police came and arrested him. He is now in an out-of-state jail awaiting his trial. He is a total loser, he is a scumbucket, and I hope he rots in hell!"

I was shocked and amazed at this woman's story. I knew it was true, because I had seen the article when it came out in the paper the previous week. "I am so sorry for your pain," I replied slowly. "I am really glad you are safe and sound. You got scabies from that pervert." She was somewhat relieved when I told her, "Your skin will be 100-percent cured, and you will have no residual scars."

What a coincidence that the woman in the newspaper article was now sitting in a white gown on the examination table in front of me. I did feel exceptionally sorry for her. In addition to curing her skin and her severe itching, I wanted to give her a little extra something. I knew she would appreciate anything, any little nugget that would give her comfort and relief from her traumatic experience. Just then, a light bulb came on.

"Ronda, you caught scabies from this slime ball. Normally I like to notify all contacts that they have been exposed to scabies. Why, they could itch for months and be really miserable if we didn't contact them."

Ronda told me the exact jail where he was being held. As I contemplated calling the prison, a wicked grin came upon both our faces simultaneously. "Ronda, just maybe I won't be calling any jail after all," I chortled.

"Good job, Doctor. I love you."

We never did call to let the prisoner know he had scabies. He had given the itchy disease to my lovely patient, along with all the other mean and nasty things he had done to her. I felt good that we were extracting a measure of dermatological justice on this low-life. We could never recover the lost five weeks of Ronda's life, but maybe we could make the loser itch for at least five more weeks. If we were lucky, maybe he would get the full seven-year itch?

Ronda was soon cured, and after one follow up visit, I never saw her again. I hope she recovered from her physical and emotional suffering. I don't know how long her abductor was sentenced to prison, but I hope it was for a long time. And I don't know how long it took before he was diagnosed with scabies, but I hope it was an eternity!

Chapter Thirty-Two:
More Hives

Leslie walked into my fifth floor office at Elmendorf Air Force Base Hospital in Anchorage, Alaska. "Doctor Naversen, I have had hives for 12 years now," she said. "Can you cure me?"

"Hives for 12 whole years?" I questioned incredulously. I tried not to frown or scowl. If I couldn't smile, at least I could attempt a neutral facial expression; any extraneous grimace would give away the gloom that overwhelmed me upon learning of her long history of urticaria. Leslie had triggered the memory an old dermatology proverb that I'd heard during my residency, less than a year before: "If you have the choice of facing a charging bull elephant at close range, or of facing a patient with chronic urticaria, you are a fool if you don't choose the elephant!"

How could I, without the help of professors or fellow residents, isolated in the frozen tundra of Alaska, possibly hope to cure someone with severe hives—much less hives of 12 years' duration? I glanced at her medical file, now thicker than a volume of the *Encyclopedia Britannica*, filled with past workups from a zillion other doctors who also probably would have chosen the aforementioned charging bull elephant rather than Leslie's mysterious hives. Her chart was like a giant whopper hamburger—I needed two hands just to pick it up.

Hey, Naversen, this is why they pay you the big bucks, I thought. (Never mind that it was only an Air Force salary.) Leslie was a demanding, heavy, blonde woman with thick glasses and a biting personality, and that is the kind version of her description. But I guess anyone could turn obese and depressed if they had to face severe itchy welts all over their body every day for 12 long years. She must've been trapped in her own personal version of the Bill Murray movie *Groundhog Day*. The hives came on slowly when she was 23 years old, lasted day after day after day, and at 35, she didn't want to play this game anymore.

"Leslie, any idea what is causing them?" I asked. "Good opening question," I thought. Why didn't I just say I couldn't help her? Naversen, bend over and take your whipping like a man, and just move on to your next patient, instead of wasting this woman's time. With chronic, severe hives like this, I thought I'd have a snowball's chance in hell of curing her.

But I heard desperation in Leslie's voice when she said, "I don't have a clue. All the doctors and nurses I have seen don't have a clue. My husband and two children don't have a clue." Frankly, at that moment, she looked suicidal.

I didn't want to give Leslie any false hope that I could cure her. So I didn't tell her that urticaria (hives) was one of my strong suits. Although I knew how challenging cases like hers could be, I'd had the opportunity to assist my old professor, Dr. Bill Akers, on a "Seminar In-Depth on Chronic Urticaria" for a few years running at the American Academy of Dermatology annual meeting. Thousands of skin doctors from the United States, and from the four corners of the earth, traveled to the meeting. I consider it the best dermatology meeting anywhere—it may even be the single best medical meeting in the world. I was impressed with its organization, scope, large attendance, the skin lasers available for inspection and purchase, the cosmetic and pharmaceutical exhibits, the medical texts available for review and sale, and the chance to take courses given by experts in any and every area of dermatology. We had 50 or so doctors attending our seminar every year. And I suspect that each of them was there hoping to learn how to cure a particular patient—a case as difficult as Leslie's.

Over the years, I had pretty much reviewed all of the available world literature on chronic urticaria. If any new article came out on the subject, I would pounce on it and add the paper reprint to the voluminous folders in my filing cabinet. There was no readily-available computer storage back then.

I decided that while we were discovering the cause of Leslie's hives, we would push her anti-histamines to the point of drowsiness, and then back off. We would really load up on her bedtime dose, since the old anti-histamines such as Benadryl and Atarax were sedating, and they might knock her out if she took them during the day. We would search for a drug cause, including prescription drugs and even aspirin and over-the-counter cold pills, vitamins, and supplements. We would check for food allergy, and we would not forget to rule out allergy to additives such as azo and benzoic dyes used to color food and pills. We would rule out respiratory dust and pollens in the air, although that seemed less likely since she had no asthma or hay fever. We would inquire about her cigarette smoking history, since even regular cigarettes and menthol brands have caused hives in case reports within the literature. We would be aware about the possibility of internal cancer causing her urticaria, but I reflected that if she had cancer, she was not likely to have survived for 12 long years; she would have passed on long ago.

In addition, we would get an ANA blood test for lupus. One in ten lupus patients suffers from hives, in addition to their characteristic lupus rash. (Modern doctrine favors an autoimmune cause for many cases of urticaria.) We would also exhaustively hunt down any silent, focal infections smoldering unknown, deep-down inside her body.

I took home her chart that night. My wife, Jane, was good at raising our three kids, and she let me do some evening work I just couldn't fit in at the busy, hectic clinic during the day. She saw me go through every page of Leslie's chart. I made a note of her lab and x-ray studies. She had already had the "million-dollar workup" by the time I saw her. I thought of a few remote possibilities that had not been covered. Since she got hives every single day, even on vacation in the "Lower 48," she must be carrying the hive-causing agent inside her body (endogenous urticaria as opposed to exogenous urticaria). So, to my thinking, a focal infection would be high on the list. Or maybe it was even some ubiquitous food additive present in our food supply.

I remembered back to my gastroenterology rotation as a medical intern at Wilford Hall in San Antonio, Texas. What disease do you get if you are female, fat, fair, 40 and fertile? That is, a female patient who is overweight, Caucasian, is in her 40s, with one or more children? That is the profile of someone likely to be troubled with gall stones! Well, Leslie wasn't 40 yet (she was in her 30s), but all the other criteria fit. I recommended an oral cholecystogram at the radiology clinic. (We would do a gallbladder ultrasound or a fancier scan in the present day, but the "OCG" was the gold standard back then to discover gallbladder disease.)

Leslie was ready for anything, and to endure any procedure that would get her cured. Although she had no fatty food intolerance, gas, bloating or pain radiating to her right shoulder blade (classic for gallbladder disease), we proceeded with the study.

I was excited when the radiologist called me: "Doug, Leslie has a gallbladder stuffed full of gallstones!"

This was big news to Leslie. She didn't have a clue about any gallstones. I speculated that the gallstones could be harboring a smoldering bacterial infection. Periodically, the bacteria would be released into her bloodstream as a "superantigen." Wham! Off would fire her mast cells located in her skin and around her blood vessels. A massive release of histamine would trigger itchy welts. Maybe this was the big break we needed after 12 long years?

I had become emotionally attached to Leslie on her visits to my clinic. I learned about her marriage, her two kids, and some of the problems she faced on her day-to-day schedule, all the while fighting the hives. But I expressed optimism: "Leslie, I can't guarantee it, but if we take out your gallbladder, there is chance your hives may be cured."

At the time, we couldn't do laparoscopic surgery for gallstones like we do now. So she would need a general anesthesia and a big operation. I didn't want to subject Leslie to the operation if it wouldn't cure her hives, but I couldn't promise her anything other than her gallbladder and gallstones would be out and gone. "But what would happen with the hives?" we both wondered.

We were blessed with a fine surgeon at Elmendorf named Dr. Dave

Anderson. (He and Dr. Garcia were young lions.) He agreed to do the surgery. As Leslie came out of surgery, I sat with her in the recovery room. I was sad when I saw that welts were still on her body, hiving merrily away. We had failed! Leslie was too groggy to talk or understand, so I just squeezed her hand and smiled. I didn't sleep very well that night.

One week later, Leslie knocked on my door at the clinic. "Dr. Naversen, my hives are gone. You cured me!" She gave me a big hug from the heart. The gallstones containing the silent bacterial infection in her body were now out of her system. She must have been forming gallstones for over a decade, but she didn't know it.

In the months that followed, we kept our fingers crossed. Would the hives recur? Leslie was excited. There was no need for any antihistamines, and there was no more itching, since the hives lied dormant.

After two years, we realized the hives were gone for good. The last ones she ever had were the ones I saw in the recovery room. Leslie was so happy to be hive-free—it literally changed her life. She lost weight, replaced the thick glasses with contact lenses, and even lost her sour disposition. The only bad part occurred when she divorced her husband. I guess they didn't match each other anymore.

Before I left Alaska, Leslie gave me a plaque which I still have on my wall in Medford. It says, "To Dr. Naversen, thanks for getting down to the true nitty gritty. Sincerely, Leslie."

Wouldn't be nice if all my cases could end like this one? It was total capitulation by the enemy, in this case the urticaria. And it was total victory for Leslie and Dr. Naversen.

Chapter Thirty-Three:
The Yellow Man

Kansas came into my office with a scared look on his face. "Dr. Naversen, I'm turning yellow!"

This visit occurred in Alaska on the shortest day of the year, December 21st, when the sun hardly shines. My office was on the fifth floor of the hospital, and I could only see the sun from 10:30 a.m. to 2:30 p.m. as it rose above and sunk down below the mountain ranges surrounding Anchorage. I looked at the pale skin on my palm, and then I looked at the apparently-jaundiced skin on his palm. He wasn't kidding—his skin really did have a yellowish tint.

One glance at Kansas' eyeballs revealed white sclera. If they were yellow like his skin, then he would most likely have had "yellow jaundice" caused by viral hepatitis of the liver. But a short medical history revealed that, at age 22, Kansas was the picture of health. He had no known diabetes, thyroid disease, liver disease or other similar medical conditions. He had not been exposed to hepatitis A, B, or C, or any other such virus. He and his family were all fair-skinned Caucasians from Arkansas. There was no Asian blood or people of color in his ancestry that could have imparted that yellow hue to his skin. If anything, he seemed overly healthy. He was a vegetarian, and he hadn't eaten red meat in years. He ingested lots of health food, and he loved eating carrots. As a matter of fact, he told me, "I eat six large carrots a day."

"Whoa, Nelly!" I stated. With this information, I felt newly confident that he had a benign condition. We sent Kansas down to the lab. The phlebotomist drew a tube of his blood and they spun it down in the centrifuge.

"By the way," I said to my corpsman, Cannie Brown, why don't you volunteer to go down to the lab and have blood drawn, too? (Could it be in the military, 'volunteer' is an oxymoron?) We need a control specimen." Seeing that I was the officer and Cannie was the enlisted man, he quickly walked to the lab for the blood donation. Maybe if Naversen had been more of a scientist, the doctor himself would have gone to be the guinea pig instead of the trusty corpsman.

Within 20 minutes, we had two test tubes filled with blood back in our office, one from the yellowish gentleman and one from the sergeant. The red blood cells were in the bottom portion of the tubes. The serum was on top. Cannie's serum was pale and straw-colored, and Kansas' was so yellow it knocked my socks off! This confirmed my suspicion, the lad didn't have any serious disease, but instead he had the benign condition known as "carotenemia."

The yellow-orange pigment from the carrots was absorbed into his stomach, and then it was slowly infused into his bloodstream. From there, the pigment trickled into his tiny capillaries in his skin where it was selectively deposited into the stratum corneum, the outer layer of his skin. This gave him his noticeable, dull-canary skin color.

Then Kansas asked the big question with fear and trepidation, "But Dr. Naversen, can I still eat carrots? I really love them a lot."

"Kansas, if you don't mind the yellow skin, you can eat all the carrots you want. You don't really have a disease. You are okay."

Kansas slumped back in his chair, smiled and yelled out, "Great, Doc. You're the best!" I could hardly believe it when he then pulled out a carrot from his pocket and he began munching on it.

As I reflected on his condition, I realized that carotenemia is more common than we think. You have probably looked at a cute little baby's skin. Although the epidermis is beautiful since it has no wrinkles, liver spots, moles or freckles to mar the baby's appearance (the baby hasn't had time to cook and fry in the sun), if you look carefully, the ears and the palms and soles often have a yellowish hue. Many infants eat baby food consisting of carrots, squash, sweet potatoes and tomatoes, which are all high in carotene. Mom and dad don't know it, but their baby may have carotenemia, just like Kansas did. The color slowly resolves as the baby's diet changes into a child and adult diet. The skin usually reverts back to normal before the parents even notice.

Lupus patients can actually benefit from carotenemia. I have placed some of them on Atabrine (Quinacrine), an anti-malarial medication that coincidentally prevents them from burning and getting rashes from ultraviolet damage from the sun. If they are on a high enough dose for a long enough time, their skin will turn slightly yellow due to natural staining inimical to the medication. By putting them on beta-carotene simultaneously, it gives them a more natural orange-red-yellow color that looks pleasing to the eye compared to the pure-yellow skin of Atabrine.

Chapter Thirty-Four:
The Lazy Norwegian

My partner, Dr. Dave Igelman, calls me "A Wegian." So maybe we should rename this chapter "The Lazy Wegian." Scandinavian humor is an oxymoron. There really is no Scandinavian humor. Norwegians are stoic people who till the fields, fish the oceans, eat lutefisk and lingonberries, and tend the oil derricks in the North Sea. They pay exorbitant taxes on liquor and cigarettes, and they have won lots of medals in the Winter Olympics—an especially-impressive amount considering they are a country of only four million people. But they don't have a lot of humor.

If you need to amputate a Norwegian's leg, just have him climb up on the procedure table. You don't even need to knock him out with a general anesthesia. Don't even consider wasting local anesthesia. Just cut off the leg, and they won't squawk. No need for lengthy, verbal, and written informed consent. And no need for the HIPAA forms that doctors and dentists and hospitals are now forced to make our patients sign. (In our government's great wisdom, they won't let us harvest timber, but the bureaucrats spew out so many rules and regulations and paperwork that vast tracts of forests have to be cut down to supply the paper.) Remember, Norwegians are stoic.

The Norwegians are familiar with herpes zoster, also known as "the shingles." They call it a "belt of roses from hell." In many cases, they are right. You get chicken pox as a kid, and the virus lies dormant in your nerves until death do you part. If you are unlucky, you will be the one out of five adults who suffers from shingles later in life.

If you do get shingles, try to contract it before age 65. You will heal faster and you will have a lot less pain. If you are over 65 (or under 65 for that matter), get on an oral antiviral bullet within 72 hours of onset to speed the healing. Although somewhat controversial, a course of prednisone by mouth for two to three weeks will cut down on immediate pain, and more importantly, it may reduce the chance of post-herpetic neuralgia (pain occurring for months after the blisters have dried up). I have seen patients who suffer with miserable pain for several years after herpes zoster, so I prefer to be aggressive with these relatively safe therapies.

The FDA just approved a new shingles vaccine, Zostavax, to prevent zoster in adults 60 and over. If you get immunized, you are only one-half less likely to get shingles, and only one-third as likely to develop post-herpetic neuralgia compared with the placebo group. It sounds like a good deal to me.

But we digress. To dispel the myth that Norwegians are totally devoid of humor, I want to tell you about my Great Uncle Enoch. He was born and lived in Stavanger, Norway, the current center for Norwegian oil and gas operations in the North Sea. Amazingly, he looked just like my dad, also named Enoch. He just looked 30 years older.

Uncle Enoch and I were walking along a country road across the bay from Stavanger, near "The Pulpit." (If you get a chance to visit Prestotoken, I would strongly recommend it.) Uncle Enoch suddenly got the call of nature. Fortunately, there was an outhouse on the side of the farmer's field just ahead. With a pained expression on his face, Uncle Enoch sprinted for the outbuilding. He looked like a woodchuck in a hurry. He frantically pulled up the toilet lid as he simultaneously leaned over and carefully checked the seat for black widow spiders. (He hated spiders!) By this time, his pants were halfway down his legs. While just about done with his final sweep looking for bugs and vermin, he watched in panic as his brand new spectacles slipped off his nose, and they fell down into the depths of the outhouse. As he peered into the bowels down below, the odor nearly knocked him down.

The sequence of events that followed was totally comical. Uncle Enoch, standing bare-bottomed and hunched over the opening of the commode, proceeded to take off his expensive Rolex watch from his left wrist and calmly dropped it down into the bottom of the pit. Then he coolly extracted his thick wallet out of his right rear pocket, and he threw that too, down to join the Rolex and his glasses.

"Uncle Enoch," I screamed, "What are you *doing?*" You just threw away your Rolex watch down into the outhouse. And you threw your thick wallet with all your credit cards and your driver's license! Dear Uncle, with all due respect, are you nuts?"

"Nephew Doug, you are young and you are American. You know not of ways Norwegian. Did you really think I am dumb enough to go down in the bottom of this foul-smelling outhouse just to retrieve my spectacles?"

So maybe there is a little Norwegian humor after all, which brings me to the title of this chapter. Just how lazy are Norwegian men, anyway? Well, rumor has it that Norwegian men are so lazy, so lazy indeed, that they will only marry pregnant women. And that is lazy!

Chapter Thirty-Five: Poison Oak

Jan scratched wildly at the red linear blisters on her arms and legs. "Jan, don't scratch," I said. "It looks just like poison oak."

"No, Doug, I don't ever come in contact with poison oak," she replied. Still, I gave her a class I, super-potent cortisone cream to extinguish the fiery dermatitis.

Jan was one of my favorite people in the whole world. She had been my next door neighbor in Anchorage, Alaska, for five years. I like to tell the story of how I didn't like my next door neighbors, Jan and Jim, on the cul-de-sac where I lived, so I bought the house on the other side of them. I moved two doors down. We were now living on the left side of their house, not on the right side.

When we moved to Oregon, I was overjoyed some years later when Jan and Jim moved a block away from our home in Jacksonville, Oregon. We quickly renewed our friendship.

For the whole spring and summer, Jan kept breaking out with what looked for all the world like poison oak. But she kept denying any exposure. That autumn, I couldn't stand Jan's scratching any longer. The long linear blisters were inflamed and sensitive. Tissue juice wept from the blisters and made her totally miserable. I vowed to make a personal field inspection at her house. Maybe she had an exotic plant like Peruvian

Lilly or English Primrose growing indoors. The leaves of the plants could "turn on" Jan, and they could make her highly allergic, similar to what happened to the Medford woman who had English Primrose on her kitchen table.

I drove down the hill to Jan's house. The cold autumn air had killed the chlorophyll in the trees and bushes. That allowed the spectacular crimson color that was Jan's pride and joy, to display all of its beauty as it adorned the grounds on her front lawn. She fertilized and washed it religiously.

I took one glance at the plant and burst out laughing. "Jan, leaves of three, leave them be. You've got the healthiest poison oak plant in the whole state of Oregon right in your front yard!"

Although Jan grew up in Wenatchee, Washington, where they must have tons of poison oak, in her two decades of living in the Great Land in Alaska, she must have forgotten what it looked like. One of the best things about Alaska is that it has no poison oak. It is too far north, and it is much too cold.

We walked the grounds of Jan's house. She must have had 20 poison oak plants in various sizes and shapes scattered on her property. The mystery was solved. Not only did Jan quit feeding and watering them, her husband Jim blasted them into the Stone Age with Round Up. Bye, bye, poison oak.

One of the sorriest cases of poison oak I ever saw was a gentleman from Grants Pass, Oregon. He was in an auto accident. As he flipped his Chevy, he was thrown from the moving car. He landed on a bunch of bushes, and luckily he lived. The ambulance hauled him out a few hours later, and he spent the next two days in an intensive care unit. Fortunately, he was not seriously injured, and he was discharged 48 hours later.

Just after discharge, he developed the most blistered, itchy eruption that he had ever experienced. His face swelled, and his crotch swelled to twice its normal size. He was totally miserable. For you see, this was double jeopardy. He survived the car wreck, but he had been thrown into a large clump of poison oak. A severe rash was his reward for surviving. A rapid-acting shot of Celestone, a prednisone chaser, some Aveeno oatmeal baths, some Atarax pills at night for itch, and Temovate cream made him a new man in less than 12 hours.

All contact dermatitis looks alike, whether it is due to poison oak, rubber, nickel, or some other allergen. Poison oak tends to be much more severe and, along with its cousins poison ivy and poison sumac, is by far the most common cause of contact dermatitis in the United States. That is why I always like to rule out the commonplace poison oak first when I evaluate a patient's allergies.

One puzzler was Chick, the jeweler, who had repeated, unexplained bouts of contact dermatitis on his hands. He must be allergic to one of the cleansers in his jewelry store, I thought. Much to our collective chagrin, our patch tests were negative to every chemical tested. His dermatitis bubbled along all summer. When would it stop?

He called me one day when the puzzle was solved. Chick loved to go motorcycling. He went riding out in the country, and he heard Mother Nature's call. Into the woods he went. He did his business, he returned to his cycle, he put on his leather gloves, and off he went. I had treated him for that episode of poison oak—we knew what had caused it—peeing in the woods surrounded by poison oak.

Chick figured out that every time he went cycling, his hands would break out 48 hours later. It was the leather gloves—bingo! He had heavily contaminated his gloves with poison oak that day in the woods. The oleoresin then contaminated his hands each time he wore the gloves, and he developed attack after attack of contact dermatitis. Chick burned his gloves and he was cured.

I feel sorry for our brave firefighters who fight forest fires out in the west. Not only are they risking their lives, but many of them get severe poison oak from walking through the woods. If they breathe the contaminated smoke from burning poison oak plants, they may develop severe facial swelling and eruptions on their exposed skin. The smoke inhalation in their lungs can be a real health hazard. I tip my hat to brave firefighters that save lives, forests, houses and buildings.

There is not really much I can say positively about poison oak. Bee keepers claim if their bees make honey from poison oak plants, the nectar you ingest it will prevent you from getting poison oak. But I doubt it!

Goats will eat poison oak, so maybe we need more goats in the United States. If we could turn poison oak into a hypoallergenic food source for humans, we could feed the world's starving masses. And if we could genetically transfer its drought resistance and amazing survivability in the wild to our domesticated agricultural plants, farmers could very easily grow crops without the need for watering, without fertilizer and without concerns for the weather and plant diseases.

I often wonder what the early settlers—Davy Crockett, Daniel Boone, Jesse Applegate, Kit Carson and John Muir—did when they got poison oak. Maybe if they suffered from severe poison oak, they would have become bank tellers in New York City, and we would have lost their enormous talents in taming and exploring the West.

A few tips for those of you who suffer from this common plant allergy. First of all, avoid it. Stay on the beaten path. As I told Jan, "Leaves of three, leave them be." Don't go out slogging through the woods if you are prone to poison oak. If you like to hike or jog or trails, stay above 4500 feet, since the plant doesn't like extreme cold and altitude. If you think you will be out in it, apply a barrier cream such as Ivy Block before you go out; afterward, wash it off within eight hours of exposure and you probably will not catch poison oak.

If you have localized poison oak, have your doctor prescribe a class I cortisone cream like clobetasol. Store it in the refrigerator for a nice chilling effect when you apply to your inflamed skin four times daily, until the rash resolves.

If you have total-body poison oak, with swelling and blistering of the face and groin, get a shot of Celestone for rapid relief. Follow up with prednisone or a Kenalog shot. A good case of poison oak can last up to 21 days, and with re-exposure to the allergen, it can keep bubbling along for days or weeks. Cool baths with Aveeno oatmeal, baking soda or Epsom salts added can be very soothing, and they will help dry up the blisters. Take a soap and water shower, and scrub out your nails if you have been exposed. Heavily-contaminated skin can be swabbed with rubbing alcohol to dissolve away the uroshiol chemical that causes the allergy. If you, your spouse, or your children have been in the woods, have them throw their clothes directly into the washing machine before they take their shower. Remember not to overbathe and overscrub your skin—just clean off thoroughly the first time you are exposed.

The "moms" of the world get some of the worst cases just by pulling contaminated clothing out of the hamper when doing the wash. Keep the dogs and cats fenced in, or wash them off after they are in the woods. We commonly get poison oak by petting our dogs and cats.

If you have active poison oak, try to sleep with full-length soft cotton pajamas covering the arms and legs. An extra layer between your skin and your fingernails will help protect from nightly scratching. And sometimes knocking yourself out with a sedating antihistamine such as Benadryl or Atarax will allow you to get a good night's sleep.

Allergy shots and immunizations are not effective. Perhaps there is a youthful, budding scientist-dermatologist out there who will someday unlock the key to developing an effective shot or vaccine. Or maybe he or she will figure out a way to eradicate poison oak and poison ivy from the face of the earth. The person who figures out the cure will greatly help humanity (and probably become fabulously wealthy with the patent). If I had the cure, I would gladly forgo the huge financial gain, just because it would be such a good thing for the millions of those who suffer.

Chapter Thirty-Six: Hot Tub Folliculitis

Mark and Becky woke up to find tender red boils peppering their bodies. They couldn't figure out why they'd both broken out within 96 hours of visiting the Naversen residence. Welcome to Jacksonville, Oregon, population 2,000!

Mark and Becky are my fun-loving brother and sister-in-law from Chardon, Ohio. They are both "lab rats" who work at the world-famous Cleveland Clinic. Needless to say, they were very interested in the contagion raging on their skin.

They loved the outdoors, the mountains, the rivers, hiking, skiing, and the giant redwood trees of Oregon and northern California. I wish they would just move here instead of just visiting us in God's country, where we have quick access to all those outdoor wonders.

On this particular visit, I was exceptionally busy at the clinic and at home. You know, trying to do all things for everyone, both at work and in my personal life. And I was especially trying to be a good host since I really liked Mark and Becky. One evening, I was so busy I didn't have time to join them in the hot tub, set in the intimate garden of my backyard. Although the ambience was sensational, I had a vague feeling that I just hadn't been getting those hot tub chemicals right lately. You know, the pH, the alkalization, the chlorine and bromine levels; maybe I had even missed a weekly "shock treatment" or two that would kill any bacterial buildup. I am no chemistry major like my partner Dr. Igelman.

The couple didn't have a hot tub back in Ohio, so it was a treat for them to soak in mine after a hard day of skiing downhill on the slopes of Oregon. And since the hot tub was mine, I could hop in anytime I wanted to. Instead, I tried to stay up on my chores and to keep my wife happy, so she wouldn't stress out. Mark and Becky hit the hot tub every night, and they found it to be great for relaxing the muscles, and even better for elevating the psyche.

They suspected something was rotten in the state of Denmark when, the next morning, they both erupted with tender red pus bumps from the neck on down, especially under the bathing suit. Since they were both college grads and pretty darn good laboratory sleuths, they suspected the problem was maybe closer than Denmark—more likely something right here in Jacksonville, Oregon.

I saw Becky in the office that Friday, as a patient. I noticed tender boils on her torso, arms and legs. The rash spared her neck and face. The sores were especially accentuated beneath her swimsuit. Being the scientist I am, I gently cleaned one of the sores with rubbing alcohol, and I pricked the boil with a sterile #11 Bard-Parker blade. I swabbed the gunk with a sterile culturette, and then my office staff submitted it to the lab. It was somewhat ironic that this was exactly the kind of lab testing that Mark and Becky did back in Ohio.

I wasn't surprised when the hospital grew a pure culture of Pseudomonas aeruginosa. It is a common cause of swimmer's ear—and hot tub folliculitis. It occurs when people soak in a contaminated hot tub. Unbeknownst to me, my ozonator that automatically killed bacteria in the hot tub had died. My second line of defense, the chemicals I added to the hot tub, also failed me. Some would use chlorine, but I chose bromine. In addition, I would add an acid or a base to keep the pH and alkalization just right. My momentary lapse in getting the chemicals "just right" resulted in an epidemic of two, with pseudomonas growing from the neck on down. The good news is, I got some awesome pictures of Becky's skin.

To this day, I still show these classic pictures of hot tub folliculitis in my dermatology lectures.

After I evaluated Becky's skin, I went ahead and filled out one of my billing superforms, charging her $1,200,000. That should just about pay for the new office, I chuckled to myself.

The cure for hot tub folliculitis is simple—vinegar soaks in the bathtub and Cipro antibiotics by mouth. Drain the hot tub, scrub it out, thoroughly rinse it, and then start from scratch.

When a patient comes in with hot tub folliculitis, the diagnosis usually takes just an instant glance at the sores on his or her skin. The appearance of the bumps is so classic that nothing else really mimics it. I casually ask, "Whose hot tub have you been in recently?"

"Doctor, how did you know? We just got a new hot tub at our house. My husband didn't think it was all that important to use the chemicals."

Another scenario is when people go to a party. They sit for hours in the hot tub sipping wine and socializing. The ones that get out quickly, and rinse their body and suit in the shower have no problems. The ones that stay in the tub the longest, and then get out but leave their swimsuits on, are most likely to be infected. Often, hot tub folliculitis occurs in mini-epidemics where ten or more people suddenly come down with the skin disease a few days after a party.

Why doesn't it get on the head and neck? Well, most of us don't stick our heads under the hot water.

Oregon was one of the first states to ban wooden hot tubs. It was too easy for the Pseudomonas bacteria to live in the cracks, fissures and splinters in the wood. We are less likely to contact it with a ceramic or molded tub, but it still happens with regularity.

If you frequent a hot tub, don't get in if the water has an odor or if it is not clear. If your gut reaction says no, they just walk away. Let the maintenance man (in this case, me) know the hot tubs needs to be checked out.

If you do get in, as soon as you get out, take a soap-and-water shower, and also wash your bathing suit. If you own a hot tub, invest in an ozonator. The circulating water is piped through an ozone layer which safely kills bacteria dead. Follow the manufacturer's recommendations about the use of chlorine or bromine, and about the use of an acid-and-base neutralizer. Change the water twice a year, and your hot-tub experience will be a good one.

At family reunions, I am often reminded how I gave trusting relatives diseases such as hot tub folliculitis. I keep thinking, if only they could have been non-lab people like Uncle Al and Aunt Sue who stepped in the tub that night. And to inflict hot tub folliculitis with Pseudomonas on two laboratory workers is the ultimate bacteriological sin. When the subject comes up at family gatherings, I just bend over and take my whipping. So what else is new?

Chapter Thirty-Seven: The Wire-Brush Effect

Years ago, in San Francisco, we dermatologists were called to the rescue. We evaluated an African American gentleman who had been involved in a fiasco. He had "warts" down in "man land." Some surgeons cut them out. Although beautiful surgery was done during the excision, the wound dehisced (pulled apart) the following week, leaving the man with a large defect on the shaft of his manhood. No problem, thought the surgeons, we will just take a skin graft from his thigh, and suture it onto the penis to cure the problem. Well, they did, and it did. The graft survived and grew like normal skin, thus covering the former large gaping hole on his proboscis.

Unfortunately, three months later, hairs sprung up all over the graft site. The surgeons had taken the skin from a hair-bearing site on his thigh, and the result was essentially a hair-transplant procedure. The hair was tough, curly, black and very irritating. Whenever he had sex with his partner, it was like a wire-brush effect on her anatomy.

That is when the dermatologists got involved. The surgeon sent him to us for electrolysis. We noted a very black, militant and hostile patient with a large afro on his head. "I don't blame him for being hostile," I thought. His significant other was a beautiful blonde woman.

We proceeded with electrolysis, but the patient found it far too painful on his delicate male anatomy. Being in San Francisco, we found a gay electrolysist that specialized in—you guessed it—hair removal from penises. The package was complete with his red neon lights illuminating his hair-removal studio.

Because of the severe discomfort of the procedure, our staff dermatologist and my good friend Dr. John Reeves had to accompany the man on all the visits. The dermatologist numbed up the penis with xylocaine before the electrolysis could be done. What an unusual scenario played out on those electrolysis sessions under the sexy red lights—a medical doctor in a white lab coat, injecting a man's penis, and an electrolysist poking a sharp, sterile, pointed needle into the hair follicles on his unit, while the blond woman held her boyfriend's hand and comforted him. After many painful visits, electrolysis knocked out the hair follicles and cured the wire-brush problem.

As best we can figure, the man never did have viral warts in the first place. He had "pearly penile papules," a normal variant that 10 percent of men have. It might have been nice to have had a dermatologist on board at the beginning so we could have avoided the catastrophe. After all, dermatologists are the only doctors that know the 2,319 different skin diseases. (There used to be only 2,318, but then came along the monkey pox virus from those darn pet prairie dogs!)

Had I seen this gentleman in 2008, my lasers could have simply and painlessly resolved the hair problem. The F.D.A. has approved the Sciton Profile hair removal laser for permanent hair reduction in all skin types, including blacks. Dark skin, since it has more pigment, has historically been more difficult to laser than light skin. We want all the laser energy to go into the pigment in the lower half of the hair follicle. It therefore destroys the hair without causing collateral damage to the rest of the surrounding skin. But, in people of color, some of the laser energy is picked off by the melanin pigment in the outer layer of skin. This could result in crusting and blistering of the epidermis. To prevent the complication, we could just use a lower energy setting, but that would cut down on the effectiveness of the hair removal. With the Sciton Profile, we just use a longer wavelength of laser light, and at a setting using a 1064 nanometer wavelength, we bypass the epidermis completely and avoid the collateral damage. And, by using topical anesthesia in a cream form, the laser procedure is virtually painless.

The government paid a lot of money to the man for his bad outcome. I don't know how much, but he deserved money for lost wages, medical costs, pain and suffering. (He had been treated at a government facility, so this was a federal case.) This unfortunately was a case of medical malpractice and he deserved a fair settlement.

Chapter Thirty-Eight:
Malpractice

Malpractice does happen, and we realize doctors need to keep medial malpractice to a minimum by talking to our patients, telling them the risks-to-benefits of a procedure or treatment, and then by doing the most excellent job we can do for them. In America, we have the best-trained and sharpest doctors in the world. We also have the highest malpractice judgments in the whole world. If genuine malpractice has occurred, physicians should be expected to pay a reasonable amount for lost wages, medical bills, supplies and needed physical therapy, other related expenses, and for pain and suffering. But with the huge cash awards being given out by juries for pain and suffering (also called non-economic damages), we are breaking the bank. Doctors are retiring early, and it is hard to attract and keep the trauma doctors and neurosurgeons that every community needs. Bright, young people are not going into medicine because they are being scared off. And newly-minted doctors are reluctant to start a practice in Oregon (or your state), because of malpractice issues.

Many family doctors and obstetricians are giving up delivering babies due to the malpractice risk. For example, in Oregon, 120 physicians who used to deliver babies are no longer doing so. One local obstetrician in Medford cut $50,000 off his yearly malpractice insurance bill by quitting deliveries. Some women on the Oregon Coast, when in labor, have to drive 50–100 miles, or even to another state to have their baby delivered, since local doctors in their town no longer do them. This is not good medicine, and it is not safe.

In Medford, Oregon, which is growing into a fairly sophisticated medical community (we just completed a 110 million dollar rebuild of one of our hospitals), we lost neurosurgery coverage on certain days of the week due to malpractice issues. I advised my patients not to have a head injury on Thursdays or every other weekend. The medical malpractice crisis had caused three of our neurosurgeons to either quit doing surgery, or to leave the area for greener pastures, because they were overworked due to the shortage.

Medford is the regional medical center for northern California and southern Oregon. The doctors here treat a huge geographical area, west to east, from the Oregon coast to Lakeview. We treat patients from as far north as Roseburg, and as far south as the California communities of Yreka, Etna, Mt. Shasta, Weed, Horse Creek, Montague, Fort Jones and Happy Camp. What happens if you or your loved ones are in a bad auto accident? If it is the wrong day of the week, you or you family could die while being transported to a distant city instead of having surgery locally. Fortunately, after a void of several years, fulltime neurosurgery coverage has been restored here in Medford with the addition of some new talent.

Wake up America—the malpractice crisis among obstetricians is a women's healthcare issue. In 1999, in Oregon, our illustrious State Supreme Court threw out a cap of half a million dollars ($500,000) for pain and suffering on medical malpractice judgments. They said it was unconstitutional. Funny, Oregon modeled its constitution after Indiana, and Indiana has a cap of $200,000. Why is the cap constitutional in Indiana, whereas in Oregon, it is unconstitutional? (Ask the lawyers who served on the Oregon Supreme Court.) Even litigious California has a cap of $250,000 on non-economic damages. Society has to put its foot down and say, "We are sorry, you were wronged by your doctor or your hospital, but $200,000 or $500,000 is a truckload of money for pain and suffering. Take the money and get on with your life."

The U.S. House of Representatives passed a national tort reform bill, but it was blocked in the U.S. Senate (also known as the "home of trial lawyers"). I urge you to contact your state and federal legislators and call for serious tort reform. Or soon, you and your loved ones may not have an OB doctor, a trauma surgeon or a neurosurgeon to take care of you in your time of need. In addition, many other states are in need of tort reform for malpractice issues. Along with Oregon, Nevada and Pennsylvania are just a few of the other states in crisis.

Chapter Thirty-Nine:
The Grand Mal Seizure

We were eating in the cafeteria at spectacular Crater Lake, Oregon's only national park. Well, I was trying to eat, anyway. I had gotten a particle of dust in my eye. I was blinking furiously trying to get it out. After 10 minutes, the blinking was getting old. My eye was irritated, red and watering profusely.

I could barely see a man walk up to our table. He was making funny faces at some stranger sitting next to us. You know how kids will grimace and contort their faces, stick out their tongues, and roll their eyeballs, just to be silly. That is what this man appeared to be doing, but I thought he was kind of old to be playing such a game. I stared through my inflamed eyeball at him, and suddenly realized he wasn't playing around. He was in the prodrome of a seizure. I sprung to my feet, and as he tottered over backwards, I lunged for him. Blam! He slammed to the floor just beyond my outstretched hands. Bummer, I had just missed him. If my vision would have been okay, I could have easily caught him, I thought.

Max proceeded to have a grand mal seizure right on the floor of Crater Lake cafeteria. I grabbed his head to prevent even more damage as I simultaneously loosened his tie. We cleared tables and chairs and people out of the area, so he would not flail into them with his arms and legs. My wife Jane assisted me, or maybe I should say I assisted her.

A crowd formed around Max as he seized and seized, violently jerking his body, grunting and turning purple. I announced in a loud authoritative voice to the on-looking crowd, "My wife is a heart nurse at Rogue Valley Medical Center in Medford, and she just got 100-percent on her advanced cardiac life support test last week!" That gave the group confidence that she knew what she was doing. I conveniently forgot to mention that I was a lowly dermatologist and medical doctor. Let Jane save the day and get the glory. Doug will go incognito this afternoon.

Jane took his vital signs. His pulse was rapid, his blood pressure was high, and his respirations were labored. We administered oxygen that came with the paramedics. After what seemed like the longest time, probably only seven minutes, the flailing was over. Max lay sweating, whipped, limp, and exhausted on the floor.

The bizarre part was his wife standing nearby while she calmly chatted with a friend, as she watched her husband have a grand mal seizure. Many loved ones would get in the way, they would become hysterical, or they would pass out or cry. Not this one—she was a cold fish. Ice Woman!

The big question was, Why did Max have the seizure? A grown man without a history of epilepsy who suddenly seized would be at risk for having a tumor. The increased pressure on the brain could induce a sudden seizure. I guess Ice Woman didn't know that.

Max woke up, and he looked embarrassed. He also looked like a wet noodle. The violent thrashing would make his muscles ache for days, and the knock on his head from the fall would result in a large hematoma, a blood clot in the tissues. Slowly, the crowd dispersed, and the paramedics took Max away in an ambulance.

As I stood up, I noticed that the speck in my eye had fallen out. I guess while kneeling over him and attending to his needs, I must have blinked the particle out of my eye. That is cleaning your eye out the hard way.

I was now able to find the table where we had been sitting. As my reward for being a Good Samaritan, the bus boy had taken my food, dessert and beverage during the 20 minutes we toiled over Max. By then I was no longer hungry, but the manager was nice enough to give me a free cup of coffee when he learned of my plight.

Jane and I walked outside to reflect on the excitement, and to clear our heads. The beautiful deep dark blue waters of Crater Lake instantly calmed us. We saw a boat carrying tourists far down below, and it was docking at Wizard Island. Up on top, we saw some handsome birds at the viewing area. They were almost the size of a crow, a light gray color with dark eyes and dark wings. They were not shy, and they would grab food scraps left by visitors.

Story has it that many years ago, two strangers approached the viewing area. One said to the other, "That's a pretty bird. Do you know what it is called?"

The other man replied, "I don't know the name of the bird, but if you look in this bird book, you can find it."

The stranger replied, "I wrote that book, and that bird is not in there." The stranger was Roger Tory Peterson, world famous bird expert and author of **A Field Guide to the Birds**. If you go to Crater Lake someday, you will probably see the Clark's Nutcracker, just as Roger Tory Peterson did that day.

Chapter Forty: Fainting

I heard a thud in the hallway of my office. The thud was Laurel's head colliding with the wooden board on the back side of a fireplace. She was knocked out cold. I rushed over to her, and she awoke. She was more embarrassed that hurt. We helped her to her feet, and we laid her down on our exam table.

"Just relax, Laurel, you will be fine," I said confidently. I felt responsible for her fall since I had just removed a mole from her shoulder. She looked good as she sat up from the procedure table, but unfortunately suffered the "delayed fall" several minutes later, upon checkout. We elevated her legs on a few pillows and put a cold washcloth on her forehead. I gently held her hand as I felt her pulse with my other hand. She had a rapid heart rate, but with a regular rhythm. After five minutes, she felt better and we had her sit up and dangle her head between her legs.

"Make sure you are feeling your oats before you stand up," I volunteered. "Most people don't faint until they see the bill," I added. Nothing like a little humor at a time of crisis. Laurel now felt fine. She left the office in good condition.

Some years later, she graduated from college with honors. So there was no brain damage. We did place a brass plaque in her honor on the board she cracked with her head. The plaque is still there to this day. And of course, we did have to charge her for the damage she did to our cracked panel (just kidding!).

Laurel had a syncopal (fainting) episode after a minor surgical procedure. A small percentage of patients in my office get light-headed or faint after a liquid nitrogen treatment, a mole or cyst removal, or just from the anticipation of getting an injection of xylocaine to numb the skin. Laurel and patients of her ilk make life interesting for us. We always have to be ready in an instant to prevent a fall, and to keep our wonderful patients from injuring themselves if they do faint.

One patient long ago had leishmaniasis on his right upper arm—a "Baghdad boil" that he contracted from a sand-fly bite in a third-world country. I ordered a protocol drug called pentavalent antimony. I got it for Kyle for free, but there was a lot of government medical paperwork to fill out for the CDC. Kyle had to read and sign so many forms about rare but possible risks and complications from the medicine that he fainted at the first sight of the syringe. He went down before I could even give him the injection! He did great on future injections, and his leishmaniasis promptly healed.

I have learned from experience that it is always best to do a procedure with the patient lying or sitting down. Early in my career, I injected a 240-lb giant of a man with cortisone to treat the psoriasis in his hand. My corpsman had gone to lunch. Robert turned as white as Casper the friendly ghost when my 30 gauge needle punctured his skin. He started to say, "Doctor, I am feeling kinda funny…" before he passed out. I lunged for him across the exam table and got a firm grip on him, but boy was he heavy! He was unconscious at this juncture, and I was hanging onto him for dear life. If I tried to get around the table to grab his torso, I would have had to let him go, and down he would fall. Robert was big enough that his hitting the floor would have registered at least a 6.5 on the Richter scale. After three or four minutes of holding him up from across the table, my hands and arms were numb with fatigue. He was slowly but surely slipping from my grasp. Mercifully for both of us, Robert woke up, and we were able to get him up on the table. I'll never make that mistake again—trying to inject a big guy who is standing on the opposite side of the table.

Another patient, Heather, wanted me to remove an unwanted mole from her neck. Shortly after I numbed her up, she passed out on the table and gave a giant, titanic, total-body heave as she went unconscious. Sure scared the bejesus out of me, but I didn't let her know that. Again, laying her back, elevating her legs, showing confidence, and giving reassurance—those acts helped bring her back to the world of the living. She did not have a seizure, just a fainting episode.

And I'll never forget a two-year-old from Kodiak, Alaska. She had a bad-looking birthmark on her back that had to come off. The little girl was named Pam, and Pam was the bravest two-year-old we ever had. Her dad held her hand as I numbed her up. She didn't cry out or whimper, and she just didn't move a muscle during the procedure. Half the way through the surgery, her dad inspected the open wound on his lovely daughter's back. Then he put his nose right in the wound! While I appreciated his attention to detail and his obvious love for his daughter, I also felt this was a bit much. In his desire to inspect the surgery site, he had now contaminated our sterile field, and he could have potentially caused a wound infection.

But curiosity wasn't the cause—William had slumped forward and fainted! The sight of his innocent two-year-old daughter's blood was too much for him. Meanwhile, my corpsman Cannie had gone to lunch (Cannie, where are you when I need you?). Keeping my gloves sterile, I picked William up with my arms and elbows, eased him onto the floor, and pushed his head between his knees. Without missing a beat, I went back to his daughter and resumed the surgery. I irrigated out the con-taminated wound and finished suturing the opening. Pam sailed through the procedure! She got a gold star that day. I am sure at family reunions for years to come father and daughter will chuckle that she was braver than her big, strong daddy on that day.

Austin was one of my best fainters. He hailed from Northern Cali-fornia. One day I treated five basal cell carcinomas on his back with electrosurgery. He joked as he told me the history of the Indian wars in Northern California. He was a fan of Captain Jack, the brave Indian Chief who outwitted a far numerically superior force of U.S. Calvary soldiers for many months.

After the surgery, Austin and his wife left the office in fine shape. I was very surprised when the wife came running back a few minutes later. Her husband was "having a heart attack," she blurted. I raced out to the parking lot with my trusty back-office assistant Sharon. Austin was slumped over his steering wheel, passed out.

I felt my adrenalin pumping. This was the big one. "Naversen, get ready for CPR," I thought, then I shouted, "Sharon, call 911!" I grabbed Austin, laid him down on the hard blacktop parking lot, and went through my "ABCs": Check the airway, check for breathing, and check the circulation by feeling the pulse. Before I had to proceed with CPR, Austin woke up. He had sweat all over his face, but his pulse was strong and he was breathing fine.

What follows is pretty embarrassing. A big fire truck pulled up a few minutes later, and out came the paramedics. Naversen is out in the parking lot in his white doctor's coat, his patient is down, the sirens are blaring, and everyone is looking at us. "Naversen killed another one," they were probably thinking.

Well, I sent the fire truck away, and a few minutes later the ambulance arrived, also with sirens blaring. I commended the rapid response we got from the two rescue vehicles, but the DLAM parking lot was the center of the universe for 20 minutes or so. Not the kind of fame and publicity we like at our dermatology practice. We took Austin inside and he was fine.

Outpatient surgery and liquid-nitrogen procedures are extremely safe. But if you ever feel faint, sit down and put your head between your knees, or just lay down. Don't be embarrassed, even if you are in a crowd or a public place. Otherwise, you could fall and break a tooth or lacerate your head.

The only thing worse than a regular faint is the "delayed faint," like Austin's. We now keep him in the office for 30 minutes after every procedure. He does great unless he starts thinking about his blood and his guts, and then he goes down. When someone faints in our office, we are ready and prepared to take care of them. But with the delayed faint, they are out of our office so we may not be able to help them. If you are a fainter, please have the common decency to faint inside the doctor's office and not outside in the cold, cruel, world. I sure would appreciate it.

Chapter Forty-One: Do I Tell?

Troy helped me find the 10 penny nails in the back of the hardware store. I tried to avoid staring at his face, but I couldn't take my eyes off his forehead. He had two very obvious basal cell carcinomas planted there. The pearly translucent papules had faint central ulcerations with fine red blood vessels radiating out from the tumor. They were non-healing sores.

Should I tell him, or not? If I do, he'll get in sooner rather than later. But he might be mad as heck at me for invading his privacy when he hadn't asked me for advice. But I reasoned he didn't know he was talking to a board-certified dermatologist. If I don't, months down the road, he could end up with large, bleeding, infected, ulcerating tumors that would require extensive surgery to cure. He might even lose an eye.

"Naversen, are you a man, or are you a mouse?" I asked myself. "Go for it!"

"Excuse me sir. I'm Dr. Naversen," I said politely. "I couldn't help but notice those growths on your forehead. Maybe you should get them checked out?"

Just then the dam broke. A torrent of words flowed from his lips. Something about, "Those World War II doctors bungled my care.... I still have bad crotch-rot to this day because of those quacks!" The strangers walking by turned their heads as his voice got louder and louder and more agitated.

"Too much information," I thought. "Sir, I am skin doctor," I said patiently. "Don't see me, but check in with any local dermatologist. You need to get those growths checked out!" I did not want to appear as though I was desperate for business or soliciting for patients in the local hardware store. It was an embarrassing moment for us as he vented his spleen on a bad experience with doctors many years ago. At least I planted the seed, and I hope he got in for a check sooner rather than later.

A beautiful redhead named Danny was helping us plan our new office landscaping. I couldn't take my eyes off her. No, I wasn't a dirty old man (perhaps a dirty young man? I was in my early 30s). The reason I couldn't take my eyes off her was the irregular mole on her left cheek, just in front of her ear. I couldn't believe that the plastic surgeon standing next to me wasn't noticing it. He must have been paying attention to the office plan. (I'm glad someone was.)

After our meeting broke up, I broached this subject with Danny. She, too, had been worried about the black mole. She was glad I brought it up. It had recently increased in size and it was itching.

I excised the melanoma in situ the following week. It was removed in the entirety, and the precancer was cured in one fell swoop. Left untreated, the black mole that was presently smoldering in the outer layer of her skin (the epidermis) could have metastasized and killed her. I didn't do so well in the hardware store, but I felt like maybe I was getting better.

While vacationing in the Garden Isle, as Kauai is often called, some family members and I had a sumptuous Sunday brunch at the Hyatt Regency in Poipu. I recommend it highly if you ever vacation in Kauai. I enjoyed chatting with my new brother-in-law, Mark, the anesthesiologist, and I could tell he was deeply in love with my sister-in-law, Emily. My wife Jane has three great sisters, and Emily was one of them. As we chatted about the great food and the wonderful views of the ocean, the trained eye of the dermatologist was again roaming. I saw a lovely 12-year-old brunette sitting at the next table. She had a very large and a very ugly mole on her right leg. It could be melanoma, and she could die from it, I thought.

I quietly pointed the mole out to our group, and Mark asked, "Doug what are you going to do?"

With the skill of a diplomat I said, "Watch this."

"Hi, I'm Dr. Doug Naversen from Oregon, and I couldn't take my eyes off your very lovely daughter," I said to the girl's parents. "Her skin is so beautiful she could be a cover girl for *Glamour* magazine." She could have been—she was lovely.

"I was just noticing that black mole your leg. Have you had it checked?"

I breathed a sign of relief when Mom said, "Why yes, doctor. She saw her dermatologist last week back in the Midwest where we live. He wants to check it again in six months." I agreed that was a great idea, and I reinforced that she should definitely keep her follow-up visit. Luckily, the teenager's dad didn't jump up and punch out my lights, and he didn't tell me to get the hell out. I was happy she was plugged into the system.

Dr. Frank Watson, a friend of mine from Medford, once told a stranger in the elevator, "You might have a melanoma on your cheek. You better get in to Naversen." Frank, thanks for the referral! The veteran pathologist had enough self-confidence to tell a total stranger that he was worried about her mole and she needed to get checked out.

She showed up in our office a few weeks later. I was impressed by the variegated dark color of the silver dollar—sized patch on her left cheek. Tina agreed to the biopsy, and I was relieved a few days later when the pathology showed only a solar lentigo, a "liver spot."

"Tina, we dodged a bullet on that one. Luckily you didn't have skin cancer. It is totally benign, and you will never die of it. But does the growth bother you cosmetically?"

"Why, yes, doctor, I absolutely hate the black smudge on my cheek. Some people come up and try to wipe off my dirty spot with a handkerchief. Can you do anything about it?"

A month after a single Versapulse laser session, Tina came in for a post-op check. The appearance of her cheek knocked my socks off. I couldn't even tell which cheek the large liver spot had been on! Thank goodness for modern q-switched lasers. It vaporized the pigment in one session without a scar. The laser energy is selective—there is no collateral damage to the normal surrounding skin or underlying structures. What a fun time to be alive, with all the modern laser advances and new technologies coming down the pike.

In my early years as a dermatologist, I was less inclined to point out suspicious lesions to complete strangers in the elevator or in the hallway. I guess I have mellowed in the 30 years since I first entered U.C. San Francisco dermatology training in 1974. I find I am more willing to risk someone's anger, ridicule, insults or unpleasantness while I tell them they have a funny growth that needs to get checked out. If I am a wimp and keep my mouth shut, my fellow human being could die of a melanoma. And you good people reading this book, if you see a friend or relative with a funny mole or growth, swallow your inhibitions and urge them to get checked out by their dermatologist. You could save their life!

Chapter Forty-Two: Humor

At DLAM, we pros like to use humor to lighten the mood, and to put our patients at ease (well, at least my three partners are pros). Here are some examples of how we keep our patients—and ourselves—laughing:

Childhood Humor

Emily was lying on my surgery table, and she had a "bad mole" that needed to come off. She appeared to my eye to be about six years old. Her mom was lovingly holding her hand as we chatted. "Emily, how old are you," I asked. "About 16?"

She laughed, "No, doctor, I am only six. You are silly!"

"Emily, you are very beautiful. You have long shiny black hair. You have pretty brown eyes. You must drive the boys wild. Are you married?"

"No doctor, I am only six years old. I am too young to get married."

"Emily you are gorgeous. If you aren't married, tell me your boyfriend's name," I said as I winked at her mother. "Is it Ron, Sam or Dwight?"

Emily blushed. "No, doctor, I hate boys. They are nasty!"

"Well, if you're not married, and you don't have any boyfriends, do you have any kids?"

"No, doctor," Emily says as she blushes.

"Well, do you have any brothers and sisters?" I asked. I have got to get at least one yes answer out of her.

Emily responded that, yes, she has one brother and two sisters.

Sharon has Emily painlessly numbed up by now. As I carefully removed the biopsy from her delicate skin, I said, "Look, Sharon, she has green blood. Once or twice a year we get a Martian and that is how you tell—green blood."

"No, doctor, I was born in Medford, Oregon, not on Mars," replied Emily.

"Well, Sharon, she is right. She doesn't have green blood, it is really blue. She is a blueblood! There must be some European nobility in the family dating over 200 years ago. At the minimum it was a duchess, but judging from the dark blue color of her blood, it was more likely a princess or queen."

"Doctor, you are talking funny!" said Emily.

I think we have broken the ice. Emily was so concerned about my worry for her future husband, her potential boyfriends, her siblings and her green or blue blood that we had the mole removed and sutured before she knew it. I encourage my employees to use humor to make our day fun, and to deflate a potentially stressful dermatological situation with a young patient.

Sharon chips in now that we are done with the procedure, "Emily, you did great. You didn't move a muscle during the biopsy. You obviously come from sturdy genetic stock."

"Why, just last year we did the same procedure on Dr. Naversen. It was the first time I ever saw a grown man cry. But he didn't move a muscle either. He obviously comes from sturdy `peasant stock!'"

"Ouch! Thanks a lot, Sharon," I replied. "What am I, chopped liver? Dermatologists are people too!"

Teenage Humor

Chelsea was troubled with noticeable acne on her face. We discussed Accutane therapy, the yellow capsule that works on close to 100 percent of patients. I told her, "We are going to put you on a medicine that will work so good, it will knock my socks off when you come in for your five month visit."

On her follow-up visit, I say, "Chelsea, we are two months into your course of therapy. You are doing so well! I am very pleased. We are going to put the final nail in the acne coffin. As a matter of fact, we can see the light at the end of the tunnel."

I pause to reflect for a moment, and then I say, "Chelsea, I am so sorry, the light at the end of the tunnel has been turned off due to budgetary constraints. There is no light at the end of the tunnel!"

Christmas Humor

A patient comes in the week before Christmas. I freeze multiple growths on his skin. "John, this will leave unsightly sores on your skin for a week or two. I want you to show these to every one. They will buy you free breakfast, lunch, and dinner. Why, as a matter of fact, I want you to milk it for all the sympathy you can get. Santa Claus will bring you extra presents this year!"

John leaves the office with his skin smarting, but he is looking forward to all the free meals and presents he will get. I didn't have the heart to tell him, "John, if you run with the same crowd I do, you will get no sympathy at all; they will probably just laugh and make fun of you. It is a dog-eat-dog world out there, and we have on milk-bone shorts."

Political Humor

It was Presidential Election Day. In honor of the tradition-laden American election process, my partner Dr. Dave Igelman and I decided we would use no anesthesia on our Republican/Democratic voters today.

Our back-office employees, Sharon, Sara, Cassie, Michelle, Tabitha, Tanya, Amy and Ronda, would somehow find out the patient's political affiliation prior to their procedure. If our patient was a Republican, we would tell them we did not use anesthesia on Democrats. And vise versa. And theoretically, if our patient happened to be sympathetic to the wrong political party, we would conceivably pull out Dr. Igelman's thick brown leather belt from the back closet. And it was rumored we might say, "Please bite on this Mrs. Jones, we have just run out of local anesthesia."

At the end of the clinic, and after seeing many patients that day, Dr. Igelman and I compared notes. We didn't have a single patient of the opposite political party the whole day! Every one of our patients got a local anesthesia. Bummer, we aren't going to save any money on xylocaine that way. And darn, we didn't get to use Dr. Igelman's thick, brown leather belt one single time.

The next day our first patient was Ilse. In the course of our surgery, blood ran down her arm after my scalpel incision. "Don't worry, Ilse, we only do bloodless surgery here at DLAM," I piped in. "We use ketchup for special effects, you know, to dramatize our surgery."

"Sharon, what brand are we using this year?" I asked.

Without missing a beat, Sharon replied, "We normally use Heinz ketchup, but being an election year and all, we have switched to Hunts."

Procedure Humor

Last month Sue came in for a skin check. She was worried about cancer. I said on her visit, "Let's go ahead and do 'mole patrol.'" Sure enough, we biopsied a suspicious growth that proved to be cancerous.

When Sue came in for her skin cancer surgery, she was obviously very nervous. "Sue, before the days of modern anesthesia, we would just have you chug this bottle of Jack Daniels." (Formerly, when a Russian-born assistant worked at DLAM, we told the story with vodka, pronounced "wodka," in her honor.) "Then we would have you bite on the silver bullet. Don't worry—it already has bite marks on it so you won't have to break off any teeth. And don't concern yourself about AIDS and hepatitis; even in times of yore we autoclaved it so you didn't have to worry about contamination."

We continued, "Sue, when you were sufficiently inebriated, we would call in four strong men, and no matter what you came in for, the leg had to come off. We would then go ahead and saw off the right leg. To add insult to injury, we would usually amputate the wrong leg. So then—you guessed it—the left leg had to come off, too. Again, don't worry, just leave the driving to us; we would have the bonfire raging in the backyard to kill any bacteria or viral pathogens. Of course, to stop the bleeding we would have to sear the flesh with a red-hot poker pulled from the center of the bonfire. Some people might complain of a strong odor. But Sharon and I prefer to just call it 'Chanel Number Sue.' We think it will be a big seller in Paris this season. And if it is as big a seller as I think it will be, the sequel next year will be known as 'Eau de Sue.' And the following year, we will name it 'Toilette de Sue.' And we will get royalties."

I kept going. "Sue, I know what you are thinking. You came in just to have the darn skin cancer removed, and now you have lost both of your legs. But there is an upshot to all this. My assistant will keep a list of people who will want to buy your shoes. And don't worry, she'll get top dollar for them."

We like to feel we have a heart, and we do like to reassure our patients here at DLAM who are undergoing stressful procedures. I could tell she was a little worried by a few drops of blood coming out of her wound. "Sue, bleeding always stops. Either we live or we die, but ultimately we get it stopped."

"Thanks for the confidence builder, Dr. Naversen," Sue responded.

"By the way, Sharon, order two units of packed red cells, STAT!" I shout. Okay, so maybe we so try to dramatize our surgery a little bit. We will try anything to uplift the human spirit (if even for just a few fleeting moments) and provide some relief.

After we removed the large mole on Sue's right back, we had to do some fancy surgery to close the lesion "primarily", without the need for a graft. She could feel us relaxing the collagen and elastic bands beneath the skin surface with our scalpel, and we did have to close the wound under some tension using many sutures. Then I said, "Sue, I don't care if we have to pull your nipple beneath your armpit, we are going to get the wound closed!"

When everything went according to plan, I said, "The wound closed beautifully. Only one problem, we had to pull your belly button up two inches and three inches over to the right!"

"But there is more: You used to be an 'innie.' Now you are an 'outie.' We just went ahead and chose an umbilical ring for you, and we placed it at no extra charge. We like to go the extra mile for our patients here at DLAM."

Luckily, when she had virtually no bleeding at all on her procedure, I cackled, "Sue, hemorrhage has been officially banned within the confines of these walls."

"Sharon, I do believe Sue did better than those 21 year old whipper-snappers," I exclaimed. Sue was a foxy-looking lady at 60, and I knew she and our older patients feel their age and maturity were an advantage in potentially stressful situations such as dermatological surgery. It is!

"Sue, sit up and dangle your feet for a minute. Make sure you are feeling your oats before you stand up. Since we removed all that tonnage from your right side, when you leave the office you will be tilting to the port side. And you will find yourself walking in circles. But don't worry, it is 'Be kind to Quasimodo' week, so you'll do just fine."

If Sue's surgery went "south" and she left the office with no legs, what would we nickname her? Sue laughed when Sharon and I cried out in unison: "Stumpy."

What would we call it when her friends took her for a walk? "They would take her for a drag."

What would they call her when she went swimming in the lake? "Bob."

What would we call her when she went water skiing? "Skip."

Soaking in a hot tub? "Stu."

Soaking in a hot tub for a week without chemicals added? (This is my favorite one.) "Hot tub folliculitis."

If we leaned her against a building? "Eileen."

If we hung her up on the wall? "Art."

If we threw her on the front deck? "Matt."

If we placed her under the tall oak trees in the brisk autumn air? "Russell." Or how about "Leaf"?

But we would never call her what? "Late for dinner."

Gardening Humor

Rob came in to my exam room, and he was obviously having back pain. "Rob," I said, "Can't you find a good orthopedic doctor, or something?"

While surveying his skin, one glance clued me in. His wife must have sent him in for the many unsightly growths known as seborrheic keratoses peppering his skin. They are black and ugly, and they itch and they just keep on growing. I told Rob, "Left untreated, this one on your abdomen will grow into the keratosis that will devour Cleveland, Ohio, and that will not a pretty sight. Maybe we better just go ahead and freeze this one today."

Rob said, "Okay, Dr. Naversen, just take care of it for me."

"As an added bonus," I said, "this will help your back pain. I like to call it the counter-irritant theory of pain. The liquid nitrogen is so cold, and it stings and it burns so much, you will forget about your back pain. It works every time." Hey, we go the extra mile here at DLAM for our patients. The man comes in for skin growths, and we help his back pain.

"Doctor, you are the best," said Rob.

Then I explained, "Rob, what you have on you back is known as 'the weeds in our garden of life.' And we are going to do some weeding with our liquid nitrogen canister today." I spray a dozen such keratoses. I end our visit with, "Rob, I don't know if you have heard, but we have pretty much given up dermatology here at DLAM. But we are doing lots of agricultural work lately." That line is always good for a laugh.

"Rob, you have a million of these keratoses. Do you know what we would call your back if you were a Native American?"

"We would call it the happy hunting ground!"

As Rob walked out the door, I told him, "Rob, go ahead and grow some more moles, or get a good itchy rash. We have got to pay for this new building somehow."

We try to make all of our patients at Dermatology and Laser feel special. A well-placed joke often makes them feel just that.

Running Humor

Sharon was in the next room with a female patient. I poked my head in and said, "If there is anyone in the room buck naked, it is okay because I am a professional." I then saw D.D., a young woman on the procedure table. I told her, "We are going to remove that lump, the dermatofibroma, from your left calf. But there is a potential risk and complication you should be aware of. You might now be known as a so called 'highstepper.' Since we will remove all that weight from left the leg, you will now lift the leg six inches higher compared to the right when you walk. No added charge."

Then we removed some benign but protruding moles from her back. "D.D., I can guarantee you that after this procedure, you will be a faster runner in the upcoming Britt Woods Fire House Run. You are now lighter of foot, and with less wind resistance, you will be at least ten seconds faster per mile, which adds up to over 62 seconds in a 10K race. But that is despicable, to actually stoop to have your moles removed so that you will be a faster runner. Shame on you, D.D.," I said, laughing and smiling.

I added, "This surgery will change your life. You will now be able to leap tall buildings in a single bound, you will be able to outrace speeding locomotives, and, why, you will be even able to catch bullets with your teeth. But don't try that at home. We are professionals here."

"By the way," I continued, "we are shooting for a mole-free America by the year 2020, and you are helping contribute to the total, D.D."

Another afternoon, I had a visit from an elderly couple. "Mildred and Fred, I have been looking at all these red spots on your torsos," I said. (They were just cherry hemangiomas, or harmless blood moles.)

"Well, Doc, what causes them?" asked Fred.

"Well, Fred and Mildred, I hate to tell you this, but they just did a study up at the medical school in Portland. They traced these red bumps to sins committed in early childhood. And judging by how many you and Mildred are getting, that sinning must have continued well into your adult life!"

Mildred and Fred break into loud laughter since they realize Dr. N is kidding them. Hey, we'll do anything to take the edge off.

I went ahead and removed a few of the hemangiomas on the wife. "Millie," I said, "go out and run five miles this afternoon as part of your post-op care. Even if you have never run five miles before, just go out and run five miles." Here is yet another satisfied DLAM patient that has had her life improved for the better by modern dermatological surgery. Just by removing a few blood moles, she is now able to run five miles without even training!

Performance-Enhancing Humor

We saw Daniel for a rapidly-growing lesion on his right ear. "Looks like a squamous cell carcinoma," I thought to myself.

"Daniel, we need to do surgery. We will get it cured, and you will not die from the skin cancer," I reassured him. "Do you the want the Van Gogh treatment, or the Mike Tyson special?"

"Sharon," I said, "the ear is a noisy area to do surgery. Why don't you put a cotton ball in Daniel's ear for comfort? Correction, why don't you just use half a cotton ball? Those things are getting expensive."

"Daniel, in the heyday of dermatology, we would have used a whole cotton ball in your ear. But what with all the Medicare and Blue Cross cutbacks, we are forced to economize. Next year we will probably cut back to one-third of a cotton ball, and the following year if you came in we would just have you stick your thumb in it."

The surgery was successful. I said to Sharon, "Come to think of it, that is a valuable half-cotton ball in Daniel's ear. Why don't you just rinse it off in the sink, and maybe our head nurse Pam could autoclave it for us so we could recycle it." Now *that* is economizing that even my thrifty partner Dr. Igelman would be proud of!

"Daniel," I said, "if you walk out of the office with that cotton ball in your ear, I'm sorry, but we will have to bill you for 'supplies.'"

By the way, Daniel was an elderly man with seven grandkids. So next I said, "Daniel, now Sharon spent quite a lot of time pre-op telling you about the two ways of doing this surgery. If we did it the one way, you could never have kids again. If we did it the other way, you could have all the kids you want. (It was funny, since all we did was to operate on his ear, and it was comical since the man was nearly 80 years old!)"

Daniel gave us a quizzical look.

"Daniel, I just want to reassure you that we used plan two, so you can still have all the kids you want."

Daniel let out with a big laugh.

As he walked out the door, I told him, "Daniel, your ear will be unsightly for a few weeks. Your friends will be extra nice to you. Don't let it heal up too soon. And for god sakes don't mention Naversen. Tell them that my partner Dr. Tribelhorn did this to you!"

Surgical Humor

Jaquelyn was a statuesque woman who merited attention when she walked into a room. I examined the growth on her back. "Jaque, that mole has to come off."

As we completed the routine surgery, I said "Jaque, by the way, what are we having for dinner tonight? And if a good-looking doctor goes to bed with you tonight, it is because I accidentally sutured my thumb to your skin. Do you think your husband will mind?"

My trusty assistant Sharon piped in, "Doc, if you keep suturing your thumb to the skin of all these good looking babes, people will start getting suspicious."

"That is true Sharon," I replied. "But when we had that good-looking hunk of a man, Dieter, in for surgery last week, why did you keep elbowing me to suture your thumb to his back? I know that even your fine husband Bobby will start getting antsy when all these strange men sit down at the dinner table with you two."

Mole-Removal Humor

J.R. was getting up in years. We had to remove a mole from his face. It was one of those large, unsightly, fleshy moles that people cart around for years. If they knew how easy they were to remove, and if they knew how good they would look in a short period of time, everyone would sign up for treatment.

Sharon said just before we started the procedure, "This is a bright operating room light we have to turn on your face. Go ahead and close your eyes." When I closed my eyes, she said, "No, not you Doc!"

"J.R., this surgery will change your life for the good," I told him. "Now, I will be responsible for the healing and the surgical result. But my insurance will not cover the ladies that will be beating down your door. With your newly-found sex appeal, you better get a cane to protect yourself from the nymphomaniacs that will be appearing in your life. As a result of modern dermatology, you are now a stud-muffin. Watch out for the Sarah's of the world." (He would marry Sarah one day.) I wish every surgery we did have the same wonderful risk-to-benefit ratio.

After I removed the moles, Sharon injected anesthesia all around a cyst on his scalp. Then she said, "J.R., if anyone calls you numb-skull, they are probably not far from the truth."

With that point made clear, I proceeded to whack out the wen. For some unknown reason, the scalpel holders flew out of my hand across the room and they clanged on the floor as doctor, medical assistant and patient all watched. I calmly said, "I never liked those holders anyway. We have plenty. Sharon, get me a new pair."

"By the way," I told J.R., "we never say 'whoops' in the operating room. Instead we say 'good.' If it is an even bigger mistake, I will say 'very good.' And if it is a colossal surgical blunder of the first order of magnitude, I will say 'excellent.' It is just poor form to say 'whoops.' Can you imagine your neurosurgeon operating on your brain, and if you somehow woke up during the surgery, and you heard him say 'whoops' during the delicate surgery on your gray matter? You would think, well, there goes a million neurons with that little flick of the scalpel blade. Easy come, easy go."

We finished the surgery on the cyst uneventfully. But Sharon and I must have been feeling a little malicious that day, because just when we placed the last suture, we shouted in unison, "Excellent!"

Laser Humor

Isaac had a tattoo placed on his left shoulder. Six months later he became allergic to the blue tattoo dye within it. Left untreated, it would have felt like living with poison oak in your shoulder—for the rest of your life.

They had a solution for such a problem in medieval Europe. In England, it was known as being "Hung, drawn, and quartered." If you ever visit the Tower of London, right outside the gates is a delightful pub with the same name, "Hung, Drawn, and Quartered." Visit both the tower and the pub if you can.

But at DLAM, we do not use the barbaric methods of the past. Modern laser surgery will cure this without the more radical forms of laser surgery.

I removed a tattoo on Bruce with one of our nine Q-switched lasers. It was an image of a crude, amateur razorback (whatever that is). He'd applied the tattoo himself with India ink, and a needle and thread, when he was teenager growing up in the backwoods of Arkansas.

Although I didn't tell Bruce this, I like to think that my laser staff of Sherry and Pauline is contributing to a "beautify America" campaign. We don't get any extra awards, but we feel good about what we do. If you have seen some of the hideously ugly, amateur and professional tattoos that are disfiguring the public's skin, you will agree with our good efforts.

Bruce started squirming around with each pulse of the laser that we likened to the snap of a rubber band. (Our special Zimmer unit sprays air as cold as minus 32 degrees Centigrade on the tattoo for anesthesia, so fortunately it is only pain like the snap of a "small rubber band".) "Go ahead, we like moving targets here at DLAM so we will be better at lasering warts off of kids. Bruce, you are good target practice!"

Hair-Removal Humor

Fernando was in for permanent hair removal with our state-of-the art hair laser, when my partner Dr. Igelman walked in. I said, "Dr. Ig, bend your head over so we can show Fernando how well our hair laser works." (I am so far behind Ig in the practical joke department, that I will use almost any opportunity to embarrass him.) When he bent over, I told him the flash of light reflecting off his bald spot was so intense it nearly blinded us.

"Fernando, he was our laser guinea pig. With just one laser treatment, Ig got a big bald spot, and we can't get it to grow back. (Of course I didn't tell Fernando that Ig had been bald there since his senior year of college.)

Self-Actualization Humor

Ron and Lou have just completed a dermatological procedure. As I sit back down, Sharon pretends to pull my stool out from under me. I get up and stand by the counter. As she reaches into the cabinet, she pretends to pistol-whip me with the cupboard door. That is why I am known as "the Rodney Dangerfield of dermatology"—I get no respect.

But, I am also known as the "Mohammed Ali of Dermatology." Yes, "I float like a butterfly and sting like a bee," with my liquid nitrogen and laser treatments.

During long, dermatological surgeries, Sharon and I have a chance to talk and joke and banter with the patients. When Sharon is getting too comfortable, I like to remind her of Maslow's basic hierarchy of needs, and the plane of self-actualization.

Basically, we need to have our basic physiological needs met first, such as air, food, water, sleep, and sex. Humans then have a successive need for safety, then non-sexual love, and next self-esteem and esteem from others. Despite obtaining all of the previous, we still have a longing for one more thing. That higher calling in life is the plane of self-actualization, and I like to remind our employees that we achieve that exalted state on a daily basis here at DLAM. The intellectual stroking our office employees derive from working in the clinic is inestimable. I tell them they get such an emotional high treating our nice patients that this year, the staff and Sharon will be working for free. Next year, they will be paying us for all of the cerebral exultation they will get.

As an added bonus, since they earn no money, they will all benefit from a free, weight-reduction diet. Without any pay, how could they possibly buy any groceries?

I have observed that, three times a year, a new miracle diet book comes down the pike. People lose weight temporarily, book authors appear on talk shows, and they earn lots of money selling their paperbacks. At the end of the year, the dieter weighs the same amount as when they started their diet. Personally, I like the version printed up in *Newsweek*, which boils down to, "Work out six days a week, and don't eat junk."

Let's call our book *The DLAM Diet*. The staff would lose lots of weight (whether they wanted to or not), and Naversen would get to be on talk shows and he would be the one making lots of money. I love that "plane of self-actualization," don't you?

Of course, the book would be a best seller. To pump up our sales, we would issue a copy to each employee and bill their VISA $29.95 (plus shipping and handling). And of course, before a patient could be seen at DLAM, he or she would have to purchase a book for themselves or their family. It would only be common decency to charge them an extra $9.95 per unit for a signed copy (plus shipping and handling). Some people might call our techniques racketeering, but we prefer to simply call it "advanced marketing."

Well, enough of the plane of self-actualization and *The DLAM Diet*. We have a busy clinic, so we better get back to work.

DLAM Humor

As Pat came into the office, I warmly greeted him by saying, "So here is my next victim—correction, *patient*."

Pat smiled, and then he said, "Doctor Naversen, I have been worried about this changing mole on my chest. But just last week I scratched at it, and it fell off."

I examined his skin, and I agreed with him. "Pat, it looks like you have cured it. Unfortunately, I am going to have to arrest you for practicing medicine without a license. But don't worry—we'll get you two to five years with time off for good behavior. And you and your lovely wife will really love those conjugal visitation rights. Remember, absence makes the heart grow fonder."

Once ready to do his complete skin exam, Sharon said to Pat, "Go ahead and get buck naked. We are going to examine you from stem to stern, from cheek to shining cheek." (Which cheeks was she referring to, anyway?) "Remember, we don't do 'peephole dermatology' here at DLAM. We are professionals. Just climb up on the table when you are ready."

Pat just had a little mole that had to come off the right side of his neck, and I saw his face flush bright red at the thought of "buck naked." I rescued him from his predicament when I said, "Pat, since that mole is just on your neck, why don't you keep your clothes on. I don't want to get Sharon all excited. She won't be worth a darn the rest of the day if she sees the unexpurgated version of Pat, a glorious site that has been seen by few mortals." Pat was visibly relieved.

As he tried to get up on the table, he stumbled slightly. "Pat, if you fall off the table, it is an automatic five point deduction, just like in Olympic gymnastics." I told him. "There is nothing that can be done about it either. We don't make up the rules here, Pat, we just enforce them."

For an ex-football player, he wasn't moving that well. After barking his shin on the corner of the table, he finally negotiated the step, and the big guy got up on the operating platform. "Pat, by the way, we promise not to biopsy either your carotid or your jugular," I chipped in, hoping to take our minds off the awkward moment when he whacked his leg. "That is considered poor form."

Sharon and I proceeded with the biopsy. There was immediately blood everywhere, including red stuff on the ceiling just above the operating room table! "Pat, you certainly are a healthy, red-blooded American boy," I calmly remarked.

Sharon and I felt like the two Far Side mosquitoes on the man's arm when one of the insects was rapidly bloating up with blood after the puncture. Sharon exclaimed, "Doctor, pull out, you've hit an artery!"

I jumped in with, "Whoa, now we have to electrocute you! No, just kidding—we are only going to electrodessicate you. Bummer, we lost two patients just last week due to that minor infraction." I got the bleeder tied off, and after that I "buzzed" a few small arterioles.

"Pat, this surgery will change your life for the better," I joked. "I am afraid your skin will heal so darn well, and you will look so youthful on the right side, that your wife will want you to come back for us to do the left side."

Then I gently squeezed a clogged pore on Pat's cheek with my two fingers. Out popped the comedone. (That is a fancy word for a black-head.) "Pat, we are having a religious experience today. I laid on the hands, and your skin was cured. This is a biblical moment, kind of like when Moses parted the Red Sea. Some people would call it a miracle, but here at DLAM we just prefer to call it modern, high-tech skin care."

I then said, "Pat, Sharon and I gave you a 'DLAM bonus.' We took the liberty of tattooing our initials on your neck. But there is more! We also gave you (at no added charge) a 'Born to Lose' tattoo on your Adam's apple. And you are now sporting a new one on your left rump that is our official dermatology motto. It states, 'We cheat the other patients at DLAM so we can pass the savings on to you.'"

"Pat, some people think we send these skin biopsy specimens to the lab, prepare a glass slide for histopathology, and then carefully examine the slide under the microscope looking for cancer. Actually, we keep a big barrel in the back office. We throw all our specimens down into the bottom, and once a week Sharon takes them over to the local hospital where they fry them up for lunch. Sharon and I strongly advise you to avoid eating 'mystery meat' on Wednesdays."

"Pat, you also have a growth on your right eyelid that has to come off. Sharon, let's go ahead and enucleate the eyeball at this time. Pat, don't worry, we have a special on black DLAM eye patches this month. You will probably recreate the fashion craze on black eye patches started decades ago by the Israeli General Moshe Dayan.

Sharon said gleefully, "Pat, we are going to light your fire!"

I chimed in, "Pat, this one might hurt a little. Sharon, why don't you just go ahead and put our hyfrecator on stun mode? No, Pat is a big boy, just go ahead and crank it all the way up to full warp drive! At that moment, the whites of Pat's eyes were so large, they could be seen from cars passing by on the I-5 freeway a mile away.

Then I said, "Sharon, I forgot to tell you. Pat is a podiatrist. Don't bother wasting any numbing on him next time. God made them just a little bit tougher."

During the middle of the procedure, I commented, "Pat you are very electric this afternoon." That was not far from the truth, considering the high setting we were using. Amazingly, Pat sailed through his procedure without incident.

But the last straw was when we biopsied one last atypical mole on his right thigh. Sharon piped in, "We wouldn't want our patient to die of skin cancer, now would we?" As Pat stood up, he fainted. We must have told one too many bad jokes, Sharon and I thought. As we helped Pat back up on the procedure table, he came returned quickly to consciousness.

Despite all the dermatological torture Sharon and I could cram into one session, I had to get in a final lick or two. As Pat walked by the checkout desk, I dead-panned, "Pat, the right leg should fall off in just about 72 hours."

Then I proudly showed him a brilliant innovation we installed on the doorknob by the checkout counter. All patients checking out need to stop by the desk, and then when their bill is paid in full they are allowed to leave.

What is our brilliant innovation? Well, we run 50,000 volts of electricity through the metal door knob. If they don't pay the bill, the staff activates the switch. Upon touching the knob, the patient is stunned, and they fall prostrate to the floor. After two or three repetitions, even the "dullest crayon in the box" will manage to find that hidden cash, checkbook or plastic to pay his or her bill.

As I escorted Pat out through our lobby (not surprisingly, Pat paid his bill in full with his Master Card), I proudly displayed the poison oak, ivy and sumac plants that adorned our plant display. We often would get repeat customers within 48 hours, which just happens to be the incubation time it takes for the ivy, oak and sumac to blister a patient's skin.

Pat wondered why we went to all the expense to ship the poison sumac all the way from Florida, when we have so much poison oak in Oregon. Easy answer Pat—some of our sophisticated patients know what poison oak looks like, but very few know what sumac looks like!

"Pat, read the sign hanging over the poison sumac," I said. It stated: "Feel free to touch the pretty leaves. They won't bite."

I said, "And Jaime, our head staff member up front, wonders if you would like to book your follow-up appointment in six weeks, or maybe just in 48 hours?"

What a practice builder! Pat might never come back to see us, but more probably he would tell his family and friends about the wild and whacky Dr. Naversen, Sharon, Lori, Tracy, Tarah, Alicia and Brittany, and they would come beating down our doors as patients. Which do you think has happened?

At Dermatology and Laser Associates of Medford, we do not have a Las Vegas comedian or writer spewing out daily humor scripts for us. We have to deal with every clinical situation as it comes up. Whether I remove a mole with my trusty #15 scalpel blade or with a punch biopsy, I will invariably say, "That's the best one I have ever done! "

Sharon pops my bubble when she shouts out, "He says that every time!"

I often respond with, "Every now and then even the blind groundhog finds an acorn. Today, we found our acorn!" As you go through life, it helps to keep your sense of humor both at home and at work. It certainly keeps us laughing and having fun.

Chapter Forty-Three: Tattoos

I love a good tattoo. They are great for business! Studies show that half of all people who get a tattoo will later regret it. If a person loves their tattoo, so do we at DLAM. However, if they don't like it, that's when we get involved. Older methods of removal, such as excision, dermabrasion, and salabrasion (repetitively rubbing a moistened 4x4 gauze covered with salt) are guaranteed to cause a scar. Over-tattooing involves covering the first tattoo with an ever larger and darker tattoo, and that is not enticing for someone who no longer likes tattoos.

Modern Q-switch lasers, on the other hand, can vaporize tattoos without leaving a scar. Acting like a "smart bomb," the laser pulse heats the colored dye (for example, black, red, or yellow) to 300 degrees Centigrade. It shatters the pigment into tiny particles that can be gobbled up by the body's immune system, and the dye is transported away through the lymphatic system. Although some amateur India ink tattoos can be cured in one laser session, professional and multicolored tattoos are harder to cure, and they may require three to even a dozen sessions. The goal is to completely remove the tattoo without causing any scar whatsoever. And in many cases, we succeed.

I did a mole check on Marilyn. She got a drape, and she removed everything but her undergarments. I spied a "Joe" tattoo on her left breast peeking just above her pouting nipple.

"How is Joe?" I asked cheerfully.

Marilyn's face turned red, and she then offered a four-letter expletive! She and Joe were not only living apart, but she now hated Joe's guts. I went ahead and removed, and biopsied, an abnormal mole on her torso, and we also got her in for a free laser session for her left breast. Since it was a crude, amateur tattoo made with India ink, it melted away with only one laser session. Fortunately, there was no residual scar. Joe finally was finally out of her life.

Relationships change, but tattoos don't. I advise against having someone's name planted permanently on your skin unless it is your mom, your dad or your child. Remember, what happens in Las Vegas stays in Las Vegas—except your tattoo!

When Sandy was 16, she had the "F word" tattooed on the top of her right hand. She actually felt that way about the world. Ten years later, she had mellowed, and she really wanted a job. The local job council referred her to DLAM. Since it was an India ink tattoo, I knew it was a slam dunk with our Versapulse C laser. It really eats up that color. After a few sessions, the tattoo had vanished without a trace, and without a scar. Sandy got a job and is now off the welfare rolls.

When we removed a Bulldog tattoo from a 21-year-old woman, I actually had a biblical experience. Some years before, Pat had a "Red Cross" tattoo placed on her right lower abdomen. She soon grew tired of it, so her tattoo artist suggested he cover up the cross with a "big black bulldog," which he did. Pat eventually realized she hated the bulldog even more than she hated the Red Cross.

"No problem," I told her. "Let's see what we can do." We used our "sweet-spot setting" at a wavelength of 1064 nanometers. The tattoo instantly turned ashen-white as the laser beam impacted her skin. We placed a sterile dressing on her abdomen, and we scheduled her for a one month follow-up visit.

Now let me tell you about our religious experience. The next month, I, my very excellent laser nurse Kathy, and our very excellent laser technicians Sherri and Pauline, gasped as Pat pulled down the corner of her panties. The black bulldog was gone, only to be replaced in the center with a Red Cross!

Pat had told the truth! She had mentioned in passing on the first visit she had covered her unwanted tattoo with the bulldog. The laser wavelength we use for dark colors is different than what we use for red ones. By erasing the black bulldog, we were able to see her original red tattoo.

So what we did was to dial in the 532 nanometer wavelength on the trusty Versa-pulse laser. After one session, the Red Cross was also gone. Because of the large size of the second tattoo, and because of the large amount of ink her tattoo artist had used, multiple sessions were required. After her last session, she called us two weeks later to report a happy event in her life. She and her husband Thomas were going to have a baby. Although our machine is so safe we could use it on a pregnant or nursing woman, we gave Pat nine months off. "Come back then and show us your new baby," I suggested.

We were excited to see the healthy, newborn baby the following year. And we were equally excited that in the interval since we had last seen her, our laser, with an assist from her body's lymphatic system, had entirely resorbed the tattoo! The right side of her abdomen looked the same as the left side. You absolutely couldn't tell which side had been tattooed. We could only dream of such success in treating tattoos five to ten years prior.

Matt was very proud of his serpent tattoo on his right leg. That is, until six months later when he became highly allergic to the red dye within it. Mercury sulfide used to be the culprit in red dye that made people allergic, but that has been banned. Unfortunately, other red and blue and yellow dyes in tattoos may result in permanent allergy.

Matt's insurance company flat-out denied paying his laser work, since it resulted from a cosmetic procedure. "Sorry, but read the fine print in your contract," he was told. So without a procedure, Matt was destined to itch like he had a bad case of poison ivy on his leg—until his dying day. To excise the large tattoo would result in disfiguring surgery that would require an extensive skin graft. What can lasers do for tattoo allergies?

We numbed Matt's skin in the usual fashion with xylocaine and epinephrine. We proceeded to use a different laser on this tattoo. Our carbon dioxide resurfacing laser vaporized the pigment along with the surrounding skin. We told Matt he would have a definite scar in the shape of his tattoo, but that chances are high the allergy and itching would be cured. We guessed it would take four weeks to heal.

"Go for if, doctor. I can't live like this for the rest of my life," replied Matt.

After all was said and done, Matt's allergic response to the red tattoo dye was cured. He keloided in the area as expected, but dilute-strength cortisone shots shrunk the scar tissue down to size. The finished result was not unsightly. It rather looked like an exotic "brand" that is popular in Africa where saliva and sesame oil are scratched into the black native skin with a sharp stick.

Although I would never recommend it to one of my patient's, Matt has one of the most unique tattoos/brandings to be found anywhere in the country. The non-allergic portion of his tattoo remains surrounded by the geographic, curved raised scar induced by the CO_2 laser. It is definitely exotic.

A few tips for those of you who entertain getting a tattoo. First of all, don't get one. But if you do, don't feel too bad, because it is good for Dr. Naversen's downstream business. (A recent survey reported on the American Academy of Dermatology website revealed that 24 percent of people between the ages of 18 and 50 now sported a tattoo!)

Most tattoos are easy to put on, but laborious, time-consuming and expensive to remove. Never put one on your face. Try to avoid names. Choose a hidden location. Please avoid profanity, controversial designs and swastikas. Just say no to green, bright blue and aqua tattoos—those are the hardest colors to remove. Talk to people who have tattoos.

If you must have one, word of mouth is the best way to find a tattoo artist. (Come to think of it, word of mouth is the best way to find a good doctor, dentist, lawyer, CPA, and the like.) Make sure the tattoo shop is clean and neat, and make sure they have an autoclave, and that they sterilize their equipment. Ask to look at pictures and designs and tattoos they have done. If you don't have a good feeling deep down in your gut about the place, just walk away. The bad tattoo you get today will not go away, but you can always get your first tattoo another day.

Chapter Forty-Four:
Dr. Wally Dunn, Alaskan

Wally Dunn was one of the best things that ever happened to me!

I had a five-year hitch with the U.S. Air Force after my dermatology residency at UCSF. I carefully filled out my official Air Force Form 90 (also known as the "dream sheet"), regarding my wishes for my next assignment. I sent it to the USAF personal center at Randolph Air Force Base, Texas. Jane and I carefully requested Florida. We wanted to get away from the high cost of living in the Bay area. We knew we really wanted to get away from the San Andreas Fault and earthquake country. And we wanted to be closer to our family back in Ohio.

Some months later, in floated an official looking letter from the Department of the Air Force. I frantically tore it open. As I read it, I went into shock. I had orders to report to Elmendorf Air Force Base, in Anchorage, Alaska! In my next life, I'll know to request Alaska when I really want to go to Florida. I knew I'd lost on all three reasons for wanting to leave San Francisco. We would suffer a higher cost of living in Anchorage, and we were near the epicenter of the largest earthquake to hit North America—the Good Friday Earthquake of March 27th, 1964. The U.S.

Geologic Survey registered it as having a force of 9.2 on the Richter scale! And we were even farther away from the family way back in Ohio.

"Maybe all is not lost," I thought. I promptly called the Air Force personal center at Randolph. Having a brainstorm, I told them, "My wife will divorce me if my family gets shipped to Alaska." (Who knows, maybe she really would.) "Talk to me about other alternatives," I pleaded.

The next week I got orders to Wichita Falls, Texas. Now Jane would *really* divorce me. I have nothing against the great state of Texas, but I had just done my internal medicine internship in San Antonio three years before. Maybe Alaska wouldn't be so bad after all? Go ahead, take a chance, Naversen.

I called back Randolph Field the next day and I appealed. "I thought we were going to have a dialogue on other choices for my next assignment. You just sent me orders to Wichita Falls, Texas. Go ahead and switch me back to Alaska, please."

Basically they told me, "If we haven't already told the poor schmuck who was supposed to go to Wichita Falls, but then was switched to Alaska, we will just switch you both back to your original assignments." They hadn't told him, so off to Alaska we went. I wonder if the air force dermatologist who went to Wichita Falls that year knew how close he was in coming to Alaska. Ignorance is bliss.

Now that we were firmly committed to Alaska, maybe I could salvage a bad situation by lining up some dermatology moonlighting opportunities to help overcome that high cost of living we had heard about. I fired off a letter to a female dermatologist practicing in Anchorage, Dr. Ollie Dunn. Little did I know, she had died two weeks before my letter arrived. I later learned she was beloved by her patients. Her death wish to her loving husband was that he help any new dermatologist who wanted to practice in the Great Land.

Two weeks after arriving in Anchorage in August, 1977, the ear nose and throat doctor Wally Dunn bought Jane and me dinner. He had been married to Ollie for three decades. He made me a ridiculous offer that I couldn't refuse. He would rent me office space at his downtown medical office for $100 a month. (The first two months were free so that I could get established.) His secretary, Linda, would schedule appointments for me. I would work Wednesday nights and Saturday mornings. He would give me, at no charge, Ollie's entire dermatology equipment complete with curettes, extractors, skin biopsy kits and her patch testing kit. I could use her trusty monocular microscope. (I still have it to this day.) After a nanosecond of contemplation, I accepted his gracious offer.

I was officially approved by the local medical society, and also by the hospital commander at Elmendorf. My talents (if I had any) belonged first to the United State Air Force and the government. I knew and understood it. If my schedule otherwise permitted, I could moonlight downtown.

The next five years were truly wonderful. Since I was the only board-certified dermatologist in the state, in addition to seeing all the military patients, the veterans, the natives at the Alaskan Native Medical Center, I could now see civilians, too. At Wally's office, my wife Jane worked as the front-office assistant, and my corpsman at the base, Joe Richardson, was my back-office assistant. We all had great fun together. Every week something unique or unexpected titillated our synapses.

Wally's assistant, Linda, scheduled appointments for us. That is "Linda Number Seven" scheduled our appointments. Whenever Wally needed a new front-office person, he would put an ad in the paper. He interviewed all applicants until the first Linda came through the door, and then he hired her. I admit it was a somewhat unconventional hiring scheme, but it worked for him. Last I heard, Wally had hired Linda Number 10 (that is, if we include Lynn and Melinda in the group) before he retired.

My wife Jane was privy to lots of the front office banter. One week we had two patients waiting to see me. One was a building contractor whose sub had not showed for work that day. (Must have been working on the Naversen residence?) The guy sitting next to him needed a job, he had a good power saw, but he had no car. Jane introduced them. By the way, the contractor drove by the unemployed man's house every day, but the builder needed a worker with his own power tools. Not only did Doug cure their rashes that day, but Jane kept someone off the welfare roles when the new sub was hired by the contractor.

There was clearly a need for a dermatologist in Alaska. Linda got desperate calls like, "If you can't get me in today for my rash, I'll jump on the plane for Seattle tomorrow." Or we might hear, "I have an itchy rash, get me an appointment ASAP or I'll commit suicide." Or, "My roommate hasn't been out of the apartment in weeks because of bad acne. She stays at home with a brown paper bag over her head. Help!"

As a matter of fact, I had enough patients for a full time civilian practice, and I didn't even have an ad in the local phone book. The patients felt lucky to get in to see me, but I knew I was the lucky one. They were great patients with interesting skin problems. And they all paid cash at the time of visit. We didn't bill insurance, but instead we gave them a "superform" to clip that on to their insurance form, and then they just mailed it all in themselves. Our collection ratio was 99-percent—almost unheard of in a medical practice!

One woman was a prominent cosmetic representative in Anchorage, and she had God-awful steroid acne. She purchased and used a strong steroid cream for a facial rash. It helped temporarily, but then she became addicted to it. When she went off it, her face flared markedly. So, back to the steroid cream she went. She was a bit like a heroin addict, only on a much nobler plane. Just like the addict needs an ever increasing dose of heroin to get the same high, so she needed more and more cortisone cream to keep her skin from flaring. And when going off heroin, the body goes into severe withdrawal.

When I greeted her, I noticed that her skin was a mess. Fine pustules dominated her face, which was bright red all over. The solution was hard for her to understand: Lay off the strong cortisone cream, use this mild one, and take oral tetracycline until the inflammation is gone. Three months later, she was back to normal and she loved me. It is okay to use a mild steroid such as one-percent hydrocortisone on the face, but avoid the strong ones if you need to use them over two weeks. And keep them away from the eyes.

One Wednesday, a good-looking, blue-eyed blond lad of 19 came to see me. Tyler had severe cystic acne of his face, chest and back. He was very clean, he washed twice daily, and his diet was excellent. The sores were so painful it hurt when he rolled over in bed. I hit him with every dermatological therapy ever invented. Nothing really helped. I mentioned that Dr. John Strauss in Iowa City, Iowa, was studying a new experimental acne drug called Accutane. Tyler jumped in his car and drove all the way to Iowa. All to no avail—the F.D.A. study was over and all paperwork had been submitted. Tyler had to wait until 1982 when Accutane was approved by the FDA. I suspect he ultimately got on the medication, and he got his skin problem cured. I wish we could have had Accutane a generation or two ago.

One Saturday morning, we arrived at the office and entered through the back door. Glass was everywhere. Some druggie had smashed the window and broken into the office. Sorry, Charlie—no drugs to be found.

Several weeks later, on a Wednesday afternoon, our clinic was ready to begin. Wally motioned Jane to join him in the lounge. He opened a "sugar jar" and with a tongue depressor he put a small amount of the powder onto her tongue. It tingled delightfully.

"Wally, what is that you put on my tongue? I like it," said my wide-eyed wife Jane.

"Cocaine," said Wally. "We hide it in the sugar container so the druggies can't find it. That is why our office had been hit, but no drugs could be found by the bad guys." Of course, ENT doctors classically use cocaine for their procedures. It numbs the nasal passages as it simultaneously dries them out. Most procedures on the delicate membranes of our anatomy cause profuse secretions which obscure the operating field. Hence, cocaine is the perfect ENT analgesic. Unfortunately, a "cokehead" uses too much of it, it dries up the inside of the nostrils, and the drug ultimately blows a hole in the nasal septum. Remember Uma Thurman in the movie *Pulp Fiction*—the gorgeous woman overdosed on cocaine and it caused bleeding from her nose.

Shortly before Christmas, a middle-aged woman came into the office. She was obviously flustered and upset. "What's up?" I asked.

Mary started sobbing. "They stole all of my Christmas presents!" Turns out, she came into Anchorage from a little town several hours away. She did her Christmas shopping, and she carefully placed the presents in the back of her pick-up truck. Somehow, the tailgate fell down, and all the presents slid out onto the road. By the time she realized it and turned around in traffic, all the presents had been snatched up by maggots who jumped out of their cars and stole her presents. So much for the Christmas spirit.

I calmed her down, and I treated her skin problem. On the way out in the waiting room I told Jane, "Nancy has been through enough today. Her visit is free." That was the least I could do to help make up for her bleak Christmas without presents. We called up a local TV station. They reported the story, and the public responded by donating money for new Christmas presents. The Christmas spirit lives!

As I said, every week something new and fun and wonderful excited us at our Wednesday and Saturday dermatology practice at 4201 Lake Otis parkway..

One Wednesday evening in our clinic, I diagnosed a woman and her children with scabies. I carefully took a scabies scrape from her finger webs with a blade. A quick exam with Dr. Ollie Dunn's microscope was negative for ectoparasites. Clinically, the patient still had scabies despite the negative scrape, and I recommended Lindane lotion for her and her family. As the patient left the office, Jane explained, "Nice scabies scrape."

"What are you talking about?" I asked. "I saw no mites or bugs on the slide."

"Not a problem," Jane replied. She showed me a perfect mineral oil prep complete with adult mite and eggs.

I'd been scooped by my wife again. It is always nice to be married to someone smarter than you.

But let's get back to my main man Dr. Wally Dunn. I feel very thankful to him. Without his help and enthusiasm, absolutely none of the above stories would have occurred. What would have happened to these patients if they hadn't gotten into a board-certified dermatologist? Maybe a Hollywood mogul will do a movie sometime on the two opposite life patterns if Dr. Wally Dunn hadn't been there. You know, like George Bailey in the great Christmas movie, *It's a Wonderful Life*, with Jimmy Stewart and Donna Reed.

Wally invited my family to his homestead property near Big Lake, Alaska. Three hundred sixty acres. Wimps need not apply. It was 30 degrees below zero in the winter. The cabin was rustic and warm with the wood stove smoking 24 hour a day.

One night, Wally said, "Doug, let's take a short trip on my snow machine."

"You're the man, "I replied.

We headed off in a mini blizzard down a narrow Jeep trail. After 20 minutes we hit a popular local tavern known as Call of the Wild, named after Jack London's famous book. Wally introduced me to the locals. We downed a few brews. We excused ourselves and headed outside into the snow. Now the ferocity of the snow had increased markedly compared with when we had first arrived. Wally drove the snow machine, and I held on and admired his Alaskan homesteading spirit. But after 30 minutes of noise and vibration, our hands and ears were downright cold. We should have been back to the cabin by now. In my numb state, visions of the Titanic, the Andrea Doria, the Edmund Fitzgerald, the Donner Party, and General Custer and the battle of the Little Big Horn all flashed through my brain. We are going down!

Remember Jack London's short story "To Light a Fire," when the poor guy and his husky froze to death when the ill-fated, incubating fire was snuffed out by snow falling from the evergreen bough above? Naversen, you don't even have matches. You and Wally are not only going to be dead meat, but *frozen* dead meat. Once the snow machine runs out of gas, we will probably walk 10 miles through the tundra, and they will find our decomposed corpses in the spring if the wolves and grizzlies haven't devoured the carcasses.

"Doug, we are here," Wally shouted through the blizzard. He woke me from my stupor. Unbeknownst to us, we had completed a big circle, and we casually walked back into The Call of the Wild. Our long-lost friends from an hour ago greeted us. "Where have you been? We missed you."

Wally and I had another brew. We again excused ourselves from the tavern. In 20 short minutes, we were back at Wally's cabin. It was toasty warm. I slept well that night. Had I had a near death experience in a blizzard near Big Lake, Alaska? We'll never know.

Chapter Forty-Five: Al the Sourdough

Al was the most interesting patient I had in my five years in Alaska, even more interesting than Smokey Bob. Come to think of it, Al was maybe the most interesting person in the whole state of Alaska!

When I first saw him in my office, with his full head of wavy white hair and his thick glasses, he reminded me of a European professor. Words gushed from his mouth as he pulled his left hand out of his pocket. I almost gasped as I saw a fungating ulcer the size of a Golden Eagle eating away at the top of his hand.

Many months before, he remembered pricking it on something in the wilds of Alaska. His job was to revegetate the 800-mile Alaska pipeline, which stretched from Valdez to Prudhoe Bay. His work crews planted grass and vegetation beneath and around the pipeline so it would be environmentally-friendly to even the most discerning bird, moose and caribou. (He must have been successful, judging by published photos of the migrating caribou herds selectively and preferentially chowing down on Al's grass.)

When Al was done with his project, he decided to get serious about curing the large hole in his hand. Matted lymph nodes swelled and disfigured his forearm up to the elbow. Al figured once they got as far as his heart, he would go belly-up, just like a dead Beluga whale in the nearby Cook Inlet. He ate every antibiotic known to humans and cattle, and all he got for his trouble was an upset stomach, diarrhea and a good old-fashioned case of hives. He became desperate, and one cold Alaskan night when it was 20 degrees below zero, he poured boiling water on his hand. Well, there is only one thing worse than a fungating ulcer on your hand, and that is a fungating ulcer on your hand that has been scalded and blistered from boiling-hot water.

Al traveled to Belize (the old British Honduras) in Central America every year to break up the harsh Alaskan winter. He consulted a British doctor who recommended the antifungal griseofulvin. Approved by the F.D.A. in 1958, it was somewhat primitive, but it was the best we had at the time. Al tried it for three months, but the ulcer seemed to laugh at him, and it would not heal. He developed more swollen lymph glands going higher up his arm. In a last-ditch effort, he went holistic, and he visited native doctors, who rubbed raw papayas and all-natural herbs on the wound. But no banana—the tender sore was getting bigger every week.

Back in Alaska, now in the spring, Al visited a surgeon. The surgeon cut the sore out and grafted it, and it looked great. That is, it looked great for about a week until it promptly sloughed. It must have gotten infected. The surgeon cut it out again, and with the same result. Slough! The ulcer was even bigger now, and more lymph glands moved up the arm closer and closer to the heart. Is the third time the charm?

One of Al's friends told him to see a dermatologist. "Some of those guys are pretty good at skin stuff," he said.

As luck would have it, Elmendorf Air Force Base served as the "territorial hospital" for active-duty personnel in the Air Force, Army, Navy and Coast Guard, and their dependent spouses and children. If a veteran had been on active duty for only one day, he could be evaluated at our facility.

Al had served in the Coast Guard in WWII, and his claim to fame was that his ship bagged a German U-boat off the eastern seaboard of the United States. This was one of the few German subs captured lock, stock and barrel by U.S. forces. Since Al was Pennsylvania-Dutch, he was the only German-speaking American on board the Coast Guard cutter. He was called on deck by the skipper to translate, while the scared German crew was interrogated. Al was a celebrity among his fellow sailors as he helped grill the German U-boat captain, the executive officer, and the whole foreign crew about war secrets. The military intelligence gleaned from the Germans could save American lives! Would the captured sailors be shot? None were, and the German sailors were repatriated after the war.

Al went home, too, and later he homesteaded 360 acres on the great Kenai Peninsula, south of Anchorage. I was proud to participate in the care of this war hero. He had definitely paid his dues.

"Al, did any of your doctors take a skin biopsy on your hand?" I asked.

"I don't believe they thought of it, Doctor, "Al replied. But Al never actually replied with just one word or sentence, it was more like a torrent of words and sentences pouring out of a vomiting swan's mouth.

I promptly did a skin biopsy with a PAS-D stain looking for fungal organisms, and found that Al's sample looked like a classic case of sporotrichosis. "I think I can help you," I told Al. "About 95 percent of these cases respond to a saturated solution of potassium iodide. It tastes like heck, but it won't hurt you. We usually get sporotrichosis from a thorn or rose prick. This 'deep fungus' goes much deeper than the superficial fungus that causes athlete's foot or jock itch. That's why a person gets mountains of lymph glands on the forearm."

Sure enough, our special stains showed fungal organisms, and the fungus culture grew colonies of pathogens. I confidently prescribed SSKI drops. But eight weeks later, absolutely nothing had happened.

Al was probably thinking, "Naversen is a quack just like all the others. No better than the native herbalist in Belize."

"Al," I said as I scratched my head, "we are taking off the kid gloves. You have 'sporo,' and I am going to cure you." By this time, he had the endured the sore eating away at his hand for a year and a half!

Amphotericin B is a potentially toxic anti-fungal poison. It may cause malaise, nausea, liver damage, kidney toxicity, allergic reactions, anaphylaxis and death. I carefully explained to Al the risks and benefits of the drug. After an infusion session, we would need to carefully observe him overnight, and then he could maybe have a day pass if things went smoothly enough. After a 20-minute discussion on a Friday afternoon, my powers of persuasion must have worked, because Al agreed to spend the whole night in the hospital after each session. I knew we would get to know each other really well the next six weeks, very well indeed.

I would hospitalize Al for amphotericin B IV every other day. After his IV infusion was done that afternoon, I felt safe leaving the hospital. I was eager to get home to start the weekend. It was only a 25-minute commute, but an hour and a half in a blizzard. Since it was nice weather, I soon pulled into the driveway leading to my igloo. (Actually, I had a nice four-bedroom home in Turnagain View subdivision. I recently visited it, and the old neighborhood looked great.) I was surprised when my wife Jane yelled out the window, "Doug you have a phone call from the head nurse."

Sure enough, Al was already chafing at the bit to start his hospital pass. So much for my 20-minute conference with Al late that afternoon.

"How does he look?" I asked.

"He looks great," replied our nurse. "And he is starting to drive the staff nuts."

I really respect the opinions of my nurses, and I almost always do what they tell me to do (kind of like when you are a new Second Lieutenant in the Air Force, you glom onto an experienced Sergeant, and you do whatever he says). Making a power judgment, I said to the nurse, "Send him on his weekend pass." If a German U-boat, the Alaskan blizzards and 40-below weather haven't killed him already, I figure I could not kill him with Amphotericin B. Al was the persistent kind of guy who, once he'd made up his mind, wore you down and got his way.

The nurse handed the phone to Al, and I told him, "Go on your pass and have fun."

Al tolerated the IV therapy surprisingly well. He amazed me. One day on rounds he might be reading *Playboy*, and the next day he was reading *Scientific American*. He could really be a deep thinker and a scientist at times, and the next moment he would be his practical, garrulous, Kenai Peninsula, sourdough, Alaskan self.

One day Al appeared for lunch in the hospital cafeteria. With his stiff, starched, white doctor's coat, and the stethoscope hanging around his neck, he looked like a university professor. That day he spoke with a thick German accent, and he had half the doctors and patients believing he was a brilliant visiting European physician on loan to the Air Force. The other half of us who knew he was just "Kenai Al" bit our cheeks so we wouldn't break out laughing and spoil it. Even our hospital commander, a physician, and a full colonel in the Air Force, sat down next to Al and played along with the gag. When the secret of Al's false identity was finally revealed to the crowd, the laughter was so loud it shook the walls almost as strongly as the 1964 Good Friday earthquake that trashed Anchorage, and severely damaged the very hospital we were sitting in.

After six weeks of therapy, Al's hand was completely healed. He formed a smooth scar devoid of ulceration and infection. Even the troublesome lymph glands in his left arm shrunk away. Al's long journey with sporotrichosis was finally over.

I saw Al every three to six months for the next five years or so, both personally and professionally. I kept a sharp eye on his left hand. I did not want a relapse. The fungus never came back!

I lost track of Al after I moved to Southern Oregon. I have not seen him in almost 20 years now. I don't know if he has passed on. I still think of him warmly from time to time, for after all, he was my most memorable patient in Alaska. Kind of like a *good* Smokey Bob.

Chapter Forty-Six: AIDS, Then & Now

The young man's name was Hutch, and he told me he was 25 years old as I examined his skin at the UCSF Dermatology Clinic in the mid '70s. He had blue-black nodules peppering his skin. They looked like large blueberries. I noticed that he wore no underwear. My clinic chief, Dr. Dave Cram, said that was a sure sign the patient was gay. (He was.) The biopsy I took from his ear revealed Kaposi's sarcoma, a rare type of soft-tissue skin cancer. Within six months, Hutch was dead.

At our quarterly meeting of the San Francisco Dermatology Society, we discussed Kaposi's sarcoma. Even back then, we had separated victims into two groups. The first, classic group afflicted elderly men of Mediterranean origin. They got Kaposi's sarcoma on their lower extremities, and they followed a benign clinical course. They usually didn't die of sarcoma, but instead they tended to have a normal life expectancy, and they often passed on from natural causes.

The second group tended to be much younger. The young men got Kaposi's sarcoma all over their skin and even inside their mouths. They usually had a rapid, virulent, progressive downward spiral. They often died of this sarcoma, or of other cancers, or of raging infection. Unfortunately, they died many decades before their time.

Fast forward seven years later to Medford, Oregon, in 1983. I was in my office Saturday morning donating my old, but trusty, x-ray machine to Rogue Valley Hospital. Although x-ray is good for curing skin cancer, patients are scared of radiation, and surgery is quicker. The x-ray machine pick-up had to be on the weekend when patients were not in the office. These machines weigh a ton or more, and we needed a professional moving company to do the job.

The answering service rang me. A patient was on the phone. He worked down in California Monday through Friday. Could I please see him today while he was in Medford? I told the service, "I look like a bum, what with my old blue jeans and t-shirt on, but sure, send him over."

Twenty minutes later, Sam was in my office. He worked in the San Francisco bay area, and he drove home on weekends to be with his wife and kids. As I examined his skin, I had a flashback to the Ohio State Emergency Room and the patient with venereal disease. Sam had the typical rash of secondary syphilis, and the skin biopsy and blood test were 100-percent diagnostic. (I don't like to label someone with VD unless I am positive that's what it is—in this case, I was.) I told him on the phone early the next week, "Sam, you have VD, and I need to treat you and your wife with penicillin shots. I don't care what you tell her, just get her in here next week."

The couple's buttocks were smarting from the 2.4 million units of penicillin G benzathine I injected into each of their gluteals. (Sam's injection was repeated in one week to insure that he was cured.) Worse than the pain of the injections was the look on Sam's wife's face when she learned her husband had VD, and she was exposed to it, and could have syphilis also. That was one of the most embarrassing moments of my life. I felt so sorry for her. It was unclear where the VD had come from.

Some months later, Sam was in an auto accident. His surgeon noted he had multiple large lymph glands. That makes sense because syphilis often gives multiple large swollen lymph glands. Back in Medford, he related his auto accident history as we performed blood tests. As his VDRL titer went back to 0, we knew he was clinically and laboratory-wise cured of his VD. His wife was too. If he was reinfected, his titer would rise fourfold from baseline, and he would need more treatment. I felt confident Sam had learned his lesson, and with the embarrassment to his wife and the stress on his marriage, he would never get VD again.

Some months later, Sam developed weird rashes, low grade fevers, aches and pains, and malaise. He developed new and even more swollen lymph glands. He knocked my socks off when he told me, "Dr. Naversen, I am bisexual. I lead a double life. In Medford, I am a happily married man with a wife and two kids. In San Francisco, I am a sexual party animal. I frequent the steamy, gay bath houses, and I have had sex with dozens of men, most of them complete strangers. That's where I got the syphilis. But I couldn't tell you or my wife. I didn't want to be staring into the double-barrel of a divorce."

In retrospect, Sam had the "gay lymph node syndrome" that ultimately led to his positive AIDS test. He had a rapidly downhill course. He got mad at me, and he fired me as his doctor after I made the AIDS diagnosis. He switched to another dermatologist, and it shocked me to learn he did not tell his new doctor he was HIV positive. The doctor could have contracted AIDS when he biopsied his skin. Talk about bad behavior!

I learned that Sam soon died of complications of HIV and AIDS. He gave the disease to his wife, and she also expired, leaving two children without any parents to take care of them.

We had little therapy to offer these patients in the early '80s. We watched and fretted and used primitive drugs and prayed for them as they went down the tubes and died on us. But at least the AIDS syndrome was now well described, we had a blood test to diagnose it, and we knew how to follow the CD4 count as a measure of its severity and the likelihood of dying of fulminating infection. We would discover the Kaposi's sarcoma virus in 1994, and we would learn that this virus was a completely different one from that which caused HIV. In fact, the sarcoma virus was found to be a human herpes-virus 8 (not herpes simplex or herpes zoster) that gay men were contracting along with HIV. That is what happened to Sam—he caught two different viruses, HIV and HHV-8, along with his syphilis. The reason he died so rapidly compared to the elderly men with Kaposi's sarcoma was the AIDS virus. What a devastating combination of diseases—once you had the newly-described

AIDS virus, with associated Kaposi's sarcoma, it was a death sentence. No known treatment anywhere on earth could cure it.

Fast forward 21 years, again, to Medford, Oregon. Mike came into my office. Right up front he let me know he was HIV positive from unprotected sex. He caught Hepatitis C at the same time. I really appreciated his sharing those important medical details with me. I would hate for a doctor or his or her staff—particularly one of ours—to suffer a needle stick and contract AIDS or hepatitis. Many dedicated health care workers across the country have died of AIDS from such sticks and slices.

The good news was, Mike looked great! In the '80s, he would have died as rapidly as Hutch and Sam did. Except for sunken cheeks due to fat atrophy, he looked so normal that no one would know that he had any disease. (When walking in San Francisco, looking at street people, sunken cheeks are a tip-off that they probably have AIDS.) Mike had been treated with "HAART" drugs—highly active anti-retroviral therapy introduced in 1996. His triple anti-viral bullets had kept his CD4 count above 700 for the whole course of his illness. An intense treatment of his hepatitis C with interferon and other therapies cured the virus that attacks the liver. The Hep C can kill a victim just as surely as the AIDS virus can.

"HAART" has in many cases turned AIDS into a chronic, long-term disease instead of an acute, life threatening disease with a rapid downhill course, and an agonizing death from multiple infections and internal and external cancers. In the peak death year in 1995, 9217 Americans died of AIDS. By 1999, the death toll had decreased to 2901 thanks largely to these new medicines. And that death rate has remained stable since then. Many AIDS patients are now passing on from natural causes, rather than from fulminating infections and aggressive cancers.

When Mike told me he had AIDS, my brain rapidly whirled and my experience with Hutch and Sam flashed before my eyes. But in giving him a skin exam, I noticed he had no less than 11 basal cell carcinomas on his nose, cheeks, torso and arms. He had been a surfer in Southern California for many years, and he often burned and cooked and fried his skin while growing up. In the early years of AIDS, we wouldn't bother treating Mike since he would soon be dead. Now, since he was in such good shape, we would proceed and surgically treat all cancer sites.

I feel fortunate to have seen the AIDS epidemic unfold, and I follow with keen anticipation the discovery of blood tests to diagnose and follow its progression. I am gladdened by the beneficial anti-retroviral therapy we now have, compared to the dark ages when we had virtually nothing. I have diagnosed and treated patients with AIDS and Kaposi's sarcoma, and I am happy that they now have a chance to live many years. With the increased longevity, I will continue to treat more skin cancer in AIDS patients in the future.

Just a few words of advice—don't make the mistake Mike did. Never fail to use adequate protection during sex. Only when you are in a stable, monogamous relationship, and when you know both partners are free of disease, can you discard the condoms. Trust me on this one.

Before leaving the topic of AIDS, I want to share one of my favorite anecdotes. I recently got a kick out of one of my 70-year-old patients. He grew up in New York City, and would often go swimming at the many public beaches he had access to. Being fair-skinned with blonde hair, he sunburned very easily. Without any good sunscreens back then, he severely damaged his face and the top of his hands in his youth, such that I would now see him every six months in my office to freeze his precancers (actinic keratoses) with liquid nitrogen.

On one occasion, he had so many keratoses we choose instead to have him apply 5-FU cream twice daily all over his face for two weeks. This would "light up" his face. The precancers would be cured, although his skin would be temporarily raw, red, and inflamed. At the two-week mark, at the peak of his unsightly appearance, Lewis got in a department store elevator. Two young boys starred at his inflamed condition. As Lewis got off the elevator, he heard the older boy whisper to the younger, "That man has AIDS." Lewis chuckled to himself.

In this day and age, anyone with an unsightly appearance might be accused of having AIDS or anthrax or leprosy or some other dreaded disease by the dermatologically-unsophisticated public. In this case, I wish we could cure AIDS as fast as we treated his precancers. Two weeks later, Lewis' skin was approaching normal, as we laughed together at his story.

Chapter Forty-Seven: Tattoo Removal, the Hard Way

Travis was a World War II veteran. He served in the Navy at Pearl Harbor. I was getting ready to admire the tattoo on his right arm. But then, as I looked closer, I realized there used to be a tattoo there, but it had been removed in a way that I was not familiar with. Which is funny, for you see, we are the tattoo experts at Dermatology and Laser Associates of Medford. Whenever someone no longer wants his or her tattoo, we laser it off. I have lasered off thousands of tattoos with the help of my very excellent laser technicians.

If it is a small one, we simply excise it. In years past, I have dermabraded them off and salabraded them off (using salt and lots of gauze and rubbing), but the Q-switched laser has proven to be the treatment of choice in the new millennium. By the way, we are very nonjudgmental here. If someone likes their tattoo, we like it. When they don't like it, that is when we get involved.

So I said to Travis, "I'm intrigued. Tell me how you had your tattoo removed."

"Well, it's a long story. It happened many years ago at Pearl Harbor, Hawaii, after the war. I was working as a civilian pipe fitter for the Navy. I was called to do a job, and I just couldn't get this one darned rusted nut off the metal fitting. But it was no problem, because we pipe fitters have a few tricks up our sleeves. I just figured I would squirt a little JP-4 jet fuel on the pipe, and I would light it with a match. The sudden burst of heat would expand the nut, and I would wrench it off, no sweat."

"My only mistake was when I spilled some of the JP-4 on my shirt and arms. When I lit the match, suddenly I realized I was on fire! The flames raced from my shirt, down my arms, and singed off all my hair. I was now a human fireball, and there was no one to help me. I knew I was going to die!"

"In confusion and terror, I staggered back away from the burning pipe. My life flashed before me. This was the big one. I was done. I was a goner!"

"At that instant, as I stumbled backwards, I was surprised that the back of my thighs were hammered by a metal rail. Although I am not a gymnast, I did a beautiful, totally unexpected back flip, headfirst into an open cesspool. It would have been a perfect 10 on the Olympic diving scale. The fire was instantly doused by the warm, foul-smelling slime that surrounded my body. The smell was unbearable as I found myself bathing total-body in human excrement and sewer water. But the guano had saved my life. In another few seconds, my clothing would have incinerated me."

"A passerby called for help, and the fire department hauled me out of the black goo. I looked like a singed scarecrow covered with black repulsive fecal gunk. It was hard to tell if the smell of my burned flesh and hair was worse than the contents of the cesspool now coating me from head to toe."

"Back then they had different health standards," he continued. "Open pits like that were allowed. In the present day, a modern sewage plant would have replaced the cesspool, and I would have burned to death."

As I listened intently to this bizarre story, Travis went on with his saga. "In the intensive care unit, I looked like black, dead-meat. There were burns all over my body, and my skin was gone. The teeming bacteria in the pit attacked the open sores on my skin. You doctors didn't have all of your modern antibiotics way back then that you have now."

"They later told me I had a very stormy course ahead of me, with chills and fever, nausea, extreme pain and, later, as it happened, profound depression. I guess I'm just an ornery cuss because I survived against all the odds. I had some skin grafts on the really bad areas that were black char. On my right arm, where I had the World War II tattoo, the burns singed it off leaving just a faint blur. That is why my arm looks like it does. I never really did like that tattoo anyway."

"Travis, that is quite a story," I said. "I am impressed. Even with our state-of-the-art techniques, we would be hard-pressed to duplicate your good cosmetic result on removing the tattoo. You are one lucky man!" And I thought, Now *that* is removing a tattoo the hard way.

Chapter Forty-Eight: Why Did It Take So Long?

Years ago, in a small town in Oklahoma, a farmer's wife developed a little pimple on her nose. It kind of healed, but not really. Then it became a bigger pimple. It always seemed to heal a little after crusting and bleeding, but the darn thing just wouldn't go away. As best we could figure, Sharon was a bona fide recluse. She would never accompany her husband into town on Saturdays. The farm was her sanctuary. She was content to do her "farmer's wife" chores: cooking, cleaning, sewing, and the other endless tasks that are part of being a good wife living out in the country.

A decade went by before any doctor laid eyes on Sharon. By the time she got in for a checkup, the tumor on her nose was huge. Its mass literally took up one-half of her nose, and it threatened the sight in her left eye. She was unknowingly doing an experiment in nature that could not be ethically be done by doctors. That is, what happens when you let a basal cell carcinoma grow for ten years, without any treatment whatsoever?

She had the classical history: A small pimple or cyst turned into a non-healing sore. It partially healed, but it never really did. Some days it would weep, and some days it would even bleed. Crusts were replaced by foul-smelling nodules and tumors. The bleeding and infection got harder and harder to control at home without any available antibiotics, and without surgery.

Back on the farm in Oklahoma, Sharon's husband died suddenly of a heart attack. The faithful wife lost her beloved husband, and she was also losing the way of life as she had known it. Gone was the farmhouse, and lost forever was her quiet retreat from the world. She was forced to go live with the kids in California.

Unfortunately, by this time her nose was so hideously deformed she scared the grandkids. They would go crying and screaming to the far reaches of her daughter's house. Whenever they saw grandma, they would just run and hide. The daughter and son-in-law had to do something!

After they took Sharon to their family doctor, he wisely referred this difficult case to a university medical setting. That is how I ended up eventually seeing Sharon in the dermatology clinic at UCSF. A skin biopsy revealed a rodent ulcer—that is, a penetrating basal cell carcinoma going deep into the tissue on her nose.

"Why did you wait so long to get in?" I asked Sharon in wonderment.

"Doctor, I was scared," she replied. "The bigger the growth on my nose got, the more scared I became. I figured I had waited so long it might be okay to wait another month or two. Maybe it would just go away on its own. Plus, I was plenty embarrassed, and I was just plain scared of the unknown. I figured I would die of natural causes before the growth on my nose got me."

We presented Sharon at the UCSF visible tumor clinic. We had dermatologists, plastic surgeons, ENT docs (like Wally Dunn), eye doctors and radiation therapists evaluate her. We decided to make a mold of her nose, just in case we couldn't save it. We decided surgery would be too radical and disfiguring on this elderly woman. The group collectively decided on seven weeks of radiation therapy. The rads were given gently, only three days a week. We took great care to protect her left eye with a lead corneal shield. The x-ray was painless for her, and we took it as a good sign when the tumor crusted, and it actually shrunk in size for the first time in over a decade.

Three months after the time I first saw her, Sharon had a miraculous cure. Although she would never win a beauty contest, the tumor was gone and the normal architecture of her nose was preserved. We did not need to use the prosthetic nose the lab had expertly made for us. She still had normal vision in both her eyes.

The moral of the story is simple. If you or a loved one has a non-healing sore on your skin, get in sooner rather than later to see your skin doctor. The earlier you get in, the less time you will have to spend worrying. If it does prove cancerous, you will need less surgery, and you will get a better cosmetic result by not waiting. Get in early, and the removal of the abnormal mole or melanoma could save your life.

I remember treating a 105-year-old woman in a nursing home in Medford. She developed a non-healing sore on her nose at age 95. They said, "She is old, let's not treat it. We don't want her to feel pain. We don't want to hurt her." It sure would have been a lot easier on everyone (patient, family, nursing staff and doctor) if I had done electrosurgery on her ten years before. I ultimately cured her with a surgical procedure, but there was no need for her to put up with that foul-smelling, festering sore for all those years when she could have been promptly cured.

Remember, since ultraviolet light from the sun and tanning salons causes skin cancer, wear a hat with a 3-inch or wider brim, tight weave clothing with long sleeves, and even gloves. Do your outdoor activities early and late in the day, not in the noonday sun. If it is hot and muggy and you do not want to wear all those clothes, use a #30 SPF waterproof (soon to be called a "very water resistant") sunscreen on your arms and hands, and reapply it hourly. Please avoid tanning salons. Studies prove they do cause basal cell carcinoma, squamous cell carcinoma and melanoma. And don't wait until age 50 before protecting your skin. Encourage the kids and grandkids to start common-sense sun protection beginning early in childhood. As an added bonus, they will have more youthful-appearing, vigorous skin with less liver spots, dilated blood vessels, sallow complexions and wrinkle lines. Enjoy the great outdoors, but protect your skin when you are out in it.

Chapter Forty-Nine: Grover's Disease

D r. Grover is a hero of mine. He made the obscure, obvious. He made the complex, simple. And he made the rare, commonplace. What is the most difficult thing? The most difficult thing is to see with your eyes, what is right before your eyes. That is what he did.

While practicing as a dermatologist in Long Island, New York, in the 1960s, Dr. Grover saw half a dozen men one summer. Most of them were over 50 years of age, and they all had been out in the sun sweating and working. They suffered from itchy, red, crusty papules on their chest, back and abdomen. Formerly, this would have been lumped together as just a heat rash. Dr. Grover had the foresight to take skin biopsies—they all showed similar and characteristic changes of "acantholysis." The cells in the outer layers of the skin (the epidermis) had for some reason lost the glue that held them together. The individual cells literally seemed to "float" in the epidermis, whereas normally they are glued together with "intercellular cement." In his honor, the term Grover's disease became the eponym used to describe this condition.

Although women can get Grover's disease, there must be some hormonal factor, since nine out of 10 patients are males. Playing tennis or doing heavy physical labor in the summer sun may trigger it. The disease may sometimes be associated with a contact dermatitis to a new fabric or chemical. Men sometimes get an itchy eruption of Grover's disease on their back after double pneumonia and a temperature of 103 degrees, while lying sweating in their hospital bed. To add insult to injury, not only do they have a serious lung infection that they could die from, but they bitterly complain about the very itchy, red crusted eruption on their torso.

The best case of Grover's disease I ever saw was in a German gentleman. Every time he would fly from Germany to southern Oregon to visit his daughter, he would suffer with red itchy bumps on his back. He stated he would usually be on the plane for 18 hours with all the different legs and transfers from Frankfurt to New York to San Francisco to Medford. Two weeks later, he would always develop Grover's disease on his back from the occlusion and sweating, with his back lying against his airplane seat for all those hours.

I never used to diagnose Grover's disease early in my years as medical doctor, since I didn't recognize the condition. Now I diagnose it daily in one or more of my patients. I suspect many non-dermatologists have never made the diagnosis, nor have they even heard of Grover's disease. We treat it with potent cortisone creams, a burst of prednisone and modification of exercise activity. I recommend exercise in an air-conditioned room, not outdoors in the heat and humidity. The patients should wear a modern fabric in their workout clothing that wicks moisture away from the skin. Paradoxically, sometimes starting the patient on light treatments in our ultraviolet box can help resolve it, also.

I have been in dermatology meetings when a distinguished professor gives a lecture, and he reviews a host of inflammatory diseases of the skin. When he gets to Grover's disease, he says, "By the way, Dr. Grover is in the audience." We all stand up and give the good Dr. Grover an ovation. Then the lecture continues.

People (especially men) have been getting itchy red bumps on their torsos for thousands of years. But it wasn't until the 1960s that we learned that actually they had Grover's Disease, also known as "TAD," or transient acantholytic dermatosis. Unfortunately, for some people it is "PAD," or persistent acantholytic dermatosis. It doesn't want to go away in just a few weeks, but it may linger for months or even years!

If you are a man over age 50 with an intensely itchy eruption of your chest, abdomen or back, you may well have Grover's disease. Check in with your local dermatologist for a definitive diagnosis and some treatment.

I like it when a doctor keeps an open mind. By using a trained eye in visualizing the patient's skin, in combination with a skin biopsy and an expert dermatopathology consultation, who knows how many new "Grover's diseases" will be discovered in future years. Maybe there will be a "Naversen's disease" just around the corner? Someday, I would love for a dermatology resident to say, "Looks like a classic case of Naversen's disease." Now *that* would be immortality.

Chapter Fifty: Tom Valley, My Best Friend

My childhood best friend, Tom Valley, was murdered by his wife and a drug dealer back on the East Coast some years ago. The two were convicted of murder one. We were happy to hear that Tom's mother got her grandchild back from the low-life mother, and raised the little guy in a loving house. Although Tom is gone, his memory lives and he is missed. This story doesn't have anything to do with dermatology and medicine. But thinking of Tom takes me back to the carefree, golden days of my youth, when I was in grade school and junior high—long before the stresses of high school, college and medical school.

One summer, Tom and I got the brilliant idea that we would walk beneath the city of Huber Heights (near Dayton, Ohio) in the sewer drain pipes. When we made it to the end of the line, where it flowed into the Great Miami River, we would be in "ball heaven." Tennis balls, golf balls, baseballs, softballs—every kind of ball you ever wanted—would surely be trapped in the mesh at the end of the sewer pipes.

Tom and I set out with high energy and a bounce in our step. Since the pipes were not high, we couldn't stand completely upright while inside them. And because the creek flowed right into the middle of the pipe, we had to waddle like ducks, with our feet on either side of the flow, or our feet would get soaked. We hunkered down, trying to ignore the darkness and the sewer smells. Would rats greet us around the next bend in the deep, dark section of the pipes?

After what seemed like hours (and actually was), our backs were aching, and we getting hungry and thirsty. But there was no end in sight. Not wanting to retrace our steps, we pushed onward. We began thinking, if we got a sudden summer Ohio downpour, the drain pipes would fill up causing a flash flood, and even if we didn't see a rat, we would drown like one.

Finally, Tom and I had a pow-wow. We had to turn back. We would have to painfully retrace our steps in the darkness. There would be no "ball heaven" for us on that day. We wouldn't even catch a glimpse of the Great Miami. To make matters worse, our flashlights were dead. We had to step carefully as we painfully felt our way through the darkness, and as we straddled the water flowing through the center of the sewer pipe. We got a little glimpse of light every block or so as the sun shown in on a storm drain entrance by the street gutters. Tom and I tried to hurry, as we knew that soon the sun would be setting. We would be left in total darkness. 30 minutes later, the sun did go down. God must have been watching the two scared boys walking slowly and clumsily straight ahead into what seemed to them the dark bowels of Hell.

After what seemed like days of straddling inside the big dark void, my back felt like it was breaking. I was famished, dehydrated and filthy. Tom was a quarter mile behind me in the sewers beneath Huber Heights. Would our legs and backs give out? Would we bump our heads and get knocked out? Would we take a wrong turn and get lost forever? Would some rodent or poisonous snake bite us in the darkness? We felt like Tom Sawyer and Huck Finn trapped and lost in the great cave back in Mark Twain's era.

As Tom and I were filled with great self-doubt, fear and trepidation, I saw the best thing I had ever seen in my life. My dad was leaning up against the inside of the sewer pipe 30 yards ahead, calmly smoking on his pipe. Although I despise smoking and tobacco because of all the cancer and heart attacks they cause, the familiar scent of my dad's favorite brand of tobacco filled me with warmth, cheer and hope.

Earlier that day, my mom Thelma wondered why Tom and I were looking for flashlights on a bright, hot summer day. We must have made some passing reference to a sewer pipe, and her mother's intuition figured out that's why we missed lunch and dinner. Her baby was lost in the sewer pipe! She was right, and the Colonel (my dad Enoch) was dispatched to rescue us.

My dad had hiked in one-half mile from the entrance, where the creek flowed into the sewer pipe. Although Tom and I were hurting, we covered the final half mile in record time. After a bath and big dinner, we were right with the world again. Mom and dad weren't too hard on us—we weren't being malicious, it was just boyish enthusiasm.

By the way, we later found out there were no baseballs, tennis balls, beach balls or any kind of balls where the sewer pipe flowed into the river. It was just a boyhood myth that could have cost us our lives. Tom and I had learned our lesson—no more getting into trouble. Well, at least not until the next month.

It was Friday afternoon, and Tom and I were packing the books we would need for our weekend homework assignments. Tom's locker was conveniently located right next to mine. I was surprised when he reached over into my locker. He pulled out one of my books, and he forcefully slammed it on the floor right at my feet.

Tom was certainly a prankster! Not to be outdone, I reached into his locker. Tom watched motionless as I threw not one but two of his books on the floor. Before we knew it, Tom and I were wrestling like noisy hogs on the floor covered with books all over our bodies. Our lockers had been completely cleaned out, which explained the clutter on the floor. We were alternately yelling, screaming and laughing in uncontrolled glee.

Just then our principal, Mr. Jett, happened to walk by. Mr. Jett was a towering six feet, four inches tall, he must have weighed 220 pounds, and he was uniformly feared by all the students. He had a reputation for sternness, and he just plain scared most of us eighth graders. Tom and I were in deep dog dung of our own doing, and we knew it.

Mr. Jett, in his authoritative voice, said, "You two boys get up. Get this mess cleaned up right away. You report to the principal's office Monday morning at 8:00 a.m. sharp. Don't be late!" He then rushed off to a meeting.

Tom and I had nightmares Friday and Saturday night. What would Mr. Jett do to us on Monday? Would we be on permanent detention until we were seniors? Would we have to do a thousand hours of community service? Maybe we would even get a public paddling in front of the student body! (Don't laugh—that happened to me in seventh grade. Teachers would probably be fired for that in this day and age. But who knows—maybe I deserved it?)

You notice I didn't mention anything about nightmares on Sunday night. What with school and our deadline with destiny looming at 8:00 a.m. sharp on Monday, why no Sunday night nightmares? Well, I came down with a God-awful strep throat that night, complete with chills, fevers, rigors, painful throat, huge tonsils and a temp of 105 degrees—the whole nine yards.

I had to go in for a big shot of penicillin first thing Monday morning. I can still remember the smell of isopropyl rubbing alcohol as it was applied to my buttock in preparation for my injection. Just like Pavlov's dogs, the odor would cause me to feel the deep burning hurt of that sharp needle before it even pierced my skin, for I knew the big slug of medicine was coming. As a matter of fact, it took quite a few decades for the same smell of the alcohol not to trigger the same fear of impending rump throbbing!

Needless to say, I couldn't go to school that day. My throat hurt so badly, plus I would have been contagious to the other kids. In addition to feeling bad from the strep throat, I felt pretty bad for my best friend, Tom Valley, who was left to face the wrath of Mr. Jett alone. With two of us, we could have shared the punishment. Misery truly does love company. But since I had deserted him, Tom would be all alone in the world without a friend as he knocked on Mr. Jett's door. Would Tom and Mr. Jett think I was faking my strep?

Tuesday rolled around, and I was still pretty sick. On Wednesday, I showed signs of life. I had an inkling that life might actually be worth living again. My mom told me I would be going to school on Thursday.

I wondered in sympathy what fate had befallen young, brave Tom who toiled alone in punishment. My fears were not just for Tom, but also for "moi"—I knew whatever Tom got, I would suffer the same punishment, just doled out three days later.

I looked for Tom at school all Thursday morning. What had happened to him? Was he in junior high jail?

I didn't discover him until noon, when I spotted him in the cafeteria munching on a sandwich. I ran across the room with anticipation. What was to be my fate? I blurted out, "Tom, what did Mr. Jett do to you Monday morning? I'm sorry I couldn't be with you. I felt so badly for you."

Tom slowly finished chewing his bite of peanut butter sandwich. That was his favorite sandwich day after day. He reflected for a moment, and then he slowly said, "Doug, I never went to Mr. Jett's office on Monday morning. When you didn't show, I freaked out. I was scared to go alone to the principal's office. I'm kinda lying low. I hope I don't run into Mr. Jett in the hallways!"

That scallywag Tom had me worrying about him for nothing. We both decided to keep a real low profile for the next month or two. Maybe Mr. Jett forgot who we were, or maybe he completely forgot about the incident as he rushed off to his Friday afternoon meeting.

Tom and I got off Scot-free on that one. We worried about it, and we stewed enough over it that our feelings of guilt were probably punishment enough. Sometimes life is not fair. Every now and then, you got tattooed for something you really didn't do. This time, the gods were smiling over me and Tom. We never were brought to justice for our boyhood transgressions in front of our lockers that day.

The golden carefree days of our youth pass far too quickly. Tom made my boyhood days both fun and memorable. Tom Valley, my best friend, please rest in peace.

Chapter Fifty-One: Glad There is a Specialist on Duty

While working in the emergency room in Anchorage, Alaska, in the middle of the night, I got a STAT call: "Dr. Naversen to OB, please!"

Although half-asleep from my day's travail, I sprinted down the hallway and up two flights of steps. For some, the running would have been heart-pounding. For me, it was relaxing. For you see, running is what I do. I had a few seconds to steel my nerves for whatever medical crisis faced me in labor and delivery.

I blasted through the doors into OB. The nurse blurted out, "A delivery is in progress. Get scrubbed up, and get in there quick!"

I had just set the world record for sprinting from the ER to OB, and I believe I also set the record for scrubbing my hands, arms and fingernails. The corpsman expertly helped me put on my sterile gown and gloves, and into the delivery room I popped just in time to catch the greasy, white, coated baby that was being born at that very moment.

The nurse attending the delivery was a pro. She told me the OB doctor on call had been notified, but that he had not arrived yet. Our patient, Adrian, decided to have a precipitous delivery, and she obviously wasn't waiting for the OB doc to saunter on in. I grabbed the little one as he emerged from the inside of mom's womb. I took great care not to drop the little guy. I know you lose big points with the head nurse and the mother if you drop the slimy little butterball on the floor.

We all noted he was a boy—and what a man he would be someday judging by his already-impressive anatomy! I gently rolled the baby upside down and patted his back, and he let out a scream that any parent would have been proud of. The nurse handed me the scissors, and I clipped and clamped the umbilical cord like an experienced pro. I pronounced an "8" out of 10 on the Apgar rating scale. It would have really only been a "7," since the "ankle-biter" was a little blue. (You can't deduct for color anymore.)

Next I delivered the placenta and afterbirth, and fortunately for me, it was routine. I noted that Mom was fine. Although I had delivered seven babies in medical school, plus I had delivered my first-born daughter, Laurel, it had been a few years since I had any OB experience. I must have fooled them all when the veteran nurse said, "Good job, Dr. Naversen, we are lucky to have a specialist on call tonight." We all laughed, including the mother. Everyone knew the specialist happened to be a dermatologist. The baby suckled contentedly on Mom's breast.

The mother and Nathan visited me routinely for "well baby dermatology visits" in the clinic. I don't know if she had decided what to name her baby before the delivery, but I was flattered nonetheless when she named the little guy Nathan, same as my only son. I also shared with her that her son Nathan had beautiful skin. That was no idle chatter—this was the trained eye of the dermatologist.

Childbirth is one of the great beauties of nature. To suddenly have a healthy newborn baby cry out after the delivery is awesome. Even the most hardened, veteran doctors and nurses are moved every time it happens. I was just happy I could play a small part in the miracle of birth in the middle of a cold winter night in Anchorage many years ago.

Chapter Fifty-Two: Porphyria

Mom and dad took their cute little baby for a stroller walk on a beautiful spring day. You know, the kind of day that elevates the human spirit and makes you happy to be alive. As soon as the sun hit the baby's face, she began crying uncontrollably. It seemed that only when she was placed in the shade, did she quit screaming. Baby Emily was very fretful that summer, always crying when outside. She developed sores and blisters on her face, hands and arms. Why, the beautiful baby's skin was getting scars. Her young hands looked like she scrubbed toilets all day long.

I saw Emily later that year in the fall when the sun's rays were weakening. Her sores and infections were healing and resolving. With a little antibiotic cream and some Aveeno oatmeal soaks, Naversen got another cure. Or so I thought.

Emily did well in the winter when the sun didn't shine. However, for the next two springs and summers she again flared up, developing infected sores and blisters on her sun-exposed skin. She was lost to follow-up, until Mom brought her back when Emily was three-years-old.

I was startled at the aged, weather- beaten appearance of the toddler's face and hands. She appeared to have acne scars on her face, but why at age three? Her poor little hands and arms were a mess. I knew Emily had to have a unique inborn error of metabolism. No normal child looked like this.

Several weeks later her blood tests came back, classic for porphyria. She had a variety of what was also known as "Werewolf's disease," named after the disfigured, hairy people back in Transylvania who only came out at night. They suffered from a particularly severe form of porphyria known as Gunther's disease. Fortunately, we knew Emily's was a milder form known as erythropoietic protoporphyria (EP). She and some of her relatives lacked a key enzyme that normally degrades porphyrin, a chemical found in everyone's body. Since she was lacking the enzyme, porphyrins would build up in her blood stream, and then they would spill into the fine capillaries that coursed just beneath the skin's surface.

Unfortunately, the chemical is a strong photosensitizer. The specific band of light from 400 to 410 nanometers, found in the sun's rays, zaps and activates the porphyrin in the skin. She would now be highly allergic to the sun. Her skin would sting, burn, blister, and then it would even scar. We know the specific wavelength can even pass right through window glass, so riding in a car with the window rolled up would offer no protection. When she was out in the direct sun, the ultraviolet light in combination with the porphyrin made her cry in the baby stroller on the bright, sunny spring day.

Fast forward a decade. Emily is in remission, now that we know what her disease is. She wears protective hats with wide brims, long sleeves and gloves. She particularly benefits from sunscreens with physical blockers, which contain zinc oxide or titanium dioxide—they block out everything, including the critical 400–410 nanometer wavelength that triggers porphyria. Regular sunscreens don't work for her since they mainly block the sunburn rays (UVB) of the sun.

Her other magic bullet is beta carotene. By dosing up on 10 pills a day every spring and throughout the summer, beta carotene photoprotects her. While she still has a few faint scars on her face, her hands and arms don't look so old anymore. Although she is at risk for having liver problems and gall stones, she most likely will live to a ripe old age. But her kids and grandkids may inherit the disease.

Of course there are other cases of sunlight sensitivity. Some medications such as diuretics (water pills), can make a person allergic to the sun. Some creams and chemicals rubbed onto your skin can react with the sun's rays and make you allergic. For example, bartenders working outside by the pool can get allergic to the lime juice on their hands. If the party was inside, they would have no sun and no problems.

Rarely, someone might have lupus, an autoimmune disease that my beautiful, but depressed, African American patient had. The most common cause of sunlight sensitivity is polymorphous light eruption, which is especially common in Native Americans. You break out in the spring, your skin "hardens" by late August and you are good until the next spring.

If you are troubled with photodermatitis, you might check in with your local dermatologist to get a definitive diagnosis, and to discuss therapy that could help. By knowing the specific wavelength that injures your skin, you can rationally choose the right sunscreen that will protect your skin from allergy.

Emily's case is astounding to me. In years past we might have thought her mother was crazy or making it all up. How could a baby be allergic to the sun? Cavemen and women surely had porphyria, but the disease was not figured out and described until the 1960s.

I suspect there are still quite a few diseases like porphyria that will be discovered in the future. Someday we will have reliable biochemical and gene markers available on routine blood tests to make a firm diagnosis, and to follow the progress and improvement of the disease. Young students out there, we need you to go to class, study hard in medical school, and come out with a trained mind and a fresh outlook on life and disease. I bet some of you will describe a new syndrome, discover a new treatment, and affect a new cure.

Chapter Fifty-Three:
The Vagabond

D r. Chick Clemmensen and I walked into a patient's room at San Francisco General Hospital. Chick was my friend and co-resident. We went way back. At the Air Force Academy, we shared pre-med classes. He went off to Harvard Medical School, while I went to Ohio State. Some years later we were delighted to link up again at U.C. San Francisco. We loved our rotation at the General. We didn't see mundane cases like acne and warts. We saw fresh cases of leprosy, deep fungus and tuberculosis of the skin, along with weird bacterial infections. The problem was, no matter how well we treated the patients, they would seldom come back for a follow-up visit. They were too strung out on booze and drugs. For some of these patients, if we didn't cure them on the first visit at the General, they would die. They had little healing reserves, what with malnutrition, substance abuse, poor hygiene and a lot of craziness thrown in.

The picture that greeted us in the patient's room was not pretty. Jim was a gentleman who looked far older than his stated age of 50. He was lying back in his bed with festering sores all over his body. He was plugged into an IV, and his docs were pumping him full of antibiotics. The antibiotics weren't working, so they gave the dermatology department a call.

The old guy lived out on the streets of San Francisco. He just got by on a small monthly check, and whatever he could get begging on the streets. His house was beneath the overhang on a local shop off of Market Street. He had a "VIP suite" since he had an old cardboard box to sleep on. He slept on half of the cardboard, and he pulled the other half over his body on the cold nights. We knew how cold it gets in San Francisco, even in the summer.

Chick and I sensed something was wrong with this picture. Why wouldn't Jim heal? He had received enough antibiotics to cure an elephant. On a hunch, I asked the RN on duty, Tanya, where were Jim's clothes? She pointed to the closet. I pulled on my exam gloves, and I slowly opened the closet door. Inside was a brown paper bag filled with the ancient one's clothes. I deftly pulled them out, and Chick and I examined them carefully.

Chick exclaimed, "There they are, Doug. Seam squirrels!"

Indeed, hiding in the seams of Jim's clothing in the bottom of the bag were body lice, too numerous to count. The mystery was solved. Jim didn't have just a simple infection; he had an infection caused by body lice known as "Vagabond's Disease." Whenever I see infection, I like to figure from whom or what it came from. I like to know if the patient is immunosuppressed, with diabetes, malnutrition or HIV, which would make them more susceptible to infection than a healthy patient.

Good personal hygiene, a daily bath, clean fingernails, a well-balanced diet and a fresh set of clothes would do wonders for Jim's skin. He finished his course of antibiotics, and we gave him a cortisone cream plus moisturizers to counteract the toxins deposited on his skin by the body lice. (In World War II, he would have been deloused with DDT powder.)

The nurses were totally freaked out by the whole scenario. They were worried that they too would get body lice, and then their families would catch it from them. We bagged his clothes in plastic, and we sent them to the incinerator for burning. But first we plucked 20 of the little guys off Jim's clothes, and we put them in a glass jar for the Friday afternoon dermatology resident's conference. In addition to the nurses, could we also freak out a few doctors by the sight of these repulsive ectoparasites all glommed together in the container? (We did!)

Jim was pretty much cleared up by the time of his discharge. But I was not optimistic. Short of a major lifestyle change, Jim would soon be back on the streets again. With his poor hygiene, he was doomed to reinfestation and more infection. At least we skin men had done what we could to help get him cured, if only temporarily.

Chapter Fifty-Four: The Seven-Year Itch

The following condition actually can last seven years, if your doctor doesn't nail the diagnosis.

Andy was a bright engineer. He was hired by an American firm to work in Japan for a year. (That's a switch—Japan produces more engineers than Krispy Kreme produces donuts.) Andy started itching just before he left the States, and it became worse and worse. Especially when he went to bed at night, when he severely clawed at his skin.

Andy consulted seven Japanese doctors in the course of the next year. He told them he thought he would lose his mind if he didn't get some relief. His Japanese language skills were about as good as the English skills of his Japanese doctors: virtually nonexistent! As best as Andy could understand, he had some peculiar Japanese allergy and he might just have to live with it. He took a succession of emollient creams, cortisone ointments, antihistamines, and even prednisone by mouth. The medications helped a little, but basically his entire skin from the neck down was an excoriated, infected rash, peppered with red bumps here and there. "At least it didn't get on my face," Andy thought.

After almost 12 months of extreme suffering, the symptoms actually improved a little. Instead of 100 percent agony, he was now in only 75 percent agony. That's when Naversen got involved. Andy walked in to see me at the UCSF Dermatology Clinic, and after a thorough exam, I noticed burrows on his finger webs, wrists, belly button, and even on his penis and scrotum. A burrow is a whitish-gray track mark on the skin surmounting a red papular bump. He had severely excoriated his skin with a dermatitis that covered his skin from the neck down. His face and scalp were free of disease.

Andy nearly fell off the exam table when I said, "Andy, you have a classic case of scabies, and I can cure you."

Andy was incredulous. "Dr. Naversen, with all due respect, how is it that seven Japanese doctors couldn't cure me, but after one quick exam, you can?" Many thoughts raced through my mind. I did not want to disparage the good doctors of the Land of the Rising Sun. This diagnosis should be an easy one for a dermatologist. I knew Andy had a common, worldwide condition. Anyone who has severe nightly itching when they go to bed has scabies until proven otherwise. The red bumps on the finger webs, wrists, umbilicus and groin are typical. Scabies spares the head and neck because of the massive amounts of sebum (oil) that we produce there. The mites have an aversion to the oil, so they stay below the neck.

I shared none of these thoughts. Instead, I said, "Well, Andy, I am lucky to get to see you farther downstream when the classic manifestations of scabies presented themselves. I am sorry you had to put up with a year of dermatological hell, but let's move on with your life and get you cured."

He applied Lindane lotion (Kwell) from the chin to the toes, and he didn't miss a square inch of his skin. He washed it off in the morning, and just to be sure, he repeated the procedure in a week. Within a few days of the application, the scabies mites were killed, and his itching resolved. Although the mites were eradicated, it took three weeks for the allergy to the mite parts to resolve. On Andy's follow-up visit, he thanked me profusely for curing his skin and making life livable again.

Lindane is no longer available in California, but we still use it in Oregon and the other 48 states. (How much Lindane were they using in California, anyway?) Elimite is safer, but more expensive. I feel both are safe when used as instructed, and don't you apply them more than twice.

Ivermectin taken by mouth will revolutionize treating scabies, since you won't have to laboriously apply creams all over your body—you can just take a pill. Ivermectin is not yet approved by the FDA.

By the way, I always treat close contacts of a scabies patient, such as spouses, boyfriends, girlfriends, children in the house, grandma, grandpa, and the babysitter. Don't forget the college kid off at school who caught scabies when home on Christmas break, but the family doesn't know it yet. And don't overlook the mistress.

Every now and then, when a certain measure of dermatological cockiness overcomes me, God, or maybe the devil strikes me down. You are only as good as your last case.

Barney was 70, and he had been itching for quite a few months. He had seen a few general practitioners, a few internists and even a dermatologist or two. But to no avail. He was itching just all day long and all night long. He was very clean and he bathed several times a day. He tried many creams and salves over the course of the previous year, and I was quite surprised when he dumped out a shopping bag onto my table showing the many potions, pills, ointments and products he had used on his skin. And that did not even include the many oral medicines he took for his internal problems.

I examined Barney's skin, and I saw no primary lesions to give me a clue as to the cause of his itching. A wheal—a swollen patch of skin—would indicate hives (remember Leslie and her 12 years of itching). A pustule centered around a hair follicle would indicate folliculitis, and antibiotics would cure that. A plaque with a thick white scale overlying it on the elbows, knees and scalp would indicate psoriasis, but Barney's didn't have that either. He didn't seem to have anything other than scratch marks and dryness from over bathing.

"Oh, no," I thought. "Not another case of pruritus (itching) of the elderly!" Just like chronic hives, pruritus of the elderly opens up a Pandora's Box of diagnostic possibilities. Just bring on the charging bull elephant, and put me out of my misery. "No incurable itchy patients for me today,"

I joked silently to myself. As the decades go by, our immune system may change and weaken. Patients in the Medicare age group may respond differently to creams and medicines than their younger counterparts. The skin dries out more readily. Their itching may be on a metabolic basis—a failing liver or kidney, an underactive or overactive thyroid, a deficiency of B12 or folic acid, or subtle anemia. The patient might have an autoimmune disease like bullous pemphigoid, also known as "chronic blistering disease of the elderly." Early on, they may just itch but have no blisters. It is easier to diagnose later, when they have large tense blisters.

They may have a rare small blistering disease known as "dermatitis herpetiformis." For every ten thousand rashes I see, only one of them is caused by dermatitis herpetiformis—but put that patient on dapsone and he or she will love you for life, since the itching is promptly cured.

Maybe Barney had a drug-caused rash or itch. Barney was on 15 medicines for his heart, lungs, arthritis, gout and other medical conditions. All were medically indicated and necessary. It is laborious to have his internist stop or change them all around. He could have a severe flare-up of angina while one was stopped and another was started. And in the back of my mind, I worried that his deep-seated itch could be caused by an internal malignancy, such as lung cancer, prostate cancer or lymphoma or leukemia. Sometimes the first manifestation of internal cancer is itchy skin. That is why I say not the eyes, but the *skin* is the window to the soul.

Hoping to avoid a mega work-up, I asked Barney, "By the way, does your wife itch?" I figured in a monogamous relationship, if the husband has scabies, the wife or bed partner would also have scabies.

"No doc, I have been married 50 years now, and she doesn't itch."

"Well, if she ever starts itching, please let me know, Barney."

I proceeded with a complete work-up of blood and urine studies along with a chest x-ray. His family doctor did a complete exam and found no evidence of internal cancer—good! We stopped or changed all his medications, all to no avail. Everything came back normal or negative on his lab studies.

"Looks like Naversen strikes out on this one, "I thought as Barney came in for one of his follow-up visits. This was one of many follow-up visits in the six months since I'd first seen him.

"By the way, doc," he said. "My wife is itching now."

"What do you mean?" I asked.

"Well, doc, you said if my wife ever starts itching, please let me know. Well, she started itching last month."

A bolt of lightening from heaven! One person itches, okay. Two people itch, think ectoparasites—a fancy word for scabies. I quickly examined Barney's skin with a bright light, and with a large magnifier placed on my head which protruded in front of my eyes.

My wife says I look like a dork when I put them on. (I do, but they sure help me diagnose skin disease.) For the first time on any of his visits, I spotted fine burrows on his finger webs and wrists. Using a #15 Bard-Parker blade and a drop of oil, I gently scraped at four sites. I placed a cover slip over my glass slide, and I practically sprinted for my microscope. Using 10-power magnification, I immediately spotted an adult mite with her legs moving back and forth. I then noted multiple eggs that Mom had just laid in the burrows.

Now, the ability to nail a positive scabies scrape is an art that separates dermatologists from other doctors. Many non-dermatologists have never seen a single mite or egg under the microscope—they just treat empirically. It is always nice to get a positive microscopic exam; then you know 100-percent, positively, for sure, right then and there, that the patient in fact does have scabies.

I'd like to thank my old professor, Dr. Axel Hoke, for showing me his bedside examination technique for finding the little buggers. After all, with magnification, the adult mite at the end of a burrow barely looks larger than a speck of dust. I raced back to the room. "Barney, we can cure you! You have scabies, and so does your wife Betty!"

He came back three weeks later, and he was beaming. "Dr. Naversen, we are both cured." They had applied the same Lindane lotion that had helped the engineer. Why did it take so long for the Betty to itch? It turned out that Barney was a snorer, and the husband and wife had separate bedrooms, and they were intimate only infrequently. Normally once you catch scabies, it takes only a month before you start itching. So this "red herring" of delayed itching from scabies threw me off on my diagnosis.

A year later I saw Barney in follow-up. He thanked me profusely for curing him of his horrible itch that had lingered so long. Fortunately, his symptoms never came back. I apologized that it took me six long months to figure out that he and his wife has scabies. Usually it takes only one visit. The message: If you have severe nightly itching, and if other family members or close contacts itch, you have scabies until proven otherwise.

Up in Alaska, I got a kick out of a third scabies scenario. I diagnosed a teenager with a typical case. I described in great detail the cause, the cure and how we could treat the patient's family and her boyfriend. I even gave her a handout describing how to do her treatments step by step.

Communication between a doctor and his patient is key, and I take pride in doing that. Later, I was surprised when the teenager's mother frantically called me on the phone and asked, "How did my daughter get 'Eskimo' scabies?"

Well, I guess everything in Alaska is bigger and better than anywhere else. I had never heard of "Eskimo" scabies myself, but I guess they must be a gigantic variety of scabies mite?

I assured the mother that there was no such thing as "Eskimo" scabies. In her excitement of learning she had scabies, the daughter imagined words I had not said. By spending an extra five minutes on the phone with Mom, I resolved her concerns.

As I mentioned above, luckily there is no such thing as "Eskimo" scabies, but "Norwegian scabies"—that does exist. That will have to wait for another chapter in another book.

Chapter Fifty-Five: This is Not Africa

Kyle and Sarah were each close to 80 years old. Unfortunately, they were probably only months away from going to a nursing home. They valued their independence, and they tried to keep up and maintain the three-bedroom house that they had enjoyed for the last 50 years. With increasing age, they were getting more and more forgetful, and more medical problems kept cropping up.

Kyle was troubled with a large stasis (circulation) ulcer on the inside of his right ankle. It weeped and oozed, it got infected, and when he rubbed 20 different over-the-counter creams on it, he suffered repeated bouts of contact dermatitis. Basically, it was a hard one to heal since he didn't have 21-year-old legs anymore.

The couple was hilarious on their visits. Despite their combined age of 160 years, they had not lost their wit and banter. They always had me and my assistant, Pat, roaring with laughter.

I recommended an Unna boot for compression, and dicloxacillin antibiotic by mouth for staph infection. A mild steroid cream known as "Tac," along with Cetaphil cream, would heal and soothe the surrounding skin. I recommended he elevate his legs on an ottoman and a couple of pillows whenever he could.

Several weeks later, Sarah called and said she thought her husband Kyle had bugs crawling on his skin.

I said, "Well, Sarah, he couldn't have bugs. This is not Africa. But go ahead and bring him over this afternoon."

An hour later, Dr. Minor Matthews, one of our fine local cardiologists, called me and said, "Doug, with all due respect, I guess it is Africa after all. I see bugs crawling on his ulcer!" It turned out on the way over; Kyle had a sudden flare-up of angina in his chest so he stopped by to see his cardiologist. Minor squared away Kyle's heart problem, and then he eyeballed the ulcer and he called me.

Thirty minutes later, I examined Kyle's leg. I tried to suppress the revulsion that hit me as soon I gently removed his dressing. Maggots were crawling in his three inch square leg ulcer! How did this happen? Well, every afternoon, Kyle propped up his leg, and he sunned his ankle on the open air porch he shared with Sarah. The usual post-prandial dullness that afflicts us all after a large lunch would strike Kyle with surety at 1:30 in the afternoons. He had his leg propped up on two pillows, and invariably he would fall asleep, gently snoring as he restored his body and mind with the needed rest.

As best we can figure, a fly landed in his leg wound when he was dozing, laid some eggs, and the maggots grew and prospered in the fertile wound bed. Since Kyle had poor vision and even worse sensation in the leg, it took several weeks before Sarah spotted the maggots. Although she freaked out when she saw the critters moving around on her husband's skin, I was glad she didn't have delusions of parasitosis by proxy. Maggots would be a lot easier to cure than mental illness.

Even as a trained professional dermatologist who had seen a zillion gross rashes, infections and infestations, the actively moving maggots sickened me. I must admit, however, this was the cleanest I had ever seen the ulcer bed! The maggots ate away all the dead and dying tissue and bloody crusts, leaving a clean wound. (Medical-grade maggots are still available for sale in the United States for tough-to-heal leg ulcers. The thought of introducing maggots into one of my patient's skin is too repugnant for me—I'll never use that therapy since I feel I have other dermatology tricks up my sleeve that will work as well or better than maggots.)

But how do we get rid of the maggots now that they were there? I don't want Kyle's grandkids calling him "Old Maggot Leg."

I could find no textbook that told me how to rid Kyle's skin of the organisms. That was a treatment of yore, maybe in the Civil War or World War I, when they had nothing better. I finally decided to apply 5FU cream (Efudex) twice daily to the ulcer. This cream works great for precancers on the face, and it eradicates them without leaving a scar. It causes a red, poison oak-like rash while zapping the RNA in the rapidly-growing precancerous cells. But would it kill maggots?

It did! After a few applications, all the maggots were dead. We gently debrided and soaked them out. After a few more months, the ulcer finally healed. I guess even in Medford, Oregon, we can still have a touch of the exotic. And yes, on that afternoon it was Africa!

Chapter Fifty-Six:
The Lost Tick

During my three-year dermatology residency at U.C. San Francisco, I had the pleasure of spending three months rotating through Kaiser, San Francisco. It was a different patient population and a different clinical set-up, somewhere between solo practice and military medicine. Plus, I had the chance to learn from superb clinicians such as Dr. Jim McGinley and Dr. Vera Price.

As is true both in dermatology and in medicine, you never know who will walk through the door next. Most patients have mundane, common clinical problems, but they are attached to a unique person. At other times, we will have a very rare "Zebra" case that we haven't seen in ten years. And the "Zebras" usually come in herds of three. Bam, bam, bam! A trio of rare cases in short order, and then we get back to the ordinary problems of acne, warts, psoriasis and eczema. We dermatologists like seeing all-comers. Although a patient might not have a rare disease, nonetheless, it is nice to help a pretty young woman with noticeable acne, or to aid a working man with psoriasis flaring so badly on his hands that he can't work.

One day at the Kaiser clinic, in walked my "Zebra." This young man told me his name was Mark. I guessed Mark was in his early 20s. He related he was hiking in Sonoma County, California, enjoying the beauty of wine country. Some days later, he noticed a bloated tick feasting on blood extracted from his right upper thigh. "I hate those suckers!" he exclaimed. Mark plucked it off, and he showed his wisdom by saving it. (By the way, the best way to remove a tick is to gently twist it with tweezers or forceps until the bulk of the tick comes out. If a tick granuloma develops, see us and we will gently numb the skin and remove the inflamed tick parts with a punch biopsy. It is no biggie).

One week later, an expanding red bull's eye eruption appeared on his leg. It moved centrifugally away from the central tick-bite punctum. It itched just a little, but Mark was otherwise healthy. He became worried as it moved on his skin just like an expanding wave generated by a rock thrown into a deep, quiet pond.

As I eyeballed his skin I thought, "Looks like a classic case of erythema chronicum migrans." Now known as erythema migrans (EM), cases had been known in the Black Forest in Germany for decades. In addition to other parts of Europe, Wisconsin and the New England states generated sporadic case reports. Although it was thought to be an allergic or toxic phenomenon from the tick venom, why did the European doctors use penicillin or other antibiotics on it? No infectious agent had been cultured or ever proven.

With my consulting staff Dr. Larry Gardner (I was still a lowly resident, green behind the ears), we decided to thoroughly investigate the case and go the whole nine yards. We wanted to find the cause, and we desired to get him cured. We knew we were sitting on top of a definite reportable case in the medical literature. For you see, this would be the first time in the United States where the tick vector of EM was positively identified! To have a medical report accepted and published in the **Archives of Dermatology**, to me that would be immortality. The paper would be there for the ages. Although we didn't know it at the time, Google and the internet would pick it up as part of our general knowledge base. The case report would be part of Larry's and Doug's legacy.

Dr. Gardner and I decided to do a full workup with a complete blood count, a comprehensive panel, urinalysis and bacterial and viral titers. A skin biopsy and special stains confirmed inflammation in the skin, but no organisms were identified and the sample was not diagnostic. As the blood work trickled back from the lab, we watched as the ring on Mark's skin enlarged, but as it also faded. It was not very visible to the naked eye early in the morning, but by the afternoon or after a hot shower or exercise, it became bright red.

We planned on treating Mark with antibiotics just after our upcoming dermatology staff conference. Seventy five board certified dermatologists, residents and medical students would examine his skin in the clinic. Certainly, 75 sharp medical minds could help solve the mystery of the cause of this disease.

We even enlisted the help of the California State Health Lab in Berkeley. They were very helpful in performing viral titers. Surprisingly, all were normal or negative except for an elevated measles titer, probably just a normal reaction to a bout with Rubeola (10 day measles) as a child.

On the day of the conference, we presented Mark to the doctors. He was poked and prodded and asked a million questions. We proudly presented the tick, also—the little guy was dead as he lay magnificently, lit up with a bright light at 10-times magnification under our Olympus microscope. Maybe this would be the most famous tick in the universe!

The case was a great success. The doctors all concurred this was classic erythema migrans. They agreed the cause was unknown, but since the German doctors use antibiotics such as penicillin or tetracycline or other broad-spectrum antibiotics, we should now proceed with such therapy. But a toxic or allergic response could not be ruled out. As the conference broke up, I walked through the crowded hallway to discuss our recommendations with Mark. Plus, I needed to retrieve that precious, unique and now famous tick. First one in the U.S. to be identified as the cause of erythema migrans! Who knows, maybe Dr. Naversen and Dr. Gardner would be up for the Nobel Prize in medicine!

When I got to Room 4, I sensed something was wrong. Mark was there, but where was the microscope and my bug!? Well, Doug, no one ever said it would be easy. Our head nurse "Mac" (bless her heart) was very efficient. With the mid-morning clinic starting soon, she carted off the microscope, tick and all. When I frantically located her and the scope, the tick was gone. Falling off the scope, maybe in Room 4, maybe in the hallway, the tick had blown a chance to be the most famous tick in the history of the world. I ran back to Room 4, told Mark what had happened, and despite a thorough search, we couldn't find the little guy anywhere. I crawled on the floor and looked for the tick with my eyes two inches above the carpet. I didn't feel very dignified as I lifted up the soles of my shoes looking for the squashed ectoparasite. (You know, just like when we were kids, we looked at the soles of our feet to see if we had stepped in dog dung.) I even checked the feet of my professors standing outside the room hoping I would spy the little guy. "Who is this Naversen resident anyhow?" my professors must have thought.

"There goes our award winning paper," I sighed. Just then our saving grace arrived from heaven. My fellow resident, Dr. Greg Jenkins, had taken a high power photo of the tick during the conference with his 35 mm camera and macro lens.

Greg was and is married to the beautiful Peggy Fleming (Olympic ice skating gold medalist). If the picture was in focus, and if we magnified it to maximum resolution, maybe our bug experts at the state lab could still identify it. Greg's picture was sharp and well- lighted. A large blow-up cost me $20 out of pocket, and in the 1970s that was a lot of money. But it was worth it! To our experts in Berkeley, we forwarded the exact date and location of the tick bite along with a copy of the photo. The entomologists let us know, yes, it was positively identified as Ixodes paci-ficus." Great! There is a God! Our paper could go forward.

The chief editor of the *Archives of Dermatology* was Dr. John Epstein of the Epstein dermatology dynasty. John was also a distinguished professor at UCSF. Although I was still only a resident at UCSF, I considered him my friend. I must have submitted the paper 20 times before it was finally accepted. A technical paper prepared for the scientific literature is tough to accomplish since it requires precise dermatology language and many detailed references from other medical articles. Dr. Larry Gardner was helpful, providing editorial guidance, which I greatly appreciated. On one version I put in the body of the report the word "rash." John Epstein wrote back, "Rash equals no good, call it a dermatitis." So I did. The submission of my first paper into the literature taught me to be philosophical. Just like April 15th, when the tax man cometh, just smile, bend over and take your whipping like a man. I knew in my head the paper had to be accepted since the case and the tick "Ixodes pacificus" were unique. When Dr. Gardner and I finally got our letter that our paper was accepted, I was exhilarated. Larry and I felt we were now immortal! Larry is now practicing in Reno, Nevada, and I owe him a beer the next time I see him.

We treated Mark with an appropriate antibiotic. What little of the rash was left promptly resolved. Shortly thereafter, I moved to Anchorage for my hitch with the Air Force. I kept in contact with Mark, who had moved north of the Bay area.

When the news trickled in about an epidemic of juvenile rheumatoid arthritis (JRA) in children living in Lyme, Connecticut, an inquisitive housewife wouldn't buy it. Her child came down with it, but why were so many other kids afflicted with this uncommon form of arthritis? With the help of some brilliant detective work by Dr. Allen Steere and associates at Yale University, the mystery was solved. A lot of the kids with arthritis had a history of a prior tick bite, and an expanding red bulls-eye rash around the bite. The syndrome was not JRA, it was an infection caused by something transmitted by the tick bite.

Later, Dr. Burgdorfer and other researchers found the infectious agent that caused Lyme disease—a spirochete! The cause of EM was identified after all these decades. The kids and adults were infected with a tick-borne spirochete called "Borellia burgdorferi." (Remember, you discover something neat like this, and they probably will name it after you. Good job, Dr. Willy Burgdorfer!) Just as syphilis is caused by a spirochete, and is cured by antibiotics such as penicillin, so is EM caused by a non-sexual, non-venereally-transmitted spirochete, and it is cured by antibiotics such as penicillin or doxycycline. Our German colleagues had it right after all!

I wrote to Mark and asked him how he was doing. He related he did have a bout of arthritis, but it resolved before he got into see his doctor. I have lost follow-up on him, so I don't know if his joint symptoms were caused by Lyme disease or if it was coincidental.

In New England, the tick causing Lyme disease and EM is "Ixodes scapularis."(It was formerly called "Ixodes dammini." As in, damn that tick!). On the west coast we know that "Ixodes pacificus" is causative. There are so many infected ticks back east that "Lyme hysteria" has set in. Anyone one with a tick bite wants to be put on antibiotics ASAP.

Could any vague joint ache, muscle twinge, headache, fatigue, depression, or whatever be caused by Lyme disease?

Lyme Rix vaccine was never a commercial success, and it was pulled from the market after several years. (I hope reports of autoimmune disease from the vaccine are greatly exaggerated—I already had my series of shots.)

Over the years I have jogged with my wonderful golden retrievers, Cassie, Bob, and Annie (and now my pup Jackson), through the hills and mountains of the lovely Applegate Valley. I would sometimes think of ticks and Lyme disease and of Mark. After one long run, Bob had 24 ticks crawling on his thick, marvelously-soft coat of hair. Cassie only had 12. And I had none that I know of. You can't see the ticks on the trail, but they hang on the ends of weeds or long blades of wild grass dangling across the path waiting for the warm- blooded deer, bear, dog or human to pass by. They jump on you, inject an anesthetic into your skin, and then start sucking your hard-earned blood without you feeling it.

Here are a few tips for you and your loved ones who have rashes, arthritis or a history of a tick bite. If you have a tick bite, remove the tick and save it. Check in with your doctor or dermatologist for prompt treatment, and for consideration of relatively safe and inexpensive antibiotics. Incubating Lyme can be cured with a short burst of doxycycline for a few days up to 14 days. "Doxy" is not used on young children because of possible teeth staining, but penicillin or ampicillin can be used instead. Blood tests for Lyme are now much more accurate compared with the early years. To see if you have the disease, your doctor can order an acute (right now) and convalescent (a month later) blood test. If the acute titer is negative or low, and if the convalescent titer rises four-fold, then you have a recent infection. If both acute and convalescent titers are elevated, you have an old infection. If both are negative, breathe a sigh of relief, because you don't have Lyme disease.

The incidence of ticks infected with "Borellia bergdorferi" is likely to increase across the country, especially on the west coast. We formerly had little Lyme disease in the U.S.; it was mainly in Europe. Now the east coast is infected, and the west coast and the rest of the country are next.

Prevention is always better than the cure. When hiking or jogging, stay on the beaten path, and avoid weeds and grasses hanging over the trail. The highest incidence is from May to August when the immature nymph forms are most active, and when the human host (me or you) is most likely to be hiking in the woods. Wear long pants tucked into the socks, and wear a long sleeved shirt. Use an insect repellent containing Deet. Permethrin, the active ingredient in such products as Nix (over-the-counter) and Elimite (prescription), kills ticks when applied to your skin or clothing. Now marketed as a tick spray that can be applied to clothing, it is stable through a number of washings. Use of both Deet and permethrin provide superior protection from tick, chiggers and mosquitoes. Check your skin and your family members after an outing. If you feel an itch or something weird on your skin, visualize it to see if it is a tick or if it is nothing. Most will be nothing.

Get anti-tick medicine for your outdoor pets from your vet or over the Internet. These drops have revolutionized treating fleas and ticks— they kill the buggers and prevent them from imbedding. Feel your dog's skin for tick granulomas. Look closely at the inflamed lump to see if there is a tick at the bottom of it. My two dogs have never complained to me about ticks, but they sure have scratched them. If your pet could talk, it would thank you for removing the parasites. And finally, stay away from deer and mice and their droppings. They are the unfortunate hosts of Lyme disease.

Chapter Fifty-Seven: The Lost Biopsy

I hate it when I lose a skin biopsy specimen! In the last three decades, there have been so few lost I can count them on the fingers of both hands. But I will fess up about a few embarrassing moments.

Strike one: Back at UCSF, one of my co-residents, Steve, had to sweet talk a little old lady named Mabel into having a skin biopsy done. She had a peculiar dermatitis that did not respond to the usual and traditional cortisone creams. Could it be lupus, or just contact dermatitis?

The procedure is quite simple, really. Just a gentle prick, and in goes the xylocaine with epinephrine. After this point, there is absolutely no pain. Then we use a tiny 3 mm punch biopsy, cookie cutter. Out comes a sample plug containing the three layers of skin, the epidermis, the dermis and the underlying fat. Two tiny 4.0 nylon sutures completed the procedure.

Mabel tended to faint, and she was known to swear like a drunken sailor when she woke up. After much coaxing, she finally consented to the procedure, but with much fear and trepidation. Things went smoothly, and for a change Mabel was on her best behavior. She didn't faint and she didn't curse like a person with Tourette's syndrome.

Steve was called out of the room on an emergency, and when he got back Mabel had already left the clinic. Thinking the nurse had processed the specimen and taken it to the lab, he finished with his patients in his afternoon clinic. Later that week he was viewing slides with Dr. Dick Goodman, our very excellent dermatopathologist. Mabel's biopsy was nowhere to be found! Lost. Gone. It had vanished form the face of the earth.

When Mabel came back a week later for suture removal, Steve realized that truth was best. He would just explain that the clinic had lost her biopsy. He cleared his throat and began talking to Mabel, "Mabel, I'm sorry to say we…"

Just then, Mabel chirped in, "Why young man, that medicine you gave me didn't help at all."

"Which medicine was that, ma'am?" said the resident.

"This clear stinky medicine in the vial that you gave me," she replied.

Steve was shocked. Mabel had mistakenly taken the vial of formalin with the skin biopsy plug hidden at the very bottom. Mabel wasn't known for her visual acuity, and she never spotted the skin plug at depth of the bottle. She dabbed the formalin on her skin twice a day, and she didn't have a clue what else was in the bottom of the little jar. I wonder if her perfume usage surged in the past week?

Steve smoothly said, "Well, Mabel, I am so sorry that our medicine didn't work for you. Just give it back to me, and I'll get you a free sample of a stronger salve from our drug cabinet. By the way, Mabel, there has been an unexpected delay. We won't have your biopsy result until next week. I'll give you a call when we get it."

With the sutures removed and the steri-tape protecting her skin biopsy site, and her free sample of expensive cortisone cream in tow, Mabel was pleased. She triumphantly rushed out of the clinic, and she bumped into the heavy door on her way out.

Steve, now out of earshot, cackled to himself. He was off Scot-free! No whipping today. The skin sample was preserved in the bottle of formalin, so he wouldn't have to talk Mabel into having another one. Halleluiah! There is a God!

Our dermatopathologist, Dr. Dick Goodman, studied Mabel's prepared glass slide under the microscope. Lots of eosinophils (allergy cells) fit well with contact dermatitis. The Lidex sample Steve gave her cured her problem. And Mabel never knew about her lost biopsy specimen.

Strike two: Years later, in Medford, Oregon, I chatted with Becky as I took a skin biopsy specimen from her arm. Suddenly we were transported at warp speed to a *Seinfeld* episode. Becky's skin specimen had somehow freed itself from my tools and began to float in slow motion through the air. I recalled how Kramer, when observing a surgery in the OR, once lost his grip on a Junior Mint, which dropped right into a patient's abdominal cavity. The surgeons on *Seinfeld* hadn't noticed the slip—and Becky hadn't noticed mine. But a dignified doctor in his stiff white coat couldn't admit that he had let his patient's skin specimen fall into the peachy, flesh-colored shag carpet on the floor.

My retired partner, Dr. Lee Harlow, was known for his thriftiness. He got a deal on the aforementioned carpet at a remnant sale. I swear it was the same color as Caucasian human skin. Although we were now in the 1980s, the shag was right out of the 1970s.

Without saying a word, my wonderful medical assistant, Pat, and I slid Becky down to the far end of the operating table, and we escorted her in a wide arc away from the table (and away from the lost specimen hidden in the shag carpet). Pat helped Becky check out at the front desk. As soon as Pat joined me back at the procedure room, the distinguished duo of Naversen and Pat locked the door, got down on our hands and knees, and scoured the carpet for 20 minutes before we found that 4 mm little sucker of skin. Thank goodness it wasn't crushed, and it wasn't dried out. It was still adequate for processing! If there are any dermatologists reading this book, I would not recommend a flesh-colored shag carpet for the office.

Strike three: Some years later in Medford, the devil threw us another curveball. Pat collected the four skin biopsy specimens we had done that day. This was a light day, since some days we take 20 biopsies. Sealed and taped as usual, Pat dropped the eight-inch, sturdy, cylindrical canister into the nearby mailbox. Off it went to Modesto Histopath Technical Lab in California. They did good work. Usually the turnaround time was less than a week. When the prepared slides returned in the mail, I would study them under my Olympus microscope and generate a pathology report. Pat would notify the patients with their results. If a biopsy showed skin cancer, we would then re-excise the area to ensure a cure.

But these biopsies never came back! After one week, we started an official trace with the U.S. Postal Service. The lab in Modesto claimed they never received our package. The post office didn't have a clue as to the whereabouts of our important specimen.

Just like Steve (the UCSF resident) had decided years ago, Naversen needed to tell his patients that their biopsies had been lost. I thought if one of these specimens was a melanoma, and if we didn't re-excise it, our patient could die.

I was cool and confident with the four patients when I let them know that their biopsies were missing. I told them I had reviewed their charts, and my clinical impression was that their lesions were benign. I told them I had looked at enough human skin lesions, and I had biopsied enough of them to get a good idea which were benign and which were malignant. I told them that the skin biopsy was still the gold standard, the court of last resort. So I apologized to them all for not having their biopsy results back. It was particularly painful for me to talk to one of our local attorneys. I had taken a biopsy on the left side of his nose. "Ken, I think your biopsy was benign. I'll let you know as soon as it shows up." Was it a "weed in our garden of life," or was it a melanoma?

We waited three long months. The glass slides for the four patients came rolling in one day in the mail, as if straight out of the twilight zone. Since the specimens were preserved in formalin, we knew they would last indefinitely, as long as they didn't dry up. I quickly read the four slides under the microscope, and fortunately they were all benign. Our patients were happy to hear their skin biopsies were indeed okay. We breathed a sigh of relief.

We later learned our postman found our metal cylinder in the bottom of a mail pouch. They had thrown the "empty" mail sack into the back of the warehouse. They didn't need the sack for three whole months.

I guess if you are a patient, you might worry about the possibility of your lab test being lost or being done incorrectly, or it being switched with someone else's specimen. Based on our experience at D.L.A.M., it is about as likely you will die from a lab mishap as that you will die from a lightening bolt striking you from the heavens. Although errors happen with repetition and human processing, our odds are so good, I recommend you don't lose any sleep over it.

We now have an in-house dermatopathology lab at D.L.A.M. We have two great histotechnicians, Linda and Angela. We don't have to mail the biopsies out of the area any longer. If it is foggy and the planes don't fly, we don't care because we get our slides the next day instead of a week later. May we never lose another specimen!

Chapter Fifty-Eight:
The Olympic Torch

A gentle snow fell from the heavens as the Olympic torch passed into my hands. I was ready to run a full marathon, and to drop dead at the end of my race (if required) as I passed the brightly burning torch to the next runner. No Naversen, this is not Greece, two thousand years ago. You will not have to reduplicate Pheidippides's feat from 490 B.C. He ran from the battle of Marathon to Athens, over 22 miles away, to let his people know The Athenian army had defeated the Persians. He made the supreme sacrifice when he cried out "Rejoice! We conquer!" before falling prostrate to the ground and perishing from his noble exertions.

I was surprised and honored when I learned I had been chosen one of Jackson County's Olympic Torch Bearers. There were only seven of us, so we all felt extra-special. We had been selected by a committee based on entries sent in by friends, acquaintances, business assistants and relatives. I am not sure exactly of all the people who nominated me, but I would sure like to thank them all. I was told I was chosen because of my gang tattoo laser removal program.

My office staff surprised me with a special luncheon just before we left Medford for the Amtrak station on the other side of the mountain.

Since a winter storm was bearing down on southern Oregon, I was ready to rush out and buy some snow chains for my tires during the noon hour. Luckily, my partner Dr. Igelman grabbed me as I was heading out the door. He clued me in to what was going on, and he told me to look surprised when they sprung the party on me. He was nice enough to rush out and buy the chains for me while the party went on.

The lunch was tasty, and the staff topped it off with cake for dessert. They presented a special miniature trophy of me with my Olympic torch. It is on my desk, and I treasure it to this day.

Jane and I braved a blizzard on the way to the venue in Klamath Falls, Oregon. As we made our way over the snowy, windy pass, missing a head-on collision by just five minutes, it occurred to me that maybe the real reason I was chosen to carry the torch was that I was one of the few who was willing to travel there in the middle of the winter and be ready to go at 3:00 a.m. the next morning.

That's right—3:00 a.m. The Salt Lake City Winter Olympic torch relay runners were to assemble at 3:00 a.m. the next morning, January 26, 2002, at our designated meeting site.

But the festivities really began the night before. We were treated like royalty by the good people of Klamath Falls. Patsy Smullin, owner of the local NBC affiliate, put on a party in our honor the night before the torch relay. I got to meet the mayor of Klamath Falls, some ex-Olympians, many excellent athletes, and lots of wonderful people who had conquered great adversity in their lives.

Safely in our hotel room that night, I sure hoped my alarm clock would go off at 2:00 a.m.—I didn't want to miss the parade, because it wouldn't wait till I got out of bed!

We didn't oversleep—I was too excited. In the wee hours before 3:00 a.m., we drank coffee to stay warm, and we snacked on breakfast rolls while we were being briefed on our role in the relay. The Olympic relay staff was highly professional and enthusiastic as they leap-frogged across the country from Amtrak station to Amtrak station. They made us feel like we were special. I know they were special. To keep that same high level of enthusiasm town after town, day after day, whether the activity was in the morning, noon or night, was incredible to see.

Each runner would be bussed to his or her starting point. I was runner number five. When the Amtrak train rolled into town carrying the Olympic flame, the first runner's torch would be lit. Each torch bearer would run to the next station, light the next torch, extinguish his or her torch, and then get back to the Amtrak station for the festivities.

As the big powerful steam train pulled into town, all eyes were on the Olympic flame. It shone brightly in the chilly, snowy night air of Oregon. The train even carried a "torchmeister" who tended to the flame and kept it going. With special engineering and design features, the flame blazed proudly. It would not be extinguished even if the train was going as fast as 70 miles an hour.

As my leg approached, I grabbed the torch, the official photographer tried to capture a "Kodak moment." He fell on his butt on the icy road. He yelled for me to wait while he got up so could regroup, but the Olympic torch official said, "Go," and so I went.

I was euphoric. Although the 32-inch, five-pound torch was long and heavy, it felt like a feather since adrenaline was surging through my body. I noticed a lovely young 19-year-old torch aid to my left. There was someone quiet, mean and lean to my right. If I had croaked on the course or been unable to finish, the aid to the left would have grabbed the torch and delivered it to the next runner without missing a beat. Although we were not expecting terrorist activity, the gentleman to my right was quietly running with us to insure our security. I saw nothing bulging on his tight uniform, but I knew he was packing iron somewhere on his anatomy. He tried to be as anonymous as his six-foot frame would allow.

I thought the streets of Klamath Falls, Oregon, would totally be deserted that winter night. But as I ran by, the avenues were lined with hundreds of applauding, patriotic Americans. The destruction of the twin towers in New York City, just four months before on 9/11/01, was still fresh in our minds. My run and the whole torch relay seemed to honor the 3,000 Americans who perished in the terrorist attack. Many Oregonians gave up hours of sleep in support of America and the Olympics that night. I got goose bumps up and down my spine as I thought about these wonderful people. The American spirit lives!

I was surprised to hear huffing and puffing behind me as I ran. I looked back and there was my good friend, Joe Eaton. I had the easy task—running with the Olympic torch. Joe had the hard task—running the same course and pacing me in the darkness, but recording it all with a steady hand on his camcorder, and without looking down at the snow and the ice at his feet. He risked tripping on the frosty road surface at any moment. He did a great job!

My great fear was that I would slip on black ice, fall on my derriere, snuff out the Olympic flame, and cancel the Olympics. At best, they would have to go back to Athens, Greece, to relight the torch and fly it back to Oregon, where the relay would continue. I would single-handedly push back the Olympics a week. Luckily, my Nike cross-country shoes held firm, and the Salt Lake City Olympics went on as scheduled.

My three blocks of running were over in a blur. As I handed off the torch, everything around me grew silent as the crowd and the lights moved on. The cold and the darkness and the snow settled in. Just then, I saw a family nearby standing under the light post. The mom and the daughter were in their warm flannel pajamas accompanied by their dad. I greeted them, and asked the young lady if she had ever seen an Olympic torch.

"Could I please hold it?" she asked, almost trembling.

"Yes, you can!" I replied.

I learned Ashley was only four years old. Her mom and dad and Ashley had braved the winter cold for what was probably a once-in-a-lifetime opportunity to be a part of the Olympic torch relay. Before we knew it, Jane and I, plus Joe and his wife, Coralee, were invited into the family's warm home, just across the street, for coffee and snacks. After a quick 15 minutes, we excused ourselves, for we needed to get back for the final ceremony at the railroad station. After our warm greeting by complete strangers in the frigid darkness of night with the snow falling, we knew the Olympic spirit lived.

Back at the Amtrak station, my 19–year-old torch aid approached me. "Dr. Naversen, I am glad you are fit. You were my only runner today."

"What do you mean, Jackie?" I asked.

"Well, I attended three torch relay participants," she replied. "My first was a walker, my second was you, the runner, and my third was a wheelchair person. If you hadn't been there, I would have had to walk to whole course." I guess they didn't choose me based on my athletic ability.

Back at the Amtrak station, the Olympic torch was now relit on the train. Its flame seemed to leap to the heavens. It was still dark and just 20 degrees Fahrenheit, and the snow was gently falling creating an ambience that could not have been matched by Walt Disney Studios. We sang patriotic songs. The mayor spoke. We heard words of optimism and wisdom from an ex-Olympic athlete.

As if in a mystical trance, I wandered around the grounds with my distinctive white-and-blue nylon Olympic torch relay suit. I clutched my Olympic torch, which was now extinguished. I talked to lots of children and adults during the festivities. I felt it was my privilege to let them share in the moving torch relay experience by examining and holding my torch.

Then I saw three lads shivering in the cold night air with the snow still falling. Their shirts were off! The one on the left had a big red "U" on his chest, the middle one had a big white "S," and the one to the right had a blue "A." As I took videos of the trio, one of them suddenly blurted out, "Dr. Naversen, don't you recognize me?"

In the cold darkness, I had honed in on their bare chests, not their faces. "Corey Charakun!" I cried out. "How are you doing?!"

I knew Corey well. He had starred in track and cross-country for South Medford High School, and he had won the prestigious Pear Blossom Scholarship Award as the outstanding male senior runner in the Rogue Valley. He had even dated my youngest daughter Leina just a month before during Christmas Break. I was glad to see a familiar face, and the kids from Oregon Institute of Technology seemed to be enjoying this Olympic moment. As I greeted Corey's friends, I thought to myself, "Corey will be a fine doctor someday." He attended medical school in Virginia.

Suddenly the Amtrak train carrying the Olympic torch lurched forward, its flame shining proudly. We all watched intently as the train and flame faded into nothingness, headed for Eugene, Portland and Seattle.

With the flame gone, we all suddenly realized how cold we were. Standing outside in 20-degree weather, with only the warmth generated by moonbeams, I started shivering uncontrollably. We headed for the local Shilo Inn, and we had one of our top-ten breakfasts of all times. After one of our top-five naps of all times, we headed west for Medford with Joe and Coralee. This was one for the ages.

Chapter Fifty-Nine:
The Stripper

Well, there were actually two strippers. Stephanie, the wife of an active-duty soldier, walked into my office at Elmendorf Air Force Base in Alaska. She had flared with psoriasis all over her body. There was no certain cause; it was just Anchorage and 20-below winter weather.

Generalized psoriasis is enough of a problem for any patient, but it affected my patient's livelihood as a dancer. When she told me she was a stripper, it surprised me. From the neck up, she looked ordinary, but from the neck down, she had a beautiful body. She told me she had to use lots of stage makeup when she performed. She had her manager turn the lights way down low, and then she did her thing on stage.

He husband, Rory, was an enlisted infantry man in the U.S. Army. As a matter of fact, she met Rory when they were both on active duty in the Army. When she left the service, she went downtown thinking she could make more money as a civilian. And make more money she did. The family enjoyed the money, but it was a real source of friction that Stephanie earned 10 times the amount her husband earned, and much of it was tax-free income.

As I discussed the treatment plan with Stephanie, I tried to be very non-judgmental. Luckily for her, our Air Force clinic had the first ultraviolet light box in the state of Alaska. Stephanie came in three days a week. We started her at 30 seconds, and we increased the duration by 30 seconds each treatment. We made sure she protected her eyes by wearing protective UV goggles. When we got up to four minutes, her tan began to cover and obscure her psoriasis. Since she was Hispanic, there was very little chance she would ever get skin cancer from the light treatments. We discussed with Stephanie that dermatologists don't like tanning for tanning's sake, but if a severe skin condition is physically, emotionally or financially life-ruining, that tips the balance in favor of ultraviolet light in moderation.

Stephanie revealed her personality, her wants, her desires and her frustrations on her follow-up visits. She was uneasy on the stage, and she was really embarrassed with psoriasis all over her body. Although she knew she was a very clean person, she felt dirty and unclean when she was dancing.

And Rory didn't like complete strangers leering at his wife's naked body. It was hard on his fragile male ego to contemplate his wife's profession. He theoretically risked his life in the infantry. His platoon faced the threat of frostbite and severe injury doing their maneuvers out in the 20 to 30-below Fahrenheit weather. If his unit was mobilized for duty in one of the world's military hotspots, he could suffer maiming or death. He thought it bizarre how our society values different occupations— how a stripper could generate a lot more income than an infantry soldier, and a prima donna pro athlete could make obscene amounts of money compared to the hardworking stiff who toiled 40 or more hours a week. He knew Stephanie wanted to quit, to get out—and he wanted her to, too—but they needed the money too much.

Luckily, their story had a happy ending. The ultraviolet rays healed Stephanie's psoriasis. Her skin went into complete remission, and she tapered and stopped her treatments. She quit stripping six months later, and last I heard she had a one-year-old healthy baby. She lived the life she wanted, that of a mom and a wife. She traded her money for morals, and both she and her family were big winners.

Years later, I saw Kari in Room One at my office in Medford. She was sitting up on the exam table with her legs crossed. If her skirt had been any shorter, the police might have arrested her. Equally hard to miss were the numerous pimples and cysts on her face. Kari told me she was an exotic dancer, and she had to use more and more pancake makeup to cover up her blemishes. The more gunk she put on her face, the more it clogged her pores, and the more she suffered from horrible cosmetic acne. Just like Stephanie, her appearance was her income. She told me she desperately needed to get her skin clear of all blemishes. She had tried various acne creams, gels and oral antibiotics with only slight improvement. That was not good enough for her. She wanted perfection.

I then told Kari about "the big A."

"Accutane has been on the market since 1982, Kari, and I have virtually never had a failure on it with my patients. If you will absolutely promise to avoid pregnancy during the five months of therapy, plus one additional month, I believe Accutane will really help your skin."

She started on this Vitamin A wonder drug, and her lips got dry and chapped as expected. She was a little achy, but ibuprofen took care of that. Her periodic blood tests were perfect. She had no depression.

Each month, her skin looked better and better. I found out Kari could only relate to men as a big-breasted sexpot. She had a string of failed relationships with men. Kari would swear off men forever if it wasn't for the money. She had a seven-year-old-child she really loved. She really hated leaving her daughter when she danced the west-coast striptease circuit, from Medford to Eugene to Portland to Seattle. Some of the women even went to Anchorage and Fairbanks , where the petrodollars flowed freely.

By the end of five months, her skin looked fantastic. Two months later, it was even better. Kari learned that she didn't have to relate to all men like she was a sex goddess. I was impressed by her love and devotion to her daughter. I wish I could have solved her problems with men. But I limit my practice to diseases of the skin. Maybe she will meet a nice man, and counseling will help them both.

I haven't seen Kari in many years now. If she is like most of my Accutane patients, her skin is gorgeous and still in remission. If you, a friend, or a loved one are troubled by acne that is cosmetically noticeable, if it causes scarring, or if it bubbles along well into adult life (the 20s, 30s, and beyond), I recommend you check in with your local dermatologist. Depression and suicide issues have been greatly exaggerated, in my mind. Knock on wood, but in 26 years of prescribing Accutane, I have never had a patient commit suicide. But beware—it may affect your psyche. You will look so sweet you will have less anxiety and depression. Your personality may blossom when there is no acne to worry about anymore!

Chapter Sixty: The Jogger

I'm not referring to myself—I am a runner. You know what separates a jogger from a runner? The great running cardiologist, Dr. George Sheehan, explained it by simply saying, "All it takes to become a runner is a race-entry form and a bib number. Run in the race and you are instantly anointed runner status." So train a little bit, and enter a local 5K or 10K run, and get your competitive juices flowing.

Which is what my next patient tried to do. As a neophyte jogger, George had set out to run longer than he had ever run before: seven miles. He was training for a 26-mile marathon. Midway though his training run, George got the call of nature, and he peeled off into the woods to relieve his bladder. His partner did not wait for him, so George hastily pulled up his rough jogging shorts into the proper position. He was not really successfully in getting a correct alignment, but nonetheless, he sprinted off and caught his jogging buddy with some difficulty. As he did, he felt his shorts biting up against his manhood.

At the end of the seven-mile run, George was rubbed raw on the delicate part of the male anatomy. Despite his infirmity, that night he made wild and passionate love to his sweet wife. Seventy-two hours later, he was admitted to the hospital because of an ulcer on his framus.

George lay forlornly on the Urology Ward, and his manhood just would not heal. The urologist tried every wound-healing technique he knew, and the ulcer worsened. George was a pretty high-strung guy to begin with, but he found the ongoing pain in his tender area, and it's reluctance to heal, embarrassing. He felt totally debilitated, and he was definitely depressed.

Dermatology to the rescue! I asked to see George in consultation, where I observed a cooperative but shy gentleman with a huge, red, inflamed erosion. "No problem," I thought. I took some bacterial and yeast cultures, and I did a direct microscopic exam of skin scrapings for bacteria, fungus and yeast. I was surprised when all the tests were negative.

I prescribed a combination of creams and salves to heal and soothe the scan. A week later, I was disappointed. Nothing had worked. I figured he must be allergic to his topicals. Dermatologists are experts in skin allergies and contact dermatitis, but so far I hadn't been able to figure out what he was allergic to, if anything. I patch-tested George to everything that had touched his skin. All creams, salves, lotions, gels and ointments were negative. His failure to heal was not on the basis of allergy.

George had now been out of action a month. One afternoon, while I was on rounds, he sheepishly told me he knew why he wasn't healing. It turns out that every night, he dreamed of his lovely wife and had a nocturnal erection. His excited manhood swelled and stretched his skin, and he felt his healing tissues being ripped asunder.

Eureka! We will put George on hefty doses of valium to calm him down and we'll see what happens. George promptly healed.

This shows the importance of a good history to complement a thorough exam. And when you want to train and run that race, purchase some well-padded shoes, and wear soft shirts and running shorts. Avoid the rough ones like George had chosen. Fabrics that wick moisture away from the skin are great. Wear a hat to protect your scalp and face from the sun. A waterproof SPF-30 sunscreen would be prudent between 9 a.m. and 4 p.m., and before long runs, Vaseline applied to the nipples, thighs, groin, and feet also helps to avoid chafing, rubbing and blistering. If you wear a tank top or a sports bra, don't forget Vaseline beneath the armpits.

By the way, what do you do when your doctor tells you to quit running? That's a no-brainer. Find a new doctor and just keep on running!

Chapter Sixty-One: Frostbite

The 20-year-old black infantry soldier wiped off his profusely sweating palms with a soft white cotton towel. I was amazed—within five seconds his palms were again sweat-laden. He wasn't exercising, he wasn't nervous—what had caused his sweat glands to produce water like a flash flood in a freak Arizona thunderstorm?

Three months before, Chuck had been out on winter maneuvers in the Alaskan interior. The weather was mild, and the troops had on their lightweight uniforms and canvas shoes. Suddenly, a weather front moved in! The temperature dropped 40 degrees Fahrenheit within a few hours. The weather was now sub-freezing as the lightly-clad troops completed their maneuvers. Frostbitten hands and feet quickly ensued. It was an act of nature, and the troops were left unprepared, with inadequate protection on their hands and feet.

The orthopedic doctors treated Chuck's acute frostbite injuries. I saw him when he developed intractable sweating; for some reason, the nerve damage induced by the frostbite caused his skin to exhibit uncontrolled perspiration, also known as hyperhidrosis. I tried every trick in my dermatological book to cure him. Cool soaks did nothing. Oral antihistamines in high doses just caused blurred vision and dry mouth. Drysol, the best topical on the market, just irritated his skin without knocking out the sweating. We even tried tap water iontophoresis by soaking Chuck's hands and feet in water for 20 minutes. The procedure involves running low dose, tingling, and mildly painful electric current in and out of his eccrine sweat glands (the structures in our skin that produce sweat). Iontophoresis and all the other treatments were complete failures.

To add insult to injury, the U.S. Army considered the soldier unfit for worldwide duty, and he was discharged from the military. The Army figured (correctly) that if he was sent back out to the rigors of the Alaskan interior, he would sweat right through his gloves and socks. His wet, wool gloves and socks would freeze, and a second, more-severe case of frostbite would develop, causing even more damage to the hands and feet.

I wish I could reevaluate Chuck and similar patients today. Perhaps Botox injections into the skin of the palms and soles could retard their sweating. We could have one of our neurosurgical colleagues perform a sympathectomy. This operating-room procedure involves cutting the nerves through an incision in the armpit, and is a last-ditch effort to surgically cure the problem. Although it may greatly control the sweating problem, it can be associated with some risks and complications.

The jury is still out on the long-term effectiveness of Botox for cases like Chuck's. If that is not the magic bullet, we will still need a handle on excessive sweating from the palms or soles or armpits. Some men and women spend thousands of dollars every year since they "pit out" their clothes. And what about the young man or woman who is courting, but can't hold hands because his or her sweaty palms feel like cold, clammy fish? Whoever solves these severe sweating problems will help men and women who suffer from hyperhidrosis. They would win the undying gratitude of thousands of patients who physically, emotionally and financially suffer from low self-esteem, just because of a simple sweating problem.

Chapter Sixty-Two:
My Dog Cassie

I have always hated dogs! When I was a kid living in Tampa, Florida, my little brother Ron was bitten by a stray dog. The memory of those painful rabies shots puncturing the skin of his abdomen gave the family nightmares.

I didn't help that I was a paperboy, first in Norman, Oklahoma, then in Kettering, Ohio, and finally in Huber Heights, Ohio. Dogs take great delight in barking and chasing paperboys and papergirls. No self-respecting dog would calmly watch a paperboy just deliver the newspaper without barking and causing a ruckus. Those dogs terrorized me for years.

Then I became a runner and a biker. I cannot tell you how many times ferocious dogs almost scared the pants off me with their wild, savage charges at my pumping arms and legs. Either I was fast, or they were just half-heartedly doing the dog thing, because they never caught me, and I never suffered a bite.

One cool afternoon at the track at Denison University in Granville, Ohio, I took my little sister Andrea for a workout on their 440-yard, outdoor cinder track at the football stadium. Suddenly, a large, snarling savage dog charged at us. Instinctively, I jumped up on a nearby brick fence out of the dogs reach. Then I looked down at my poor sister who faced the wrath of the mean dog all by herself. Luckily, the dog was all bark and no bite, and my little sister was okay. However, at family re- unions, she still reminds me of my cowardice that day back at Denison. Okay, little sister, it was every person for himself. Call it survival of the fittest. It was just a quick reflex action of a superior athlete. No jury in the country would convict me. Besides, the statue of limitations has long since expired.

With that background, you can understand why I didn't like dogs, and why I was afraid of them. Nevertheless, I must have been drawn to them on some level, or at least wanted to conquer my fears. Because early in my marriage, I once actually asked Jane, "Say, honey, do you want to get a dog?"

"Get a dog?!" she said incredulously. "I don't want no dog! I have you and a child to take care of. Forget the dog."

Which I did for about two decades. But one night, while having din- ner in my home in Jacksonville, Oregon, my wife shocked me when she said, "Doug, why don't we get a dog?"

"What?" I exclaimed. "That's what I asked you years ago! You shot me down, big-time. Honey, why the change of heart?"

"Well, Baby, I have been thinking. Two of our three kids have left the nest for college. We are down to only one, and when she heads off to college in two years, we will be alone. We need a dog!"

After a pause I said, "Okay, Honey, you win." Secretly, I suppose I still wanted that dog after all those years. "But just remember, Jane, I hate dogs." I was trying my best to sound like a modern-day Scrooge, to jok- ingly rain on Jane's dog parade.

And then came Cassie! Her formal name was Cassidy, but we all called her Cassie. She was the cutest golden retriever pup I had ever seen. Jane got her from Sunshine Golden Retrievers, the fine kennel in Dexter, Oregon. The breed had a great reputation for being gentle with kids, and they were athletic, loving dogs who tried hard to please their master.

I was impressed with breeder Debbie Berry's love and knowledge of dogs. The floors of her house were so clean you could eat off of them.

She had a newborn dog litter in her second bedroom, one in the laundry room, and one in the large closet. Her cup runneth over with adorable little golden retriever pups! They were the most loveable things you could ever see.

That first day in Jacksonville, the three Naversens—me, Jane and my youngest daughter, Leina—bonded with Cassie. She had real personality, and it is amazing the inordinate amount of time we wasted while observing her every antic. She was a laugh a minute. Cassie grew very quickly, and after a year or so, she became my regular jogging partner. If we saw a strange dog, I never had to worry about being bitten. Cassie was the peacemaker. She would run up to the intruder, sniff it, make friends, give it a dog kiss, and then off we went on our adventure.

Once we ran around Applegate Lake—all 18 miles of it. Jane gave me heck when she found out I had singed off Cassie's four foot pads. "I didn't know we would encounter such rough, abrasive footing, darling," I said to Jane. The next few days, I felt so guilty that I took Cassie to work with me, and I carried her outside in the courtyard for her potty breaks. She could not really walk on her four bloody pulps. But Cassie loved all the attention the ladies on my office staff gave her. Even though her feet were raw and tender, she was panting with joy and her tail was wagging with all those pats and nice neck scratches she got that week. By the way, that was almost the last time I singed off her foot pads. (Hey, I didn't know how rough that volcanic trail was between Fish Lake and Lake of the Woods!)

One of my favorite runs was up Stein Butte Trail up to the old fire watch. At 4,400 feet in altitude, it was a good workout for Doug and dog. We would run on a big loop that took us from Oregon, into California, and back into Oregon to the waiting car. We would run past huge, old-growth madrone trees that must have been 250 years old. We cruised past inviting gold mine shafts, and we experienced panoramic views of the surrounding mountains in two different states. Cassie never complained about those two-hour jogs—we always had great fun.

One weekend Cassie saved my life. At the last minute, my son Nathan invited me to watch the Cincinnati Bengals (my team) play the San Francisco 49ers (his team) at Candlestick Park (now called Three Com

Park). After my clinic work was done on Friday, I jumped into the car for the six-hour ride to San Francisco, where my son lived. Fortunately, Cassie loved being in moving cars, and she always liked to ride shotgun. She accompanied me on the trip down south that night. It got real dark, and I got real sleepy. Unfortunately, I was the driver. It had been a long, tiring week in my dermatology practice. I would scratch Cassie's neck, and the force of her dog personality literally kept me awake. I am convinced I would have fallen asleep, and we would have had a bad car wreck were it not for her companionship.

When my daughter Laurel was home from college for the summer, she taught Cassie to swim when the dog was still a pup. Golden retrievers are naturals in the water, and Cassie soon was a strong swimmer. She and her younger brother Bob, whom we adopted the next year (if one golden is good, two are even better), loved swimming in rivers and lakes and going after sticks. As a matter of fact, the dogs were never happier than swimming in the Applegate River, even if on a cold, gloomy, January day.

One summer we put a human lifejacket on Cassie. We busted a gut laughing while she tried to squirm out of it. It had to be one of the all-time funniest moments in the history of the planet. Not to be malicious, we soon let Cassie out of her misery by unclipping the life vest. She jumped out, and we gave her a few large dog cookies for her trouble. Cassie had unconditional love for us. She did not hold a grudge. After she downed her cookies, her tail was wagging, and she was friends with us again like nothing had happened. Wouldn't it be nice if humans were like that?

The highlight of my day would be coming home to excited, barking dogs as Cassie and Bob greeted me. Then a ritual began that lasted almost a decade. After dinner, I would sit at the table discussing the day's events with my family. When my beverage was done, I would clang the ice cubes against the glass trying to get every last drop out. This was Cassie's signal to start barking furiously. Out I would rush with the two dogs for some serious Kong-ball action. For 30 minutes or so, I would throw the ball for the two retrievers. When they were dog tired, I would give them some cold water to quench their thirst, and then I would treat them to their obligatory dog cookies. It definitely was a highlight of every day for both man and dogs.

When camping outdoors under the sky in the Applegate Valley, Cassie was always on perimeter duty. Although we could not see what was out there, Cassie knew—she could smell the raccoons, skunks, possums, foxes, beavers and even cougars and black bears that live in abundance there. With our trusty watchdog on duty, we didn't have to worry about animal or human varmints disturbing us in the middle of the night. We always slept well.

A pleasant but unforeseen advantage of having a cute dog like Cassie was that my kids would always come home for Thanksgiving and Christmas. Although spread out geographically from Providence, Rhode Island (Brown University), to New York, New York, to Orlando, Florida, Leina, Laurel, and Nathan would return home to play with the dogs (and get their Christmas loot). If they spent a few minutes of quality time with Mom and Dad, well, that was considered gravy.

We never had to worry about Cassie and Bob running away. They knew a good thing. I always felt my wife treated them better than me. With a warm roof over their heads, two square meals a day, lots of hugs and scratches on the neck, and activities like throwing Kong balls, running and swimming, they must have felt like they were in dog heaven. The dogs must have slept 20 hours a day while waiting for the master to return home. I was always amazed at how, upon hearing a noise, the dogs could go from what appeared to be a near coma-like state while laying on the floor to an instantaneous, 60-mile-an-hour sprint.

At night Cassie would lay at the side of the bed, and I would scratch her neck while I was half asleep. I knew she enjoyed it, because even though she was also half asleep, I could hear her tail swishing back and forth with a thump-thump as it hit the side of the bed. And sometimes she would even join us by jumping right up on the bed to keep our feet and bodies warm on those cold Oregon winter nights.

A decade went by rapidly. Cassie was a loyal, loving part of the Naversen family on her 10th birthday on October 22, 2004. Three days later, Jane called me at the office in what proved to be an ironic twist of fate. One of my patients had a flare of psoriasis—can I squeeze him in that Monday? Hey, he was a great guy. Despite the active psoriasis and the arthritis that came with it, Caleb managed to run his own carpet-cleaning business. I had the utmost respect for his doing such hard manual labor, despite his debility. He always did a great job for us.

I got him squared away that morning at the clinic, and he left for his first job in the day. It turned out he headed directly to the Naversen residence to clean our living room carpet. Great—it needed it, and Caleb would do his usual excellent work.

Just before the start of my afternoon clinic at 1:00 p.m., Caleb put in an urgent call to me. "What is going on?" I thought.

When I picked up the phone, Caleb was half-crying. He blurted out "Dr. Naversen, I am sorry! When I was done with your job, I got in my truck, and as I backed out, I ran over Cassie. She is gone. I killed her dead. I so am sorry!"

"Could this be a joke or a mistake?" I wondered. "I just spent a wonderful Sunday with Cassie at the river yesterday. How she could be gone so suddenly?"

It was gut-check time. I thanked Caleb for calling me. I pointed out it was an accident. No one was blaming him.

I called Jane at Cardiac Rehab where she worked at Rogue Valley Medical Center in her job as an RN. She would want to know. She was shocked, too, but we both had full clinics that afternoon. "Be a professional, do your job, and get home as soon as you can"—it was what both of us knew we had to do.

When I got home at 6:00 p.m., I saw Cassie's body beneath the blue tarp on the back of the driveway. I gently uncovered her. She still looked beautiful. There was no blood or guts to be seen. Her golden coat shone in the late afternoon sun. I figured this had to be a mistake. Cassie looked too good to be dead.

"She is just asleep," I thought. As I touched her coat and patted her, I almost expected her to wake up. But her body was cold and stiff.

My other dog Bob came up and wagged his tail. "Get up, Cassie, come and play, Dad is going to throw the Kong ball for us now," Bob would have said if he could talk. But Cassie didn't get up.

I loved Cassie because she truly appreciated the outdoors. She would sit outside in the driveway by the garage for hours both on sunny days, and even on cool nights. We should all love the beauty of the outdoors like my dog Cassie did. She had been a little sick and a little stiff lately, and maybe she was getting a little hard of hearing. Was that the reason why she didn't jump clear of the truck tire as the vehicle backed up?

My son-in-law, Jim Geraghty, and I buried her the next day at her favorite place in the world—the Applegate River. We dug a deep hole just the right size. We carefully chose a spot that would be free of rocks. We didn't want a shallow grave that varmints could dig up. I carefully clipped a piece of her hair, and I put it in a plastic bag for Jane. I checked to make sure her collar and chain were off; she always hated the way they felt on her neck. Luckily, there was no collar and no chain on Cassie's neck that day. I positioned her head and body just right. If she had been alive, she would have been able to look at the house and the lovely Applegate River to the west. I told Jim, "Let me put the first shovel of topsoil on her."

With her body wrapped in a bright blue tarp, I carefully placed the first spade of earth over her head. Jim and I then solemnly covered her body with the rich soil, and we filled in the hole. Midway through our efforts, we placed some concrete blocks over the soil on top of Cassie. We didn't want any animals disturbing her gravesite. After raking the surface, no one would have known my loving pet was buried there except for the cross I placed on top. It said, "Cassie—R.I.P." We were both teary eyed, but we wouldn't admit it. Her gravesite was surrounded by evergreens and a giant oak tree for shade in the summer.

Jim and I shared a beer at the gravesite. I toasted, "To the best dog a man could ever have."

My life was greatly enriched knowing and living with Cassie for 10 years and three days. After years of fearing dogs, Cassie taught me to love them. I know how to act around strange dogs now. If you show authority, and if you are in charge of the situation, the dogs will back off and they will not bite. Many ferocious dogs turn out to be friendly after all. Soon they are wagging their tails as you pet them.

Recently, I ran the Pioneer Run, a nine-miler which is the oldest footrace in southern Oregon. A vicious dog came running out of its driveway headed for my legs with its razor-sharp teeth. I merely held out my hand, and I said "Stay!" The dog stopped in his tracks, and I got safely by. Several other runners in front of me and behind me were bitten, and the savage dog drew blood on at least two of them. Cassie, I owe you for saving me from a bad dog bite!

Dogs teach us about the life cycle seven times faster than what we get in human time. Puppy dogs, teenage dogs, adult dogs, and then senior citizen dogs flash by with their lives. We see the old-age ailments that can afflict both animals and humans. If our children have pets, an accident or a death in the animal prepares them for real life when Granddad has a heart attack or a big brother is in an auto accident.

The Naversen household was saddened with Cassie's death. I was impressed with the outpouring of sympathy from our teary-eyed friends, neighbors, and co-workers who knew of Cassie and of her doggy passion for life. We will always have a warm place in our hearts for that wonderful, golden retriever. When we get to heaven, I believe Cassie will be waiting for us at the pearly gates with her tail wagging. She will run to meet us just like she was a puppy again.

Cassie, rest in peace!

Chapter Sixty-Three:
My Other Friend Tom

You met my best friend Tom Valley in a previous chapter. I want to tell you about my other best friend, Tom Burnham.

Tom and I had been jogging buddies for years. Although 12 years my senior, I knew he would whip me in a footrace if I didn't show up in tiptop condition. As a busy building contractor in Steamboat Springs, Colorado, he was an avid skier and outdoorsman. He didn't discover what a stud runner and biker he was until he moved to southern Oregon in the mid '80s. He knocked off 5Ks, 10Ks, 10-milers, and marathons, and he usually won his age group. He would go on 100-mile bike rides for fun. No big deal, he thought.

Tom didn't know it on that fateful day in southern Utah at Zion National Park, but he had been training his whole life for this very moment. Tom and his old Colorado buddy Denny Swenson met at Zion to do some backpacking and renew their friendship. They shared fond memories of Steamboat Springs, where they had hiked and skied together for two decades. They planned a 14-mile hike along the west rim trail, but to go both ways would be 28 miles, longer than a marathon. Although they wanted to savor the entire spectacular trail with the vistas of the towering cliffs, deep red canyons and mesas, common sense dictated that they should just go out seven miles, and then retrace their steps to repeat the second seven. Bummer, they didn't like hiking the same trail twice, and missing the far half they had never seen before.

About halfway through their glorious hike, they met some strangers coming from the opposite direction. They had parked their car on the far trailhead (opposite Tom and Denny), and they, too, wanted to see the whole length of the 14-mile trail.

Upon learning they were marathon runners from the Minnesota, Tom and Denny immediately bonded with the strangers. "Why don't we just trade car keys, and each group would get to see all 14 miles without backtracking?" one of the hikers asked. Whenever they got to their respective trailheads, they would find the other car waiting for them; they could drive it off, and then meet back in Springdale before night to exchange cars.

I guess you could call the scene at Zion with complete strangers from different states "marathoner's madness." If you think the "runner's high" is unique, this strange car pact in the wilderness puts that to shame. And they weren't even in oxygen debt! Just because a guy or girl runs the 26.2 miles of a marathon, and because he or she is from Minnesota, doesn't mean they must be a noble chap that can be trusted with your car keys. Burnham, those conmen are scamming you, and they are going to steal your car! What are you thinking?

Clearly, Tom wasn't thinking about that. With high expectations of even more fun on the fresh trail that had just been given to them, Tom and Denny left the strangers with new energy and a spring in their step. (Well, Tom was in his 60s by now; who knows how much spring he had left in his step anymore?)

They enjoyed the incredible vistas in the beautiful national park, each turn and twist in the path opening up spectacular view after awesome view. "It doesn't get any better than this," they thought to themselves. Suddenly, their thoughts were disturbed by a disheveled, sobbing, panic-stricken lady who appeared on the trail just ahead of them. Her hair was a mess, and tears streamed down her face. She looked to be in her young 20s. She blurted out, "Help! My friend Agnes fell in a slot canyon up the trail. We need to get her out now, or she will die."

Chills ran up and down Tom and Denny's spine. "Life or death is staring us in the face," they thought. "Let's stay calm, or this young lady will really lose it."

Being the cool heads they were, and relying on their years of experience in the wilds of Colorado and Oregon, their steady demeanors reassured the woman, whose name was Pamela Price. After she calmed down, she explained she was camping with her friend Agnes Przeszlowska. Agnes went to explore the sights, and when she tried to get a better view of the bottom of a nearby canyon, she felt her feet slipping.

"No problem," Agnes might have thought. "I'll just grab onto a bush or tree or shrub to stop my slide." But sadly, there was to no bush or tree or even a root to glom onto. Faster and faster she found herself sliding toward the edge of the precipice. She must have traveled an agonizing 100 feet, and then at the rim of the canyon, she looked down, and the Grim Reaper stared her directly in the face. Pamela watched in disbelief as her friend Agnes then plummeted vertically another 100 feet straight down into the bowels of hell, to an almost certain death at the canyon floor.

Agnes must have felt extreme horror as her body impacted the dry, parched, rocky earth, which probably ripped her body asunder. Agnes and her friend Pamela had just experienced the danger and sudden terror of the slippery slope.

But Agnes was not dead! She cried out in agony from the distant floor of the canyon, "Get me out! I need help! I am going to die!"

As Agnes sunk into shock, her friend Pam couldn't believe what had just happened right before her eyes. There was no way she could get down into that dangerous spot to rescue her friend. If she tried, Pam would probably die too.

After quickly pondering all the scenarios of Agnes' rescue, Pam yelled at the top of her lungs, "Agnes, hang on, I am going for help. Hang on. Don't die on me!" And off Pam went at a half-running, half-walking pace down the trail, praying that her friend would not perish before help arrived.

When Pam saw the two men walking on the trail, she thought they must have been sent by God. After hearing her story, Tom and Denny quickly followed her as she retraced her steps to the site of the tragedy. The men figured out she had gone the wrong way. She had a 10-mile hike for help in the direction she was going, versus a four-mile hike in the other direction. But then had she gone the other way, she wouldn't have met the men from Colorado and Oregon.

Sure enough, when they arrived at the slot canyon, they saw Agnes lying in obvious pain far down below. She wasn't dead yet, but it was just a matter of time unless they extracted her ASAP. The group knew they had to run for help!

This could be Tom's finest hour. Although both men were athletes in their own right, Tom was in competition form. They both knew he would be the one to race for her life.

Since it appeared to Tom and Denny that the accident site was closer to the Minnesota-mobile, Tom would go in the same direction as they had gone all day on their hike. Tom cried out as he began racing along the unfamiliar trail for the mythical car that maybe awaited him at the far end of the path, "I'll be back soon. Keep her alive until help comes!"

Tom started off fast, real fast. As the sweat poured down his brow, the veteran runner knew he needed to slow down, to pace himself, and to run within himself. He knew he didn't have to set a world record, he just needed the fastest time possible between point A and point B. If he ran at a fast, even pace, maybe he could save a life.

Even though Tom was in top shape, he soon felt his heavy hiking boots weighing him down. Where were those wonderful Nike Air Pegasus shoes when he needed them? He missed his thin, lightweight, breathable athletic shorts, instead of the heavy-duty hiking pants that were rubbing and chafing his skin. Tom knew that if he got a hot spot or a blister, he would just have to run through the pain.

Incredibly, Tom covered the four miles in record time. (No one had ever run that exact course from that particular slot canyon to this specific parking lot before, so it was a world record!) As he looked ahead to the parking area, a big grin came upon Tom's face. It was a miracle. "Damn, that Minnesota car is here just like it was supposed to be!" Tom yelled out loud. Sure enough, the auto was parked in the specified location, waiting for his arrival, just as promised. The hikers were not car thieves after all!

Tom frantically punched the key into the lock, and the door wonderfully opened. He felt a surge of power as he cranked the ignition and the engine roared. Off he went, screeching and laying rubber on the dry, Utah landscape.

He flew along the road for help, feeling clueless as to where help might actually be. As he tore down the asphalt, he forced himself to ease off the accelerator pedal. Tom wisely thought, "If I kill myself on this lonely highway, Agnes will die."

Some miles down the thoroughfare, he spotted a rustic house. As he frantically banged on the front door, he realized no one was home. "They probably don't even have a phone," he surmised. "If only I had a cell phone that worked in the middle of nowhere."

Back on the highway, Tom spotted an oncoming car. He flagged it down without being run over. The driver said after questioning, "No, I don't have a cell phone. But if you do down the road five or six miles, and take the turnoff, maybe you can find a ranger. That is where they like to hang out."

So Tom again raced down the road on his life-or-death mission. The gods must have been smiling, for he soon found an experienced mountain rescue medic just where the woman said he might be. The rangers had just completed a controlled burn in the area, and they just happened to have a helicopter at their disposal. What luck!

Tom quickly recounted the happenings of the day, and shortly a chopper was launched for the slot canyon. Regulations did not permit Tom to ride in the government helicopter, so he resigned himself to driving, then walking the trail back to the accident scene. He did not know what would await him—life or death?

As darkness began to set in, Tom hiked and ran back along the trail to see if Agnes was still alive. He did not find out about the exciting events until he ran into Denny on the poorly-lit trail later that night.

Denny recounted the events that transpired once the chopper located the canyon where Agnes lay moaning in pain. The medic laboriously lowered himself down into the bottom of the canyon. When he got to Agnes's body, he yelled out, "She is still alive!"

He quickly assessed her wounds and broken bones, and unfortunately, there were many. He expertly pumped her body full of morphine with a slow, intravenous injection to give her relief from her excruciating pain. Agnes felt the incredible throbbing subside. She thought as she fell in and out of consciousness," Will I make it out of the deep canyon before morning? Will I make it out at all?"

The crew of rangers was able to ratchet her stretcher up the side of the steep canyon inch by inch. Luckily, there were no falls, slips or disasters during the perilous rescue operation. Of course, a helicopter wouldn't fit in the narrow canyon, so a manual rescue was mandatory.

Even thought it was now nightfall, a helicopter rescue flight from Las Vegas was authorized. The ranger later told Tom they usually didn't fly at night—it was too dangerous. But they sensed that Agnes would die if she had to spend the night in the canyon. The ranger also told Tom that there were very few survivors in a fall of this height. Would she be one of the lucky ones?

After the chopper had successfully picked up Agnes, Tom and Denney ran into each other on the now dark trail. Denny quickly filled Tom in on the details of the rest of the afternoon and the evening, Tom realized that he had covered 18 miles that day! He had run at least four of the miles in a sheer panic, with the girl's life on the line. Now that the adrenaline was no longer pumping, he felt total-body fatigue set in.

Before the rescuers finally got back to Springdale that night to exchange cars, the Minnesotans thought they had been had by the slick-talking Tom and Denny. Where were those guys anyway?

The men waiting impatiently back at the motel were relieved when they finally heard a knock on their door. What a story the adventurers shared with the disbelieving Midwesterners. After hearing their saga, Tom and Denny were off the hook as alleged car thieves. They all slept well that night, especially Tom.

Two years later, in Steamboat Springs, Colorado, I had the good fortune to ski with Agnes. Yes, she somehow survived the slippery slope that day. In talking to her, I found a delightful, vivacious young lady, a true survivor. She had broken over a dozen bones, including a spiral fracture of her leg, and she even suffered a broken tooth. She had many orthopedic pins inserted into her bones, and she wore metal braces, and she required a wheelchair for at least six weeks. As you might expect, she had undergone multiple operations and many hours of physical therapy.

I learned that Agnes was born in Poland, and she came to the States as a child. She was presently studying at Colorado Sate University in Ft. Collins, and when she found that Tom and Nancy Burnham would be skiing in Steamboat with Denny, she welcomed the opportunity to see them, thank them, and relive the excitement of the accident.

I felt lucky to meet this brave woman who cheated death in Zion on that slippery slope. And after skiing with Agnes, I began thinking, "If she is the one with all the broken bones and who has been in all those hours of physical therapy, why is she the one skiing so smoothly and effortlessly? Why am I in her snow wake, and why is she leaving me far behind?"

Now you know the story about my best friend, Tom Burnham, the hero. The man ran and walked 18 miles that day, and he wasn't even tired! He saved Agnes' life. Tom—you are a stud. Nice job!

Chapter Sixty-Four: That Bastard Sikorski!

A sudden "Oh, Crap!" pierced the air. It must have been a very loud cry, since I could hear it over the roar of my large, powerful, Husqvarna riding lawn mower. Out of the corner of my eye, I saw my brother-in-law Mark going down the steep cliff that would drop him and my mower into the Applegate River 40 feet below.

"That bastard Sikorski!" I thought. After all, he was about to destroy my pride and joy, my big, beautiful, brand-new, bright orange "Husky." I had just purchased it for $7,000, and it wasn't even a month old. I knew at the bottom of the Applegate it would be ruined. That swimming hole is probably 15 feet deep, and there is no telling how we would extract a lawn mower from the bottom of the river.

I have been blessed with great brothers-in-law, up to this point. There was Uncle Dwight in San Diego, Uncle Al in New Jersey and Big Uncle Mark in Phoenix. But now, Original Mark Sikorski from Chardon, Ohio, had crossed the line. (With two in the family named Mark, we call them "Original Mark" and "Big Mark.")

I had entrusted the ZTR (Zero Turn Radius) Husky to Mark. He generously offered to cut the lawn for me on his visit from Ohio, convincing me that it would be fun for him to ride on the Big Unit. I figured with his five acres and all his experience cutting his own lawn back in the Buckeye state, he should have no problem doing Uncle Doug's lawn.

Why, Mark and his lovely wife Becky had introduced me to the concept of the ZTR in the first place. On a previous visit to Oregon, they had practically hurled epithets at me after mowing my lawn with my trusty, but old, Montgomery Ward's riding mower. Just because Ward's had gone belly up, they thought my machine was a junker. And I guess those wide-cutting turns were too imprecise for the Sikorskis. Mark and Becky would only cut their lawn with a ZTR. And they probably felt smug because they had spent an extra $300 on something called a "striper." (I later found out a striper is a mower add-on that allows you to make pretty crisscross lines like in a major league ball park.) "Where do you live, inside Jacobs Field in Cleveland or something?" I joked with them. "My team, the Cincinnati Reds, has won many World Series in our lifetime. Your team, the Cleveland Indians, hasn't won since 1948!"

Don't tell Uncle Mark, but the lawn mower incident might have been partly my fault. Mark had just finished cutting the lawn for me, and I thanked him for the beautiful job he had done. But then as I surveyed the back yard, I noted, "Mark, I believe you missed several rows of grass on the lower part of the lawn." (As you might have guessed, that was the steep part of the hill right next to the cliff, where Mark's gut told him not to cut.) The grass was probably still a little wet and slippery from the automatic sprinkler earlier that morning.

With both his lawn-mowing ability and his manhood on the line, Mark reluctantly climbed back on the Husky. Shortly thereafter, he found himself launched on his wild ride straight south, headed directly for the river!

As I saw Mark headed for the cliff—and the almost certain destruction of my 1,100 pound machine, advertised as "The Commercial Lawn Care Equipment of NASCAR," since it could easily go 14 miles-an-hour across a lawn—I figured he was just getting even with me for giving him hot tub folliculitis on his last visit to Oregon.

In the space of those several seconds, Mark's life must have flashed by. But then, as I watched with horror from off in the distance, the mower stopped. The Big Unit had gotten hung up on several large rocks.

Mark and I were astonished that the mower was now suspended at a 45-degree angle, just feet from the precipice overlooking the river. My mower would not be destroyed after all!

As Mark gingerly jumped off the big, crippled Husqvarna, he checked his arms and legs, and when he noted that everything on his anatomy was okay, he let out a "Whoop!" There were no broken bones, no mangled arms, and no head injuries. He realized he had dodged a big bullet. Except for the issue of saving the Husqvarna from its riverside perch.

The next day, Mark and I planned a detailed extraction of the over half-a-ton vehicle from the steep hillside. We had borrowed a winch, and we had some strong metal cable. As we prepared for the job, I examined the Husky up close and muttered, "That bastard Sikorski!"

After nearly dying, for some unknown reason, the man had forgotten to turn off the ignition yesterday on the stalled-out vehicle. He had drained the battery dry. If we were to rescue the mower, we would need some of the power from its mighty, 25-horsepower Kawasaki engine to get it up the hill.

Twenty-four hours later, my trickle charger had restored energy to the depleted battery. After several hours of winching and serious male bonding, Mark and I had the Husky up the hill and out of danger. Even though it was dirty and dusty, we admired the magnificent, sturdy ZTR machine now that it was up on level land.

This was one of those dumb, stupid accidents that can happen to any of us. I had a friend and patient that tipped over her riding mower when cutting across a slope, instead of up and down. Unfortunately, the weight of the mower crushed her dead. Mark was right in getting off the mower the first time, before tackling the hill.

If the grass is wet, don't mow because the wheels will slip and the mower can take off downhill like a runaway locomotive. Try cutting the grade by backing up on it, if the topography is favorable. When reversing your field, try turning the wheels uphill, not downhill. You might want to take some extra time and just weed-eat those hilly parts of your lawn. Slopes are prime reasons for loss of control and tip-over accidents. Keep all movement on slopes slow and gradual. If you have a bad feeling in your gut about the hill, just don't do it. Thank goodness we can now laugh about Uncle Mark and how he nearly ruined Uncle Doug's Husky mower.

Maybe the accident was the best thing to happen to our clan. There is no longer confusion at our family reunions amongst the two Marks; we now have "Big Mark," and "That Bastard Sikorski!"

Chapter Sixty-Five: John

A doctor gets the opportunity to treat many fascinating patients over the years. But if lucky, he gets one or two unique patients that touch his soul. In Alaska, a patient named Al, who had a hand ulcer, had been my most interesting patient ever. And then John walked into my Medford, Oregon, clinic.

John was a year or two older than me, and about the same height. But when I first gazed at him, I tried not to stare at his face. For you see, in one glance you knew that something very, very bad had happened to him. It looked like gunpowder had exploded directly into his face, giving him a bizarre, hideous, spackled appearance that made me feel very sad for him. The explosion had obviously affected other body parts, too.

John told my staff and my partner, Dr. Dave Igelman, his poignant story. Three weeks before his 21st birthday, John was a nurse working in a hospital pharmacy for the U.S. Army in Washington State. As he mixed two chemicals together (picric acid and silver nitrate, not really gunpowder)—BLAM!—an explosion ripped at his face and clothing. He was blinded in both eyes, his right thumb was blown off, and his skin was peppered all over with black pigment. In the blink of an eye, his life had been changed forever.

John was told by others (since he couldn't see himself) that the pigment on his face darkened over the next few months, especially after he'd been out in the sun. He was told both his eyes were damaged beyond repair—he was blind for life. To add insult to injury, the violent explosion was so powerful it had even blasted right through his shirt, tattooing his abdomen with the same black stain that disfigured his face.

After moving to the small town of Murphy, Oregon, John resigned himself to a life of total darkness, despair and disability. His first daughter Heidi was born three weeks later; he would never see her face. Two years later, the family was blessed with another child, Holly. John knew he would never see her, either.

John told us more as we stood spellbound, listening to his tale. One day, many months after the accident, his wife Anita took him into a nearby town, and as John got out of the car a cop stopped him and said, "Sir, before you come into our fair city, would you have the common decency to please wash your face?" At that moment, John felt like he was two inches tall. This was definitely a low point in his life.

The remarks continued over the next three decades. While eating in restaurants, people would walk up and say, "What happened to you!? Are you going to a Halloween party or something?" These sorts of remarks were becoming the norm, not a rarity.

John was physically disabled, but the emotional challenge might have been worse had he actually been able to see what he really looked like. His wife Anita was a wonderful, nurturing angel. John's support group included her, his two daughters, and his great friends and neighbors. They would take him deer and elk hunting, and by their pointing his rifle at the animals, he was even able to bag some game. He developed his sense of touch, and judging from the photos of all the trout, salmon and steelhead he caught, he became a far better fisherman blind than I ever was with two good eyes. John even raised livestock and had a small pig farm.

Day after month after year after decade went by—nothing really changed his frightening appearance, nor restored his sight. A doctor in nearby Grants Pass valiantly tried surgery and multiple full face dermabrasions, but they failed to normalize his appearance.

Three decades later, John had the good fortune to be examined by an ophthalmologist named Dr. Scott Cherney in Eugene, Oregon. After a thorough exam, the doctor said, "John, I may be able to help the vision in your left eye. We might be able to do a corneal transplant."

Some very nice person who had passed on consented to donating their cornea. Was it an auto accident, a fall or some other medical malady that resulted in the untimely death of the donor? Would the transplant result in the gift of sight for John?

Post-op, when the heavy bandages around his left eye were removed, John waited with keen anticipation. Would his vision be restored?

As the dressing came off, John gasped—he could see light and shapes and forms. John could see out of his left eye! It was the miracle of sight after 31 long, hard years.

He had always imagined himself to be a lad of 20 years, but when he peered in the mirror for the first time since the accident, he saw an old guy who looked just like his dad, but who was covered in black soot. "How can anyone stand to be around me?" he wondered to himself. "How could my wife and kids live with me with my hideous appearance? If I would have known how awful I looked, I would have committed suicide long ago!"

But he didn't! People around him loved him not for his looks, but for who he was. His kindness, compassion, grit and toughness were to be admired, not scorned.

A few years later, a physician in Grants Pass, Oregon, referred John to our clinic. The doctor knew of our interest in lasers, and maybe there was some new invention that hadn't been available in the past.

After hearing John's poignant story, Dr. Igelman and I performed a physical exam and did a skin biopsy. The pigment, as seen under the microscope, revealed the dark globs to be very superficial, only 0.1 mm from the skin surface. We knew our Versapulse-C laser made by Coherent Corporation (now Lumenis), could easily penetrate through the outer layer of the epidermis, into the mid-layer of the dermis, and almost to the fat. Maybe modern lasers that had not even been conceived in 1968 would be able to help John.

Dave and I did some test-firings with the laser on John's skin. Using a long wavelength at 1064 nanometers, we knew we would get deeper penetration. The powerful pulse of the infrared light lasted only three billionths of a second. Everyone in the room had laser goggles in place to protect their eyes. (We carefully protected John's left eye with an external lead eye shield.) Of course, infrared light is invisible, so we relied on the bright red helium-neon marking beam built into the system to guide our laser surgery. Despite some local pain as the "magic wand" shot through his skin like a smart bomb, John didn't move a muscle. We applied a sterile dressing, and my front-office assistant Sandy scheduled him a follow-up visit. We waited with baited breath for four long weeks until his return.

The day finally came, and our entire staff was astounded to see beautiful, flesh-colored skin, with no scarring, where our spot test firings had impacted his skin. I gleefully said, "John, I think we can help you. Let's schedule a full face laser procedure on you in four weeks."

John replied, "Doc, I have been living with this condition for 33 years now. Can I come back in two weeks?"

I thought for a moment, and then said, "John, you can come back any time you want." Everyone in the room, including me, tried with varying degrees of success to hold back their tears.

You are never going to believe what happened next. Medicare and the Veteran's Administration denied his proposed laser surgery in my office, claiming it was "cosmetic!"

"This *isn't* cosmetic," I wrote to them in a strongly-worded letter, "this is his *whole* life. John was injured when on an active duty assignment in the United States Army. You need to have a heart, you need to step up to the plate, and you just need to do the right thing."

John was fighting mad, and he was ready to call his Senator and Congressman. We knew the sessions would be intensive, costly and prolonged over many months if we had any hope of bringing his skin back to normal. John didn't have the resources to pay for the laser surgery out of pocket. But if worse came to worse, we would have gladly treated him for free.

Someone in the Veteran's Administration did have a heart, and we finally got full approval to proceed. In the next 24 months, we fired up our lasers 35 times in one-hour sessions. We took great care to protect John's invaluable left eye. Most sessions involved an external lead eye shield. But due to noticeable black pigment peppering his upper and lower eyelids, on some sessions we needed to numb his eyeball with drops, and then we placed an internal eye shield on top of his eyeball to protect his delicate cornea. We took great care to use lots of lubrication, and to avoid scraping or damaging his sole remaining eye. I didn't want this to turn into a Greek tragedy: He loses his vision and appearance, he gets his vision back, but while restoring his appearance with our laser, we burn his cornea and blind him again.

John's treatments are pretty much completed now, except for an occasional laser touchup. He is truly a handsome man, but no one knew it before because of the black pigment disfiguring his face. In addition, I have found that he is kind, appreciative and noble. He shares his experiences with school kids. He tells his tale to community and civic groups such as the Lions Club and the Rotary. Why, John has even written a book about his long journey (**Never Give Up: a Veteran's Journey to Sight and Healing**; available on the web at www.amazon.com). A portion of each sale goes to the Oregon Lions Sight and Hearing Foundation. His story was presented to a national TV audience on Memorial Day in 2004. NBC's **Today Show** did a touching recap of his hardships, his winning attitude, and the dramatic resolution of his blindness and disfigurement.

One day, John came into the office with an extremely big smile on his face. Some folks might even call it a "S.E.G." I knew he was bursting to tell me something. I said, "Okay, John, tell me what's up. You hide your emotions as well as a little kid does."

"Well, Dr. Naversen, today I was down at the Department of Motor Vehicles sitting amongst all the 16-year-olds. I was trying to get my driver's license. I passed my test with flying colors, and I drove myself over to your office! This is the first time I have driven a car in over three decades—since 1968 to be exact." Life is good for John again.

Now that John is driving, it makes it easier for him to raise awareness among the public for people to donate their corneas and organs for the medically-needy. I've checked off on my Oregon driver's license card that "Upon my death, I want to be an anatomical donor." That means I will donate my cornea and organs after an untimely accident. (Now that I am 60, no one will probably want Naversen's ancient eyeballs or decrepit innards for a transplant.) John and I hope you will check "yes" on your driver's license, too.

Whenever I think I have a problem in my life, I think about John. Then I realize I have no problems at all. John is a wonderful man, he has been to hell and back twice in his life, and he can still smile about it. He is my most memorable patient. May John and his family find only goodness, prosperity and fun for the remainder of their days on earth. They deserve it!

Made in the USA
Middletown, DE
27 June 2015